KB264115

TEPS in TEPS

990문법

박기혁

서울대학교 졸
(현) 메가스터디 어학센터 TEPS 강사
(현) SLA 학원 TEPS 대표 강사
(현) 중앙일보 영자 신문 중앙 데일리 교육 분야 객원 논설위원
(현) 한국 생산성 본부 영어 전임 강사
(현) PTT(Park's TEPS Teacher's Group) 대표 강사
-TEPS의 최고를 지향하는 강사들의 모임

박성호

W.M.I.T(Melbourne, Australia), Trinity College(Melbourne, Australia)

(전) 국제 어학당 교수부장
(전) 앤도버 어학원 교수부장
(전) 학림학원 대표강사
(전) 다솔 아카데미 어학 연구소 실장
(현) 박정 EDi 어학원 교수부장 · 부원장
(현) PTT(Park's TEPS Teacher's Group) 강사
-TEPS의 최고를 지향하는 강사들의 모임

TEPS in TEPS 990 문법 2nd Edition

저자 | 박기혁 · 박성호
초판 1쇄 발행 | 2009년 8월 14일
개정 3쇄 발행 | 2017년 1월 16일

발행인 | 박효상
총괄이사 | 이종선
편집장 | 김현
기획 · 편집 | 박혜민
디자인 | 손정수
마케팅 | 이태호, 이전희
디지털콘텐츠 | 이지호
관리 | 김태옥

Special Staff

표지 | 장선숙
내지 | 홍수미
편집 | Susie Park
조판 | 한현식

출판등록 | 제10-1835호
발행처 | 사람in
주소 | 121-839 서울시 마포구 양화로11길 14-10(서교동) 4F
전화 | 02) 338-3555(代)   팩스 | 02) 338-3545
e-mail | saramin@netsgo.com
Homepage | www.saramin.com

:: 책값은 뒤표지에 있습니다.
:: 파본은 바꾸어 드립니다.

ⓒ박기혁 · 박성호 2009

ISBN 978-89-6049-180-9 13740
     978-89-6049-175-5 (세트)

사람이 중심이 되는 세상, 세상과 소통하는 책 **사람in**

TEPS in TEPS

990 문법

박기혁·박성호

사람in
saram in.com

머리말

Preface

영어 시험을 둘러싼 여러 가지 환경 변화에 의해서 TEPS의 중요성은 나날이 강조되고 있고 그 특징 또한 뚜렷이 변화를 겪고 있다.

첫째, 갈수록 문제가 다양화되고 있고 더욱더 세련되어지고 있다.
둘째, 시험을 치르는 대상 연령층이 자꾸 낮아지고 있다.
셋째, 특목고나 외고, 로스쿨이나 의학전문대학원 진학 등 그 쓰임새가 더욱 광범위해졌다.

이러한 세 가지 변화에 발맞추어, TEPS 교재도 다양화되고 진화되어야 하는데, 현재의 교재 시장은 그러한 가시적인 변화에 능동적으로 대처하지 못하는 것이 사실이다. 이에, 이번 TEPS in TEPS 시리즈를 통해서 진화하는 TEPS에 가장 적합한 패러다임을 제시하고자 한다.

TEPS는 참으로 복잡하고 미묘한 시험이다. TOEFL처럼 학문적인 점에 초점을 맞추는 것도 아니고, TOEIC처럼 실용 언어적인 측면만을 강조하는 시험도 아니다. 어쩌면 이 둘의 장점만을 모아 놓은 시험이라 할 수 있겠다.

학문적인 내용들을 풀어가되 좀 더 현실성을 부여하여 실용적으로 쓰이는 영어들을 묻는 것이다. TEPS가 최근 시험 시장에 지각 변동을 일으키고 있는 이유는 이런 장점이 토대가 되었다고 볼 수 있다.

TEPS는 실제로 회화를 하다가 혹은 네이티브가 보는 외국 신문 등을 읽다가 느끼는 애로사항을 잘 해결해 줄 수 있는 시험이다. 어휘력의 측면에서 보아도 실생활에서 우리는 이런 어려움을 겪는다. '단어 하나하나의 해석은 되는데 왜 전체적으로는 독해가 안 되고 해석이 안 될까?', '이 상황에서 저 말은 대체 무슨 뜻으로 쓰이는 걸까?'

그것은 바로 간단한 단어라도 초보적으로 배웠던 사전적 지식 외에 실생활에서는 다양한 뜻으로 활용되기 때문이다.

이처럼 네이티브와의 가장 적절한 의사소통에 초점을 둔 TEPS는 지극히 영어수험과 영어실용의 접목이라는 공인영어시험의 목적에 가장 합당한 인증시험이라 하겠다.

TOEIC이 점수 인플레로 상위권 수험생의 변별력을 상실했다는 비판이 많다. TEPS는 TOEIC과 같은 패턴의 지속적인 반복만으로는 해결할 수 없는 시험이다. 이에 학습자들도 이런 TEPS에 대한 관심과 욕구가 더욱 늘어나고 있는 현실이다.

필자는 좀 더 실용적이고 영어 실력 향상에 도움이 되는 TEPS에 대한 관심이 높아지고 있는 것은 고무적인 일이라 생각한다. 그리고 그런 TEPS를 연구하고 학습하는데, 이 'TEPS in TEPS 시리즈'가 선구자적인 역할을 하길 진심으로 바라는 마음으로 문제 하나 설명 하나에 세심한 신경을 쓰면서 작업에 임하였다.

혼자서는 할 수 없었던 작업에 언제나 도움이 되었던 분들께 감사의 마음을 전할까 한다. 늘 미안한 마음이 드는 가족들과, 사람인 출판사의 박효상 사장님, 김상호 팀장님, 조승주 대리님 그리고 이 책의 출간에 물심양면으로 도움을 주신 류건 선생님, 신일섭 조교, 윤이랑 조교에게도 아울러 감사의 뜻을 표하고 싶다.

PPT(Park's TEPS Teacher's Group) 대표 강사

박 기 혁

TEPS in TEPS

학생들의 자습서와 학원 교재의 성격을 둘 다 가질 수 있게 만들었다. 그래서 학원에서의 강의는 물론 독학용으로도 사용하도록 준비했다.

1. 상세한 해설을 통해 정답을 공략하는 법과 함께 오답을 피할 수 있는 Skill들을 제시하여 좀 더 높은 점수로의 도약이 가능하게 하였다.

2. TEPS의 4대 영역(독해, 어휘, 청해, 문법)과 기준 점수대별로 학습 목표와 가장 효율적인 방법들을 제시하여 좀 더 전문적이고 체계적인 학습자 맞춤형 학습이 가능하도록 하였다.

3. 애매모호한 이론이나 군더더기 설명을 최대한 배제하여 학습 시간 대비 효율성을 극대화 하도록 구성하였다.

TEPS in TEPS

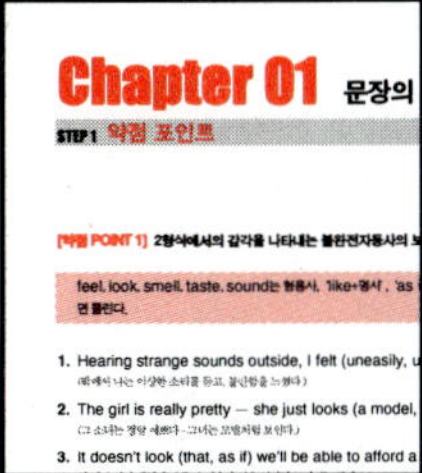

1. TEPS 문법 고득점의 방해 요소들을 제거한 약점 Point

TEPS에서 고득점자들이 자주 틀리는 문법 요소들을 선별하여 Point 별로 제시하였다. 핵심 만을 정리한 설명은 물론 모든 예문의 문제화로 학습 효율을 극대화하였다.

2. 약점 포인트를 적용해보는 Exercise

약점 포인트에서 정리한 부분을 가장 효율적으로 체크할 수 있도록 하였다. 자신의 이해도를 점검해보고 미처 알아두지 못했던 부분은 다시 한 번 정리할 수 있도록 하였다.

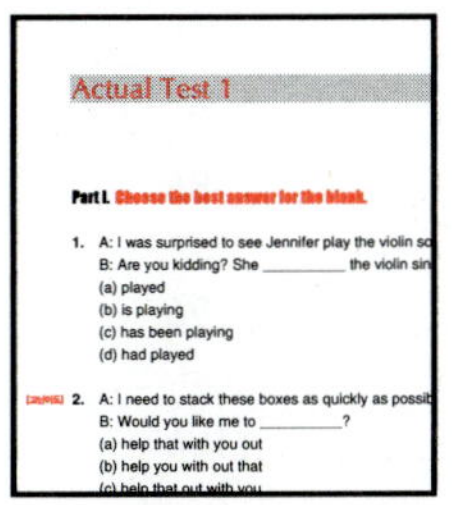

3. 자신만의 노하우를 만들어가는 Actual Test

TEPS 문법 문제에 자주 나오는 것들로 구성된 random한 테스트를 통해서 각 Chapter 별 문법 요소만이 아닌 고난이도 문제까지 다양한 연습을 할 수 있도록 하였다.

4. 실전보다 더 실전 같은 Final Test

TEPS와 가장 가까운 문제들만을 엄선하여 학습자들로 하여금 실전 감각을 최고조에 이를 수 있도록 하였다. 기존의 TEPS 문제들에 대한 대비는 물론 출제가 예상되는 부분들까지 반영하여 완벽한 연습이 가능하도록 하였다.

Contents

Chapter 01

문장의 형식과 종류

Chapter 01 문장의 형식과 종류

STEP 1 약점 포인트

[약점 POINT 1] 2형식에서의 감각을 나타내는 불완전자동사의 보어

> feel, look, smell, taste, sound는 형용사, 'like+명사', 'as if절'을 보어로 취한다. to be나 that절이 연결되면 틀린다.

1. Hearing strange sounds outside, I felt (uneasily, uneasy, to be uneasy).
(밖에서 나는 이상한 소리를 듣고, 불안감을 느꼈다.)

2. The girl is really pretty — she just looks (a model, to be a model, like a model).
(그 소녀는 정말 예쁘다 - 그녀는 모델처럼 보인다.)

3. It doesn't look (that, as if) we'll be able to afford a vacation this year.
(우리는 이번 해에 휴가를 갈 여유가 있을 것처럼 보이지는 않아요.)

4. That doesn't sound a very practical plan. (○, ×)
(매우 실용적인 계획인 것처럼 들리지는 않는다.)

5. He felt like a fool. (○, ×)
(그는 바보같이 느껴졌다.)

[약점 POINT 2] 2형식 불완전자동사의 보어

> 변화(go, run, fall, come, grow, turn, make, become), 유지(remain, keep, stay, continue, hold, lie, rest, stand), 감각(feel, look, smell, taste, sound), 판단 · 판명(seem, appear, prove, turn out)의 보어는 형용사 또는 명사가 오며, 부사가 오면 틀린다.

1. She grew (impatient, impatiently) with his constant excuses for not doing his task.
(그녀는 그가 임무를 수행하지 않는 데에 대한 계속되는 변명에 인내심이 바닥났다.)

2. The boys were wearing leather jackets and doing their best to look (manly, strongly).
(그 소년들은 가죽 자켓을 입고 있었고 남자답게 보이기 위해 최선을 다하고 있었다.)

3. He appears a little more nicely in that suit. (○, ×)
(그는 그 정장을 입으니 조금 더 멋져 보인다.)

[약점 POINT 3] 금지 · 방해의 3형식 완전타동사

'타동사 + 목적어 + 전치사 from -ing' 을 쓰는 경우와 to부정사를 쓰는 경우의 구별

- prevent, keep, stop, prohibit, inhibit, hinder, deter, restrain + 목적어 + from -ing
- dissuade, disable, discourage + 목적어 + from -ing
  cf. forbid, persuade, enable, encourage + 목적어 + to + 동사원형

1. They prohibited shopkeepers (to sell, from selling) cigarettes to children.
(그들은 가게 주인들이 어린이들에게 담배를 판매하는 것을 금지하였다.)

2. The hard wind kept us (to continue, from continuing) with the game.
(거센 바람이 우리들이 경기를 계속하지 못하도록 했다.)

3. Tom wanted to join the army, but was dissuaded to do so. (○ , ×)
(톰은 군대에 들어가고 싶었지만, 그렇게 하는 것을 단념하게 되었다.)

4. We were forbidden from entering the house. (○ , ×)
(우리는 그 집에 들어가는 것이 금지되었다.)

[약점 POINT 4] 전치사와 함께 쓰면 틀리는 3형식 완전타동사

다음 타동사들은 전치사와 함께 쓰면 틀린다.
- reach(=get to, arrive at · in · on), approach, enter(들어가다), attend(참석하다), address, attack, greet, oppose(=object to)
- discuss, mention, consider, answer, emphasize(=stress)
- resemble, marry(=be married to), accompany(=be accompanied by · with), face(=be faced with · by), confront(=be confronted by · with)
- await(=wait for), inhabit(=live in, reside in), leave(=start from, depart from)
  cf. leave의 경우, 타동사와 자동사로 쓰일 때가 있기 때문에, 자동사로 쓰이는 경우 leave from, leave for 같이 전치사와의 결합이 가능하다.

1. Dark storm clouds were approaching to us from the west. (○ , ×)
(검은 폭풍우 구름이 서쪽으로부터 우리에게 접근하고 있었다.)

2. We will (discuss, discuss about) the matter in more detail later.
(우리는 나중에 그 문제를 더 자세히 토론할 것이다.)

3. The government will not (answer, answer about) the criticism that it has done nothing about the homeless people.
(정부는 노숙자들에 대해 아무런 조치도 취하지 않았다는 비판에 대해 대답하지 않을 것이다.)

4. They have produced a cloth which (is resembling, resembles with, resembles, is resembled by) cotton closely.
(그들은 거의 면과 유사한 옷감을 생산해 왔다.)

5. The volunteers (are facing with, are faced with) many problems.
(그 자원봉사자들은 많은 문제에 봉착하고 있다.)

6. "Thank you for your help." "Don't mention about it." (○ , ×)
("당신의 도움에 감사드려요." "별 말씀을요.")

7. They will leave from Seoul this weekend. (○ , ×)
(그들은 이번 주에 서울을 떠날 것이다.)

8. She left for Japan unexpectedly last night. (○ , ×)
(그녀는 어젯밤에 예기치 않게 일본으로 떠났다.)

9. Animals of many species inhabit in the tropics. (○ , ×)
(많은 종의 동물들이 열대 지방에서 서식한다.)

[약점 POINT 5] 준보어(=유사보어)

1형식 문장에 추가되어 쓰이는 보어를 말한다. 2형식 동사처럼 형용사와 명사를 보어로 취하며, 부사(**-ly**)가 오면 틀린다.

1. We came back home (angry, angrily) after fighting traffic for two hours.
(우리는 2시간 동안 교통체증을 겪은 뒤에 화가 난 채 집에 돌아왔다.)

2. He married pennilessly. (○ , ×) (그는 무일푼으로 결혼했다.)

[약점 POINT 6] 재귀대명사를 목적어로 취할 수 있는 3형식 완전타동사

재귀대명사를 목적어로 취하는 형태와 그 수동태의 형태를 주의하자.
convince oneself of · that(=be convinced of · that), concern oneself with · in · about(=be concerned with · in · about), accustom oneself to(=be accustomed to), acquaint oneself with(=be acquainted with), seat oneself at · on · down(=be seated at · on · down), dress oneself in(=be dressed in)
cf. present oneself at(=be present at), absent oneself from(=be absent from), pride oneself on(=be proud of, take pride in)

1. She (was convincing, was convinced) that her brother was still alive.
(그녀는 남동생이 여전히 살아있다고 확신했다.)

2. He (concerned about, concerned himself about) the pollution problem.
(그는 오염 문제에 대해 걱정했다.)

3. I can't (accustom, accustom myself) to living in the United States.
(나는 미국에서 사는 것에 적응할 수 없다.)

4. He (seated, seated himself, was seated, was seated himself, sat, was sat) down.
(그는 자리에 앉았다.)

5. She remained (seating, seated) until he woke up. (그녀는 그가 깨어날 때까지 앉아 있었다.)

6. We entered the room and took a seat. (○ , ×) (우리는 방에 들어가서 자리에 앉았다.)

Answer

P4　1. X (to 삭제)　2. discuss　3. answer　4. resembles　5. are faced with　6. X (about 삭제)　7. O (leave 가 자동사의 의미를 지니는 경우, from과 함께 쓰여 '~에서 떠나다'라는 의미로 쓰인다.)　8. O　9. X (in 삭제)

P5　1. angry　2. X (pennilessly → penniless)

P6　1. was convinced　2. concerned himself about　3. accustom myself　4. seated himself, was seated, sat　5. seated　6. O

[약점 POINT 7] 통고 · 알림의 3형식 완전타동사

inform, remind, convince, assure, advise, warn, accuse + 〈목적어 + of〉 또는 〈목적어 + that절〉 구문에서 of와 that이 함께 쓰이거나, of 뒤에 절(S + V)이 이어지면 틀린다.

1. He notified us of he would resign. (○, ×)
(그는 그가 사퇴할 것이라고 우리에게 알렸다.)

2. They've informed me of that your application was rejected. (○, ×)
(그들은 내게 당신의 지원이 거절당할 것이라고 알려줬다.)

- They agreed to that the plan is too short of time. (×)
(그들은 그 계획이 너무 시간이 모자라다는 데에 동의했다.) ❶ to 다음에 절이 올 수 없다.
- There is a good chance of that she will recover completely. (×)
(그녀가 완전히 회복될 가능성이 크다.) ❶ of와 that이 함께 쓰일 수 없다.
- Because of he was ill, he could not finish the assignment. (×)
(그는 아팠기 때문에, 숙제를 끝낼 수 없었다.) ❶ because of 다음에 명사상당어구가 와야 한다.

[약점 POINT 8] 유사형태의 자동사 · 타동사의 구분

문맥의 의미를 통해 수동의 의미로 쓰이는지 능동의 의미로 쓰이는지 파악한 뒤 적절한 시제의 동사로 맞춰야 한다.

| lie-lay-lain | rise-rose-risen | arise-arose-arisen | sit-sat-sat |
| lay-laid-laid | raise-raised-raised | arouse-aroused-aroused | seat-seated-seated |

1. I didn't feel well so I laid down on the bed and rested for some while. (○, ×)
(나는 몸 상태가 좋지 않아서 침대에 누워 얼마간 쉬었다.)

2. She lay great emphasis on the point. (○, ×)
(그녀는 그 부분에 강한 강조를 두었다.)

3. The retirement age has been (risen, raised) to 65 for both men and women.
(퇴임 연령이 남자와 여자 모두 65세로 상향되었다.)

4. His resignation is certain to (arise, arouse) new fears about the company's future.
(그의 사임은 회사의 미래에 대한 새로운 우려를 불러일으킬 것이 분명하다.)

5. We should deal with the problems as they (rise, raise, arise, arouse).
(우리는 문제가 발생하는 즉시 그것들을 처리해야만 한다.)

[약점 POINT 9] 타동사로 착각하기 쉬운 자동사

우리말에서는 목적어와 함께 쓰인 것처럼 해석되기 때문에 타동사로 착각하기 쉬우나, 영어에서는 전치사구를 목적어로 취하는 자동사들로 전치사와 함께 알아두어야 한다.

graduate from	arrive at	wait for(on)	participate in
account for	listen to	complain of	object to
talk about	consent to	assent to	dissent from
apologize to	add to	reply to	rely on
refer to	speak of	subject to	sympathize with
interfere with	tamper with	meddle in	operate on
border on	infringe on	trespass on	
connive with	acquiesce in		

He graduated from Cambridge University with a degree in law.
(그는 케임브리지 대학에서 법학 학위를 받았다.)

We eventually arrived at our destination.
(우리는 마침내 목적지에 도착했다.)

Would you like to participate in our blood drive?
(헌혈 운동에 동참하시겠어요?)

Everyone sympathized with Bruce.
(모두가 Bruce를 동정했다.)

1. Would you (object to, object) my turning on the radio?
   (제가 라디오를 켜도 될까요?)

2. Nowadays, we increasingly rely computers. (○ , ×)
   (요즘 우리는 점점 더 컴퓨터에 의존하고 있다.)

3. Don't interfere with him while he's working. (○ , ×)
   (그가 일을 하고 있을 때에는 방해하지 마라.)

4. The committee chairman had to account for how the money was spent. (○ , ×)
   (그 위원회의 위원장은 어떻게 돈이 쓰였는지 설명해야만 했다.)

Answer

P7 1. X (of → that) 2. X (of 삭제)
P8 1. X (lay: 눕다 의 의미로 쓰였으므로 lie의 과거형인 lay가 와야 한다.) 2. X (laid) 3. raised 4. arouse 5. arise
P9 1. object to 2. X (on computers) 3. O 4. O

[약점 POINT 10] 4형식을 3형식으로 전환하지 않는 동사

take, cost, save, forgive, envy, spare는 간접목적어(IO)와 직접목적어(DO)의 순서를 바꿔 쓰지 않는 4형식 수여동사들이다.
The trip took me an hour. (○)
The trip took an hour to me. (×)
It took an hour for me to make the trip. (○)

1. The holiday package tour will cost (you lots of money, lots of money to you).
(휴일 패키지 여행은 너에게 많은 돈이 들게 할 것이다.)

2. (I envy you your success, I envy your success of you).
(나는 너의 성공이 부럽다.)

[약점 POINT 11] 5형식 불완전타동사의 목적보어 : 동사가 목적보어로 올 때(목적어와 목적보어가 수동인 경우)

타동사와 목적어 간의 관계를 고려하여 수동인 경우 수동 형태로 써야 한다.

- 5형식 동사 + 목적어 + 과거분사
- 미래동사 + 목적어 + (to be) 과거분사
- let + 목적어 + be + 과거분사

1. He wanted the report (typing, to type, typed, to be typed) double-spaced.
(그는 그 보고서가 한 행씩 띄어서 타이핑되기를 원했다.)

2. As the movie was full of fun, it made the audience (fascinate, to fascinate, fascinated).
(그 영화는 재미로 가득 차 있었기 때문에, 관객들을 매료시켰다.)

3. Please keep me (inform, informing, to inform, informed) while you are touring in Europe.
(네가 유럽을 여행하는 동안에 내게 소식을 알려주렴.)

4. I will never let this humiliation (forget, to forget, forgotten, be forgotten).
(나는 이 모욕을 결코 잊지 않을 것이다.)

[약점 POINT 12] 부가의문문 : 긍정문 뒤에는 부정, 부정문 뒤에는 긍정

상대방이 부정으로 물을 때에 긍정하는 대답은 No, 부정하는 대답은 Yes.

1. That's the woman who threw away the empty bottles, didn't she? (○, ×)
(저 사람이 빈 병들을 버린 여자지, 그렇지?)

2. A: Didn't he give a refund of this sky-blue T-shirts?
(그가 이 하늘색 티셔츠를 환불해주지 않았니?)

B: Yes, he didn't. I think I'll report that to consumer protection center. (○, ×)
(그래요, 그는 그렇지 않았어요. 저는 소비자 보호센터에 이 사실을 신고할 거예요.)

[약점 POINT 13] 4형식 수여동사로 착각하기 쉬운 3형식 완전타동사

'explain, introduce, suggest, propose, mention, say, announce, describe + 목적어 + to + 사람'
또는 'to + 사람 + 목적어' 구문에서 사람 앞에 전치사 to가 빠지면 틀린다.

1. The chairman explained (us, to us) that the two sides meet again the following day.
(그 회장은 우리에게 양측이 다음 날 다시 만날 것이라고 설명했다.)

2. He suggested (me an idea, to me an idea, an idea to me, an idea me).
(그는 내게 견해를 제시했다.)

3. He explained (it to me, to me it).
(그는 내게 설명했다.)

4. I will introduce to you my wife and my kids. (○, ×)
(내 아내와 자식들을 당신에게 소개하겠습니다.)

5. She said me that she would stay there for a few days more. (○, ×)
(그녀는 그곳에 며칠 더 머무를 것이라고 내게 말했다.)

6. They explained me how to operate it. (○, ×)
(그들은 내게 그것을 작동시키는 법을 설명해주었다.)

Answer

P10 1. you lots of money 2. I envy you your success
P11 1. typed, to be typed 2. fascinated 3. informed 4. be forgotten
P12 1. X (didn't she →isn't it) 2. X (Yes, he didn't →No, he didn't)
P13 1. to us 2. to me an idea, an idea to me 3. 둘다맞음 4. O 5. X (said me →said to me) 6. X
(explained me →explained to me)

- **thank**는 사람을 목적어로, **appreciate**는 감사의 내용을 목적어로 취한다.
- **rob**은 사람을 목적어로, **steal**은 훔치는 물건을 목적어로 취한다.
- **suggest, demand, hope, say** + 목적어 + **to**동사원형의 형식은 틀리다.
- **borrow**(빌려 쓰다)는 3형식 동사이고, **lend**(빌려 주다)는 4형식 동사이다.
- **say**(…라고 말하다)는 3형식 동사이고, **tell**(…에게 ~을 전하다)은 4형식 동사이다.

1. He (thanked, appreciated) me for the advice.
(그는 조언해준 것에 대해 나에게 감사해했다.)

2. I'll (thank, appreciate) it if you come to help us move out.
(네가 우리들이 이사하는 것을 도와주러 온다면 고마울 거야.)

3. The burglar (stole, robbed) the traveler of his money.
(그 도둑이 여행자의 돈을 훔쳤다.)

4. He was stolen of his money on the way home. (○, ×)
(그는 집에 오는 도중에 돈을 도둑맞았다.)

5. We (hope, want, suggest) you to stay for dinner.
(우리는 당신이 저녁식사를 위해 머무르기를 원해요.)

6. They demanded me to tell everything. (○, ×)
(그들은 내게 모든 것을 말하도록 요구했다.)

7. Will you (borrow, lend) me some money? I'm asking if I can (borrow, lend) some money from you.
(내게 약간의 돈을 빌려주겠니? 너에게 돈을 빌릴 수 있는지 묻고 있는 거야.)

8. He (said, told) me an interesting story and then (said, told) to me goodbye.
(그는 내게 재미있는 이야기를 해주었고, 그런 뒤에 내게 작별인사를 했다.)

[약점 POINT 15] 4형식을 3형식으로 전환할 때 간접목적어(IO) 앞에 쓰이는 전치사

동사에 따라 동반되는 전치사가 다르므로 이 점을 주의하여 알아두어야 한다.

- give, show, allow, offer, hand, lend, pass, pay, promise, sell, send, teach, tell, wish + 직목 + to 간·목
- make, buy, do, find, choose, get, prepare, fix, cook + 직·목 + for 간·목
- ask, require, request, inquire, demand, beg + 직·목 + of 간·목
  cf. play + 사람 + a trick = play a trick on + 사람

1. They do not normally give discounts (for, to) private customers.
(그들은 보통 개인 고객에게 할인을 해주지 않는다.)

2. He bought a ring (to, for) her, and she made a cake (to, for) him in return.
(그는 그녀에게 반지를 사주었고, 그녀는 보답으로 그에게 케이크를 만들어 주었다.)

3. They asked immediate departure (to, of) us.
(그들은 우리의 즉각적인 출발을 요구했다.)

4. I will do everything that is required (to, for, of) me.
(내게 요구되는 모든 것을 할 것이다.)

Answer

P14 1. thanked 2. appreciate 3. robbed 4. X (stolen →robbed) 5. want 6. X (demand는 사람을 목적어로 쓰지 않는다. demand + 목적어 + to do의 형태로 쓰이지 않으며, demand + 목적어 + 전치사 + 명사의 형태나 demand to do의 형태로 쓸 수 있다. demanded me to tell →demanded telling everything from me) 7. lend, borrow 8. told, said

P15 1. to 2. for, for 3. of 4. of

[약점 POINT 16] 5형식 불완전타동사의 목적보어 : 형용사 · 명사가 목적보어로 올 때

- 5형식 불완전타동사의 보어는 형용사 또는 명사이며, 부사(-ly)가 오면 틀린다.
- consider, take, regard, see, describe, treat, define + 목적어 + as 형 · 명
- think, consider, find, believe, guess, suppose, assume + 목적어 + (to be) 형 · 명
- think of, look upon, refer to + 목적어 + as 명 · 형
- take(=mistake) him for his brother, take ~ for granted

1. Their reaction made me (sad, sadly).
(그들의 반응이 나를 슬프게 만들었다.)

2. I found it (difficult, difficultly) to get the agreement from them.
(나는 그들로부터 동의를 얻는 것이 어렵다는 것을 알았다.)

3. People (think, think of) learning a language as a natural process.
(사람들은 언어를 배우는 것이 자연스러운 과정이라고 생각한다.)

[약점 POINT 17] 감탄문의 어순

구분	어순	예문
What 단수	What + a(an) + 형용사 + 단수명사 + (주어 + 동사)!	What an interesting story it is! What a pretty flower this is!
What 복수	What + 형용사 + 복수명사 + (주어 + 동사)!	What kind girls they are! What wise boys they are!
How	How + 형용사(or 부사) + (주어+동사)!	How fast he swims! How interesting story it is!
	How + 형용사 + 관사 + 명사 + (주어+동사)!	How wise the boy is! How kind the girl is!

* 기원문 : 'May + 주어 + 동사원형' 이나 '주어 + 동사원형' 의 어순.

May long live the queen! (여왕폐하 만세!)

God bless you! (신의 축복이 있기를!)

May you succeed! (부디 성공하기를!)

1. How wonderful the life is! (○ , ×)

(인생은 얼마나 멋진가!)

2. What fast boys they are! (○ , ×)

(얼마나 빠른 소년들인 가!)

[약점 POINT 18] 5형식 불완전타동사의 목적보어 : 동사가 목적보어로 올 때

타동사 + 목적어 + to부정사가 오는 경우와 -ing가 오는 경우를 구별하자.

- 요청(ask, beg, request, require), 바람(want, need), 설득 · 강요(encourage, persuade, compel, drive, force, get, oblige, order, tell, urge), 허용 · 유도(allow, permit, cause, enable, entice, entitle, induce, lead), 기타(advise, promise, forbid) + 목적어 + to 동사원형
- 지각(see, watch, look at, feel, witness, observe, sense, notice) + 목적어 + 동사원형 + -ing
- 사역(make, have, let) + 목적어 + 동사원형   *cf.* help + 목적어 + (to) 동사원형
- 유지(keep, leave), 발견(find, discover, catch), 상상(imagine, remember) + 목적어 + -ing

1. I used to love watching my sister (to draw, draw, drawn) pictures.

(나는 내 여동생이 그림 그리는 걸 보는 것을 좋아하고는 했다.)

2. I wanted to watch the film but my parents made me (to do, do, doing) my homework.

(나는 영화를 보고 싶었지만 부모님께서 내가 숙제를 하게 만드셨다.)

3. The earthquake (had, let, made) all the windows shake.

(지진이 모든 창문을 흔들었다.)

4. They left us (wait, to wait, waiting, waited) outside.

(그들은 우리를 바깥에서 기다리게 했다.)

5. I'm really sorry to have kept you (wait, to wait, waiting, waited) so long.

(매우 오래 기다리게 해서 정말 미안해.)

6. If they catch you (sell, to sell, selling) alcohol to a child, you'll lose your job.

(만약 당신이 어린이에게 술을 판매하고 있는 것을 그들이 적발한다면, 당신은 일자리를 잃을 거예요.)

Answer

P16 1. sad 2. difficult 3. think of

P17 1. O 2. O

P18 1. draw 2. do 3. let 4. waiting 5. waiting 6. selling

- 의문사가 쓰인 의문문의 경우: 의문사 + 주어 + 동사

  He asked <u>when</u> <u>the questionnaire</u> <u>would be finished</u>.

  　　　　　　　　의문사　　　　　　주어　　　　　　　　동사

  (그는 언제 이 설문조사가 끝날지 물었다.)

  Tell me where you live.

  (당신이 어디 사는지 내게 말해주세요.)

- 의문사가 쓰이지 않은 의문문의 경우 : if(whether) + 주어 + 동사

  Jenny asked if the USA quiz was finished.

  (제니는 USA 퀴즈가 끝났는지 물었다.)

  I don't know if I turned off the light.

  (내가 불을 껐는지 안 껐는지 모르겠다.)

- 의문사가 문장 첫머리에 위치해야 하는 경우

  주절에 think, believe, consider, wonder, suppose, imagine, guess 등 생각을 나타내는 생각동사가 쓰인 경우 의문사는
  문장의 첫머리로 나오게 된다.

  '의문사 + do you think + 주어 + 동사'

  <u>How</u> do you <u>suppose</u> <u>they solve the problem</u>?
  의문사　　　　　　생각동사　　　　　　　종속절

  (그들이 어떻게 그 문제를 풀었다고 생각하시나요?)

  Where do you <u>think</u> she met Mr. Lee?

  (그녀가 이 선생님을 어디서 만났다고 생각하시나요?)

  How old do you <u>guess</u> he is?

  (그가 몇 살이라고 생각하십니까?)

  Who do you <u>think</u> he is?

  (그가 누구라고 생각하십니까?)

1. I don't know where the campus is. (○ , ×)
(나는 캠퍼스가 어디 있는지 모른다.)

2. She has been wondering why did you quit the job. (○ , ×)
(그녀는 네가 왜 그 직장을 그만두었는지 궁금해해왔다.)

3. Why do you guess he is innocent? (○ , ×)
(왜 그가 결백하다고 추측하는 거니?)

4. I don't care who are you. (○ , ×)
(나는 당신이 누구인지 상관하지 않아요.)

Part I. Choose the best answer for the blank.

1. A: ___________ involves a lot of traveling.
   B: That's okay. I love to travel.
   (a) The post you applied
   (b) The post you've applied
   (c) The post you've applied for
   (d) The post you've applied in

2. A: Can you tell me whether ___________ come to Seoul?
   B: I'm not sure about that.
   (a) is he going to
   (b) he is going to
   (c) he will be
   (d) does he

3. A: I thought you were having car trouble.
   B: Yes, but I ___________ this morning.
   (a) had it fix
   (b) had it fixed
   (c) had it mine
   (d) had fixing it

4. A: What did you do to your legs?
   B: I ___________ when I was learning how to rollerblade.
   (a) hurt me
   (b) have hurt me
   (c) hurt myself
   (d) have hurt

Part II. Choose the best answer for the blank.

5. ___________ provided a living for Johnson's family for a long time.
   (a) Making films were
   (b) What was making films
   (c) Making films was what
   (d) What making films

6. Lower rates of taxation encourage people ___________ harder.
   (a) work
   (b) to work
   (c) working
   (d) worked

7. They are trying to force the government ___________ more women to senior positions.
   (a) appoint
   (b) appointing
   (c) appointed
   (d) to appoint

Part III. Identify the option that contains an awkward expression or an error in grammar.

8. (a) A: I didn't know Susan is already 35 years old.
   (b) B: How old did you guess is she?
   (c) A: I thought she would be much younger than 30's.
   (d) B: It's true that she looks quite younger than her age.

Part IV. Identify the option that contains an awkward expression or an error in grammar.

9. (a) These days, many celebrities tend to publish their own books. (b) Famous actress Shin and popular actor Jeon's biographical novels are going to be issued this month. (c) Besides, two more politicians are set to follow in their footsteps in coming weeks. (d) And they are expected to invite high-profile figures to the book launch to be demonstrated their connections and influence in the political and social arena.

Chapter 02

동사의 시제

Chapter 02 동사의 시제

[약점 POINT 1] 현재시제의 형태로 예정된 미래의 일을 나타내는 경우

- 왕래발착(往來發着)동사: go, come, start, leave, arrive, depart, meet, return, sail, ride나 시작을 나타내는 begin 등의 동사는 미래를 나타내는 부사, 부사구와 함께 현재시제의 형태로 예정된 미래의 일을 나타낸다.

  He starts(=will start) for Seoul tomorrow morning.

  (그는 내일 아침 서울로 출발할 것이다.)

- 시간, 조건 부사절에서 미래 대용

  when, until, before, as soon as, by the time, so long as, once 등과 같이 시간이나 조건을 나타내는 접속사가 부사절을 만들 때는 미래(미래완료)를 대신해 현재(현재완료) 시제를 사용한다.

  We have only five minutes before the train starts.

  (기차가 떠나기 전까지 우리는 겨우 5분 남았다.)

  If she comes home, will you give me a call?

  (만약 그녀가 집에 온다면 나에게 전화를 해줄래?)

- when이 명사절이나 형용사절로 사용되거나 if가 whether의 의미로 사용된 명사절에서는 미래표현을 그대로 사용한다.

  I don't know when he will come back. ➡ 명사절

  (나는 그가 언제 돌아올지 모른다.)

  The day will come when you will regret it. ➡ 형용사절

  (네가 그것을 후회하는 날이 오게 될 거야.)

---

1. She leaves for Paris the day after tomorrow. (○, ×)

(그녀는 모레 파리로 떠날 것이다.)

2. Jane returns home this coming vacation. (○, ×)

(제인은 이번 방학에 고향에 돌아올 것이다.)

3. If it is going to rain tonight, we'll cancel our flight. (○, ×)

(만약 오늘밤 비가 내린다면, 우리는 항공편을 취소할 것이다.)

4. I heard that he would leave for Seoul after he will graduate from college. (○, ×)

(나는 그가 대학을 졸업한 뒤에 서울로 떠날 것이라는 것을 들었다.)

5. I'm not sure when Susie will come back. (○, ×)

(나는 수지가 언제 돌아올지 잘 모르겠다.)

6. I asked him if he will come to the party. (○, ×)

(나는 그가 파티에 올지 안 올지 그에게 물었다.)

[약점 POINT 2] 부사절에서 시제의 대용

시간, 조건의 부사절에서 미래시제는 현재시제로, 미래완료시제는 현재완료시제로 대용된다. 그러나 형용사절과 명사절에서는 원래대로 미래시제와 미래완료시제로 사용한다.

1. Don't forget to turn off the heat when the water will boil. (○ , ×)
(물이 끓을 때 불을 끄는 것을 잊지 말아라.)

2. Do you know when the last concert will be held? (○ , ×)
(마지막 콘서트가 언제 열리는지 알고 있니?)

3. Can I borrow the book for a day or two if you have finished reading it? (○ , ×)
(만약 네가 그 책을 다 읽었다면, 내가 하루나 이틀 동안 빌릴 수 있을까?)

Answer
P1 1. ○ 2. ○ 3. X (If it is going to rain →If it rains) 4. X (after he will graduate →after he graduates)
    5. ○ 6. ○ (명사절 : =whether)
P2 1. X (the water will boil →the water boils) 2. ○ 3. ○

[약점 POINT 3] 주의해야 할 현재시제

- 불변의 진리, 사실, 속담
  The earth moves around the sun.
  (지구는 태양의 둘레를 회전한다.)
  Honesty is the best policy.
  (정직이 최선의 방책이다.)

- 옛사람, 옛날 책에 쓰인 말을 인용할 때
  Dryden says that none but the brave deserve(s) the fair.
  (용기 있는 자만이 미인을 얻을 수 있다고 Dryden은 말한다.)
  My father said 'Honesty is the best policy.'
  (나의 아버지는 '정직이 최선의 방책이다.' 라고 말씀하셨다.)

※ 불변의 진리, 사실, 속담, 옛날에 쓴 말 등을 인용할 때에는 현재형 시제를 쓴다.

1. Some plants give off bad smell to protect themselves. (○ , ×)
  (어떤 식물들은 자신을 보호하기 위해 고약한 냄새를 방출한다.)

2. My mother used to say, 'The early bird caught the worm'. (○ , ×)
  (어머니께서 말씀하시기를, '일찍 일어나는 새가 벌레를 잡는다.' 라고 하셨다.)

[약점 POINT 4] 진행형으로 쓸 수 없는 동사

동작을 나타내는 동사가 아니라면 원칙적으로 진행형을 쓸 수가 없다.

- 존재(be, exist)나 상태(seem, look, appear, resemble) 등을 나타내는 동사
  He resembles his father. (그는 아버지를 닮았다.)
  He is resembling his father. (×)
  He resembles with his father. (×)
  He is resembled by his father. (×)
  resemble은 진행형을 쓸 수 없으며, 타동사이므로 전치사 **with**도 쓸 수 없고, 수동태로 바꿀 수도 없다.

- 주어의 의지가 포함되지 않은 지각(feel, see, smell, hear, taste)을 나타내는 동사
  I see her swimming in the pool.
  (그녀가 수영장에서 수영하고 있는 것을 본다.)

see가 의지동사로서 '구경하다, 면회하다' 의 뜻일 땐 진행형이 가능하며, hear가 '청강하다' 의 뜻일 때 진행형이 가능하다.

They are hearing lectures.
(그들은 청강하는 중이다.)
I am seeing the sights of Seoul.
(서울 경치를 구경 중이다.)

look at은 의지동사로서 '~을 보다' 의 뜻이므로 진행형이 가능하며, listen to 역시 의지동사로 '귀를 기울이다' 의 뜻일 때는 진행형이 가능하다.

● 소유(have, belong, possess, own)를 나타내는 동사
  I have some money with me. (O) (나는 수중에 돈을 가지고 있다.)
  I am having some money with me. (×)
  cf. **I am having breakfast. (O)** (나는 아침을 먹는 중이다.)
  ◐ have가 소유의 뜻이 아닌 다른 의미로 쓰이면 진행형이 가능하다.

  This house is belonging to me. (×)
  ◐ belong to는 '~에 속하다, ~의 소유이다' 의 뜻이므로 진행형을 쓸 수 없다.

● 인식(know, believe, understand)을 나타내는 동사
  I am knowing the fact. (×)
  ◐ know는 아는지 모르는지의 인식동사이므로 진행형을 쓸 수 없다.

1. I'm not understanding what I have learnt. (O , ×)
(나는 배운 것을 이해하지 못하겠다.)

2. He is really differing from his brother. (O , ×)
(그는 형과 정말로 다르다.)

3. I feel sorry for him who is lacking some competitiveness. (O , ×)
(나는 경쟁력이 부족한 그에 대해 유감스럽게 생각하고 있다.)

Answer
P3   1. O 2. X (caught → catches)
P4   1. X 2. X 3. X (who is lacking → who lacks)

- 과거시제 부사어구 : last night, yesterday, two months ago(=two months back), just now(=just ago), the other day, then, at that time, (in) those days, What time~?, When~?, the first(last) time, in+년도

- 현재완료시제 부사어구 : lately(=of late), up to now, so far, till now, as yet, to date, for(during, over), the last(past)+숫자

- 과거완료시제 부사어구 : long before, two months before

- since의 특별 용법
since는 그 의미(~이래로 쭉~)의 특성으로 인해, 주절에는 반드시 현재완료시제가 와야 한다. (단, 비인칭주어 It이 주어로 쓰인 경우에는 현재형이 와도 무방하다.)

I have been ill since last week.
(나는 지난주부터 계속 아팠다.)
It is ten years since she died.
(그녀가 죽은 지 10년이 지났다.)

= Ten years have passed since she died. ● 주절에 '현재완료＋since＋과거시제'

1. She's just now arrived in Incheon international airport. (○ , ×)
(그녀는 인천 국제공항에 막 도착했다.)

2. Jake has lost his wallet last Sunday. (○ , ×)
(제이크는 지난 일요일 그의 지갑을 잃어버렸다.)

3. The group members have been expected to stay at home not long ago. (○ , ×)
(그 단체 회원들은 얼마 전에 집에 머무르기를 기대했다.)

4. There were a lot of serious talk about a merger lately. (○ , ×)
(최근에 합병에 관한 심각한 논의가 많이 있었다.)

5. When did you last have something to eat? (○ , ×)
(언제 마지막으로 먹을 게 있었니?)

6. What time have you waken her up? (○ , ×)
(언제 그녀를 깨웠니?)

[약점 POINT 6] 현재시제와 현재진행시제의 차이점

- 일반적이고 반복적인 일을 나타내는 현재시제는 '매일 아침'이라고 하는 every morning이라는 표현을 삽입해도 어법에 맞는 말이 된다. 그러나 현재진행형을 every morning과 함께 쓰면 틀린 문장이 된다. 그렇기 때문에 현재진행형에는 '오늘, 지금 상황' 만을 나타내는 this morning과 같은 부사구를 문장에 넣어주면 된다.
  이런 차이 때문에 현재시제는 종종 'always, usually, habitually, often' 과 같은 부사들과 함께 쓰이기도 한다.

1. Gregory is eating breakfast every morning. (○ , ×)
(그레고리는 매일 아침에 밥을 먹고 있다.)

2. John is eating breakfast this morning. (○ , ×)
(존은 오늘 아침에 밥을 먹고 있다.)

[약점 POINT 7] 현재완료 용법을 쓸 수 없는 경우

- 명백한 과거시제 표시 부사(구, 절)
  yesterday, last~, in 1950(과거 년도) 등이 있는 문장

- ago가 있는 문장

- 의문사 when, what time이 있는 문장

- just now가 있는 문장
  ❍ just는 현재완료와 함께 사용하나 just now는 반드시 과거시제와 함께 사용해야 한다.
  He has just come back home. (○) (그는 방금 집에 돌아왔다.)
  → He came home just now. (○)
  → He has come home just now. (×)

1. I have been to Seoul last month. (○ , ×)
(나는 지난 달에 서울에 다녀왔다.)

2. He has had an accident ten days ago. (○ , ×)
(그는 10일 전에 사고 났었다.)

3. When have you finished the work? (○ , ×)
(너 언제 그 일을 끝냈니?)

Answer

P5 1. X (just now → just) 2. X (has lost → lost) 3. X (have been expected → were expected) 4. X (were → have been) 5. O 6. X (have you waken her up → did you wake her up)

P6 1. X 2. O

P7 1. X 2. X 3. X

[약점 POINT 8] 미래시제 표현과 미래 의미의 관용어구

Shall의 용법
- 단순미래 : **I shall graduate from the college this year.** (나는 올해 대학을 졸업한다.)
- 예언 : **We shall overcome someday.** (우리는 언젠가는 곤경을 극복하고 말 것이다.)
- 의지 : **You shall have this book.** (이 책을 주겠다.)

미래 의미를 내포한 관용어구
- **be going to** + 동사원형 : ~할 예정이다
- **be due to** + 동사원형 : ~할 예정이다
- **be supposed to** + 동사원형 : ~할 예정이다
- **be about to** + 동사원형 : 막 ~하려고 하다
- **be to** + 동사원형 : ~할 예정이다

1. I am going to buy a new car tomorrow. (○ , ×)
(나는 내일 새 차를 살 예정이다.)

2. The president is due to speaking tomorrow. (○ , ×)
(회장은 내일 연설을 할 예정이다.)

3. She is supposed to arrive tonight. (○ , ×)
(그녀는 오늘 밤 도착할 예정이다.)

4. He is about to leaving home. (○ , ×)
(그는 막 집을 떠나려고 한다.)

5. John and Jane are to get married. (○ , ×)
(John과 Jane은 결혼할 예정이다.)

[약점 POINT 9] 상태를 나타내는 동사일지라도 '일시적인 상태' 를 나타낼 경우 진행형으로 쓸 수 있다.

1. I'm understanding what I have learnt. (○ , ×)
(나는 내가 이제까지 배워온 것들을 이해하고 있다.)

2. He is really differing from his brother. (○ , ×)
(그는 정말 그의 남동생과 다르다.)

3. I feel sorry for him who is lacking some competitiveness. (○ , ×)
(나는 그가 경쟁력이 얼마간 부족하다는 것에 대해 유감이다.)

4. My children are having a great time in their grandmother's home.(○ , ×)
(내 아이들은 그들의 할머니 맥에서 좋은 시간을 보내고 있다.)

5. Rose is being quite ugly today. (○, ×)

(로즈는 오늘 꽤 못생겨 보인다.)

[약점 POINT 10] 과거완료의 경우 과거완료시제를 필요로 하는 부사(up to that time, by 1990 …)가 나오는 경우에 쓸 수 있다.

과거완료는 기준시점인 '과거시제 부사어구' 를 수반하며, 연속되는 동작의 경우를 '과거 + 과거' 로 나타내는 것과는 구별해야 한다.

1. I had been waiting for an hour until he returned. (○, ×)

(나는 그가 돌아올 때까지 1시간을 기다렸다.)

2. By the time the war broke out, most of the people already left. (○, ×)

(전쟁이 발발할 때쯤, 많은 사람들이 이미 떠났다.)

3. Hardly did he arrived at the hotel before heavy snow came down. (○, ×)

(그가 호텔에 도착하자마자 폭설이 내렸다.)

4. I often heard about her before I met her. (○, ×)

(그녀를 만나기 전에 나는 종종 그녀에 대해 들었다.)

[약점 POINT 11] 미래완료는 기준시점인 '미래시제 부사(구)' 를 동반하고 특히, 완료의 by에 유의한다.

해석상 미래완료를 써야 하는 경우와, 형태상 'by + '미래 의미의 명사' , 'by the time + 주어 + 동사(미래시제 대용의 현재형)' 이 나오는 경우, 주절에는 반드시 미래완료를 써야 한다.

1. You shall have finished your homework by the time your mom comes back. (○, ×)

(너는 너의 엄마께서 돌아오시기 전까지 숙제를 끝마쳐야만 한다.)

2. Medical science will advance to a considerable degree by the end of this century. (○, ×)

(의학은 이번 세기 말이면 상당한 정도에까지 진보할 것이다.)

3. Jack will be an accountant by the time you get back to Korea. (○, ×)

(잭은 네가 한국에 돌아올 때쯤이면 회계사를 하고 있을 것이다.)

Answer

P8 1. ○ 2. X 3. ○ 4. X 5. ○

P9 1. X (I'm understanding → I understand) 2. X (He is really differing → He really differs) 3. X (who is lacking → who lacks) 4. ○ 5. ○

P10 1. ○ 2. X (most of the people already left → most of the people had already left) 3. X (Hardly did he arrived → Hardly had he arrived) 4. X (heard → had heard)

P11 1. ○ 2. X (will advance → will have advanced) 3. X (will be → will have been)

Part I. Choose the best answer for the blank.

1. A: I thought you said that you were going to study last night.
   B: I ___________, but my mom suddenly fell ill.
   (a) was supposed to
   (b) am going to
   (c) will
   (d) am

2. A: Anne, why are you so upset?
   B: Well, the fridge broke down and all of the food ___________.
   (a) goes bad
   (b) gone bad
   (c) has gone bad
   (d) going bad

3. A: Do you know what happened to his only daughter?
   B: Oh, she ___________ a performance artist.
   (a) is becoming
   (b) has became
   (c) became
   (d) had become

4. A: Is that man beside the vending machine new here?
   B: Oh, you mean Mr. Stone? He ___________ here since 1990.
   (a) worked
   (b) has worked
   (c) was working
   (d) had worked

5. A: Would you mind if I ___________ before you? I've got to make a very urgent call.
   B: Er... No, go ahead.
   (a) will go
   (b) went
   (c) have gone
   (d) had gone

6. A: Professor Cox, when is our final exam?

B: It ______________ on Friday.

(a) are

(b) is

(c) was

(d) were

Part II. Choose the best answer for the blank.

7. The girl ______________ going to the movies with her boyfriend this Saturday.

(a) will

(b) she always was

(c) she is

(d) is

8. Sally asked her father when ______________ leave for Italy.

(a) will he

(b) he will

(c) he would

(d) would he have

9. Of the 15 films Jason ______________ to date, the latest seems the best.

(a) made

(b) had made

(c) has made

(d) was making

10. The teacher ______________ his experimental paper on the table, then.

(a) lies

(b) lay

(c) laid

(d) lays

11. Slightly over half of the population of that region ___________ both English and French.
    (a) said
    (b) will speak
    (c) speaks
    (d) says

12. He ___________ the forum 5 times by next year.
    (a) had attended
    (b) will be attending
    (c) has attended
    (d) will have attended

13. Unless economic conditions improve next year, ___________ widespread unrest in Korea.
    (a) there would be
    (b) there should be
    (c) there is
    (d) there will be

14. He got very upset when the little boy ___________ his vase.
    (a) breaks
    (b) broke
    (c) has broken
    (d) is breaking

15. Don't forget to unplug the television before you ___________ to bed.
    (a) go
    (b) will go
    (c) went
    (d) have gone

16. When it is complete, the new sports arena ___________ 50,000 spectators.
    (a) seats
    (b) will seat
    (c) is seating
    (d) has seated

Part III. Identify the option that contains an awkward expression or an error in grammar.

17. (a) A: How long have you been in Korea?
    (b) B: Since September.
    (c) A: Oh, so by Christmas you will be here three months.
    (d) B: Yes, two months have passed since I came here.

18. (a) A: Do you know Korea is in a difficult economic situation?
    (b) B: Yes, I do. It's quite strange that the prosperous country faces economic difficulties.
    (c) A: I agree. However, Korean people are well educated and they have great potential.
    (d) B: So you are certain that all the difficulties have ironed out.

19. (a) A: Hey, Mike. Why didn't you attend the meeting this morning?
    (b) B: I'm sorry, but I get up late again.
    (c) A: I think you'd better go to bed earlier.
    (d) B: I think so, too.

Part IV. Identify the option that contains an awkward expression or an error in grammar.

20. (a) Concern has mounted for the safety of two American climbers who are missing in the Andes. (b) Their three companions, all French, raised the alarm when the climbers fail to arrive back at their base camp two days ago. (c) It is now becoming clear that a number of avalanches hit the area last week. (d) Local experts are blaming them on the unusually warm conditions for this time of year.

Chapter 03

수동태

Chapter 03 수동태

[약점 POINT 1] 수동태로 쓸 수 없는 타동사

- have, let, cost, resemble, lack, become, undergo…는 수동태로 쓸 수 없다.

- 사역동사 let과 have의 수동태 전환 : let → be allowed to, have → be asked to
  He had me sing. (그는 나에게 노래를 부르도록 시켰다.)
  → I was asked to sing by him. (나는 그에 의해서 노래를 부르라는 요청을 받았다.)
  He let me go. (그는 나를 보내 주었다.)
  → I was allowed to go by him. (나는 그에 의해 가라는 허락을 받았다.)

cf. have가 '얻다, ~을 입수하다'의 의미를 나타낼 때에는 수동형 to be had의 형태를 쓸 수 있다.
The book is nowhere to be had.
(그 책은 어디에서도 구할 수 없다.)

1. John's son is resembled by John. (○, ×)
(존의 아들은 존을 닮았다.)

2. Computer skill is lacked by him. (○, ×)
(그는 컴퓨터 능력이 부족하다.)

[약점 POINT 2] '당하다' 라는 표현

I had my purse stolen.
(나는 지갑을 훔침당했다-도둑맞았다)

'have (get) + 목적어 + 과거분사': …을 ~당하다, …을 ~시키다

1. I had my hair cut. (○, ×)
(나는 이발을 하도록 시켰다.)

2. I had my watch mended. (○, ×)
(나는 내 시계를 고치라고 시켰다.)

3. I had my wrist operating (○, ×)
(나는 허리 수술을 받았다.)

[약점 POINT 3] 'to + 동사원형' 이 수동의 뜻을 가지는 경우

a book to read = a book to be read
a house to let : 셋집
water to drink : 음료수

1. He is to blame. (○ , ×)
(그는 비난을 받아야 한다.)

2. We need something to believe in. (○ , ×)
(우리는 무언가를 믿어야 한다.)

[약점 POINT 4] 해석에 유의해야 할 완전자동사

do(충분하다), work(통하다, 효과가 있다, 운영되다), pay(=pay off)(이롭다, 득이 되다), matter(=count)(중요하다), go(=run)(…이다, …라고 하다)는 수동태로 쓰이면 틀린다.

1. It sometimes is paid to be humble in an interview. (○ , ×)
(때때로 인터뷰에서 겸손한 것이 이롭다.)

2. We'll probably never learn who stole the books, but it won't (matter, be mattered) for the time being.
(우리는 아마도 누가 그 책들을 훔쳤는지 알아내지 못할 테지만, 그것은 당분간은 문제가 되지 않을 것이다.)

<u>**Answer**</u>
P1   1. X (is resembled by →resembles) 2. X (is lacked by →He lacks computer skill.)
P2   1. O 2. O 3.X (operating →operated)
P3   1. O 2. O
P4   1. X (is paid →pays) 2. matter

[약점 POINT 5] 수동태로 표현하면 틀리는 자동사

> • disappear, vanish, expire, emerge from, occur to, last, consist of · in · with, resign from, retire from, result from · in, belong to, apologize to, object to, contribute to, experiment on · with, remain, appear, seem 등의 자동사는 수동태(be + p.p.)로 나타내지 못하며, 또한 전치사 없이 명사에 연결시킬 수 없다.

1. She (retired, was retired) from her company before her contract (expired, was expired).
(그녀는 계약이 만료되기 전에 회사에서 퇴직했다.)

2. The release of the two hostages (resulted from, was resulted from) the secret talks with the kidnappers.
(두 인질의 석방은 납치범들과의 비밀 면담에서 비롯되었다.)

3. The United Nations (consists of, is consisted of) more than 200 individual nations.
(유엔은 200개가 넘는 국가로 구성되어 있다.)

4. All my worries have been completely disappeared. (○ , ×)
(나의 모든 걱정이 완전히 사라졌다.)

[약점 POINT 6] 기타 수동태를 사용하지 않는 경우

> • that절은 수동태의 주어가 될 수 없다.
> • 간접목적어(IO) 앞에 to를 쓰는 동사 중 pass, hand, send, sell, write, read와 간접목적어 앞에 for를 쓰는 동사는 사람(간접목적어)을 수동태의 주어로 쓰지 않는다.
> • make와는 달리 사역동사 have와 let은 수동태로 쓰이지 않는다.
> • 재귀대명사는 수동태의 주어가 될 수 없다.
> • 소유동사 have, possess, belong to와 상태동사 resemble, lack, become(=suit, fit)과 같은 무의지 동사는 수동태로 나타내지 않는다.

1. That Jill is ill is said by them. (○ , ×)
(그들이 Jill이 아프다고 말했다.)

2. She was bought a watch by him. (○ , ×)
(그는 그녀에게 시계를 사주었다.)

3. I was passed the salt by Jack. (○ , ×)
(잭이 내게 소금을 건네주었다.)

4. Jack was had to promise never to discuss the subject again. (○ , ×)
(잭은 그 주제를 다시 토론하지 않기로 약속했다.)

5. Jack is let to go by Jill. (○ , ×)
(질은 잭을 가게 내버려 둔다.)

6. Herself is enjoyed by her. (○ , ×)
(그녀는 즐거운 시간을 보내고 있다.)

7. Its father is resembled by the kid. (○ , ×)
(아들은 아버지를 닮는다.)

[약점 POINT 7] 타동사구의 수동태 전환

- 타동사구(자동사+전치사) : wait for, object to, reply to, laugh at, look at
  → be동사 + 자동사 + p.p. + 전치사 + by + 명사
- 타동사구(타동사+명사+전치사) : pay attention to, take care of
  → be동사 + 타동사 + p.p. + 명사 + 전치사 + by + 명사

1. Jack was very shy but couldn't stand being laughed at. (○ , ×)
(잭은 매우 수줍은 성격이지만 비웃음당하는 것은 참지 못했다.)

2. While his mother was away, Jack was taken care by us. (○ , ×)
(그의 어머니가 안 계셨을 때, 잭은 우리에 의해 보살펴졌다.)

Answer

P5　1. retired, expired　2. resulted from　3. consists of　4. X (have been disappeared →have disappeared)

P6　1. X (that절은 수동태의 주어가 될 수 없다.)　2. X (간접목적어 앞에 to를 쓰는 동사 중 pass, hand, send, sell, write, read 와 간접목적어 앞에 for를 쓰는 동사는 사람(간접목적어)을 수동태의 주어로 쓰지 않는다.)　3. X　4. X　5. X　6. X　7. X

P7　1. O　2. X (taken care by → taken care of by)

[약점 POINT 8] 타동사구의 수동태

타동사구는 수동태에서 한 단위로 취급된다. 따라서 이중 전치사가 등장하거나 전치사로 끝나는 문장이 나오게 된다.

- 자동사 + 전치사 = 타동사구
  He laughed at me. (그는 나를 비웃었다.)
  → I was laughed at by him. (나는 그에 의해서 비웃음을 당했다.)
- 타동사 + 추상명사 + 전치사 = 타동사구
  They took good care of the child. (그들은 그 아이를 잘 돌보았다.)
  → The child was taken good care of (by them). (그 아이는 그들에 의해 좋은 보살핌을 받았다.)
  → Good care was taken of the child (by them).
- 동사 + 부사 + 전치사 = 타동사구
  The villagers looked up to the doctor. (마을 사람들은 그 의사를 존경했다.)
  → The doctor was looked up to by the villagers. (그 의사는 마을 사람들에게 존경을 받았다.)
  They speak well of Mary. (그들은 Mary를 칭찬한다.)
  → Mary is well spoken of (by them). (Mary는 그들에게 칭찬받는다.)

1. I was spoken by someone there. (○, ×)
(누군가가 거기서 나에게 말을 건넸다.)

2. He was taken good care of by his mother. (○, ×)
(그는 그의 엄마에 의해 보살핌을 받았다.)

3. The old doctor was looked up by the patients. (○, ×)
(환자들은 그 나이든 의사를 존경했다.)

[약점 POINT 9] 4형식의 수동태 전환

직접목적어(DO)를 수동태의 주어로 쓰는 경우, 능동태에서 4형식을 3형식으로 전환할 때 간접목적어(IO) 앞에 쓰이는 전치사를 그대로 쓴다.
(S + V + I.O + D.O → S + V + D.O + 전치사 + I.O)
- to 사용 동사 : send, tell, lend, give, offer, bring, owe, teach, show, write, read 등
- for 사용 동사 : buy, make, find, choose, get, cook, build 등
- of 사용 동사 : ask, inquire, require 등

- 간접목적어만 수동태의 주어가 될 수 있는 동사
  envy, call, kiss, answer, save, spare 등은 간접목적어만 수동태의 주어가 된다. 직접목적어를 수동태의 주어로 하는 경우 틀린 문장이 된다.
  They envied him his luck. (그들은 그의 행운을 부러워했다.)
  → **He was envied his luck by them.** (그는 그의 행운에 그들의 부러움을 샀다.)

1. That watch was bought for her by Jill. (○ , ×)
(그 시계는 질이 그녀를 위해 사준 것이었다.)

2. To attend the meeting in time, immediate departure was asked us. (○ , ×)
(제시간에 회의에 참석하기 위해서, 즉각적인 출발이 우리에게 요구된다.)

[약점 POINT 10] 5형식의 수동태 전환

- 능동태에서의 목적보어(OC)가 그대로 수동태의 주격보어(SC)로 쓰인다.
- 지각동사나 사역동사의 원형부정사 목적보어는 수동태에서는 ' to + 동사원형' 으로 쓰인다.

1. Jill was made marry a man she never knew. (○ , ×)
(질은 그녀가 알지 못하는 남자와 결혼하게 되었다.)

2. Jill was supposed to feed the pets while parents were abroad. (○ , ×)
(질은 부모님이 해외에 계시는 동안 애완동물들에게 먹이를 주기로 되어 있었다.)

3. A lot of breakthroughs were witnessed to be happened in the 1980s. (○ , ×)
(많은 발전이 1980년대에 발생하였다.)

Answer
P8 1. X(spoken →spoken to) 2. O 3. X(looked up →looked up to)
P9 1. O 2. X (asked us →asked of us)
P10 1. X (made marry →made to be married to) 2. O 3. X (to be happened →to happen)

[약점 POINT 11] 타동사의 수동태 의미 전용

사물 주어 + **sell**, **read**, **write**, **photograph**, **shrink**, **wash**, **drive** + 양태부사 구문에서 동사가 수동태로 쓰이면 틀린다.

1. Their new model car (is selling, is being sold) like hot cakes.
(그들의 신형 차는 불티나게 잘 팔린다.)

2. The road sign is read as follows. (○ , ×)
(도로의 표지판은 다음과 같다.)

[약점 POINT 12] 직접명령문을 수동태로 고치는 경우

직접명령문을 수동태로 고치면 간접명령문의 형태가 되기 때문에, 'Let + 목적어 + be + 과거분사' 의 형태를 사용한다. 이때 부정명령문의 형태는 'Don't let + 목적어 + be + 과거분사' 와 'Let + 목적어 + not + be + 과거분사' 두 가지가 있다.

1. Do it at once. (당장 그 일을 해라.)
  → (It, Let it) be done at once.

2. Don't touch the stone. (돌을 만지지 마라.)
  → Don't let the stone (is, be) touched.
  → Let the stone (not be, doesn't be) touched.

[약점 POINT 13] 자체에 부정 의미를 갖고 있는 주어의 경우

단어 자체에 부정의 의미를 갖고 있는 주어는 'by + 목적격' 으로 바꾸어 쓸 수가 없기 때문에 다음과 같이 바뀌어야 한다.

no → not + any	nobody → not + anybody
never → not + ever	nothing → not + anything
neither → not + either	no one → no + anyone

Nobody believed that she was rich. (아무도 그녀가 부자라는 것을 믿지 않았다.)

→ That she was rich is not believed by anybody.

→ It is not believed by anybody that she was rich.

→ She is not believed to have been rich by anybody.

1. It is believed by nobody. (○ , ×)

(그것은 아무도 믿지 않는다.)

2. That he was rich is believed by nobody. (○ , ×)

(그가 부자였다는 것을 아무도 믿지 않는다.)

[약점 POINT 14] 행위자를 나타내는 전치사를 by로 쓰지 않는 경우

능동문의 주어는 수동태에서 대개 전치사구로 나타나는데 그때의 대표적인 전치사는 **by**이지만, 동사에 따라 다른 전치사가 오는
경우가 있다.

- **with**　　be covered with~ : ~로 덮여 있다
　　　　　　be filled with~ : ~로 가득 차 있다
　　　　　　be satisfied with~ : ~에 만족하다
- **to**　　　be known to~ : ~에게 알려져 있다
- **at**　　　be surprised at ~ : ~에 놀라다
- **in**　　　be interested in ~ : ~에 관심이 있다
- **from**　　be made of~ : 완성품을 보고 원료를 추측할 수 있는 물리적인 변화
　　　　　　be made from~ : 완성품을 보고 원료를 추측할 수 없는 화학적인 변화

　　　　　　Most people don't realize that white wines, including champagne, are actually
　　　　　　made from red grapes.
　　　　　　(대부분의 사람들은 샴페인을 포함하여, 백포도주들은 실제 붉은 포도로 만들어진다는 사실을 깨닫지 못한다.)

1. The mountain is covered __________ snow.
　　(산이 눈에 뒤덮여 있다.)

2. The case is filled __________ beautiful flowers.
　　(꽃병이 아름다운 꽃들로 채워져 있다.)

3. I'm satisfied __________ my grade.
　　(나는 내 점수에 만족한다.)

4. The poet is known __________ everybody.
　　(그 시인은 모두에게 알려져 있다.)

5. I was surprised __________ his sudden death.
　　(나는 그의 갑작스런 죽음에 놀랐다.)

6. I am interested __________ this book.
　　(이 책은 나의 관심을 끈다.)

[약점 POINT 15] 동작수동과 상태수동

be동사 대신에 'become, grow, get + 과거분사'의 형태가 되면 '~하게 되다, ~당하다'의 뜻으로 어떤 일이 일어나는 동작을 나타내므로 동작수동이라고 한다.

I am acquainted with him. ◐상태
(나는 그와 알고 지내는 사이이다.)
I became acquainted with him at the party. ◐동작
(나는 그 파티에서 그를 알게 되었다.)

이와 다르게, 상태수동과 동작수동이 동시에 가능한 경우도 있다. 이때는 문맥에 맞게 해석하면 된다.
The gate is shut regularly at 6 p.m. every day. ◐동작수동
(문은 매일 규칙적으로 저녁 6시에 닫힌다.)
The gate is shut until 6 a.m. ◐상태수동
(문은 오전 6시까지 닫혀 있다.)

또한, 문장을 다시 능동태로 바꿀 때 상태수동은 행위가 이미 완료되어 있는 상태이므로 과거 관련 시제가 된다.
Our house is painted every year. ◐동작수동
(우리 집은 매년 도색된다.)
= They paint our house every year.
(그들은 매년 우리 집을 도색한다.)

Our house is painted white. ◐상태수동
(우리 집은 하얗게 칠해진다.)
= They have painted our house white.
(그들은 우리 집을 하얗게 칠했다.)

Part I. Choose the best answer for the blank.

1. A: You're late again. What's the matter with you?
   B: I'm sorry, but I got stuck ___________ traffic this time.
   (a) to
   (b) with
   (c) in
   (d) of

2. A: Since his wife's death, Cox has changed beyond recognition.
   B: Yes, he doesn't seem to care ___________ anything at all these days.
   (a) at
   (b) in
   (c) about
   (d) with

3. This restaurant is famous for its spaghetti. More than one million plates ___________.
   (a) have been served
   (b) have served
   (c) served
   (d) were served

4. Many people ___________ by the typhoon that hit the country in 1984.
   (a) killed
   (b) died
   (c) were died
   (d) were killed

5. Classicism which ___________ in Greece and continued in ancient Rome was the principal
   contributor to that aspect of our life which is usually referred to as secular.
   (a) was originated
   (b) originated
   (c) originates
   (d) originating

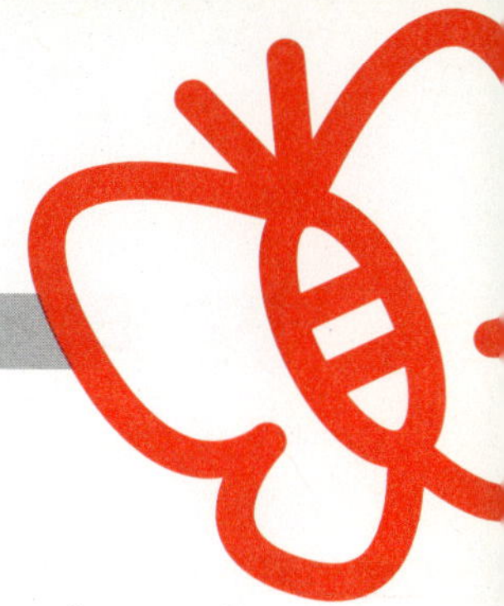

6. It was agreed that the prisoner ___________ the right to see living people and to receive letters and newspapers during imprisonment.
    (a) deprive of
    (b) deprived of
    (c) would deprive of
    (d) would be deprived of

7. The advantages of computerized typing and editing are now ___________ to all the languages of the world.
    (a) being extended
    (b) being extending
    (c) extending
    (d) extended

8. Cox has suffered from diabetes for several years, and now Jill ___________ a similar problem.
    (a) faced
    (b) face
    (c) faces
    (d) was faced

9. The government ___________ about the dangerous levels of exhaust pollution in city centers.
    (a) has concerned
    (b) has been concerning
    (c) has become concerned
    (d) was concerning

[고난이도] 10. Any change in address should be ___________.
    (a) notify the bank
    (b) notified to the bank
    (c) notified for the bank
    (d) notifying for the bank

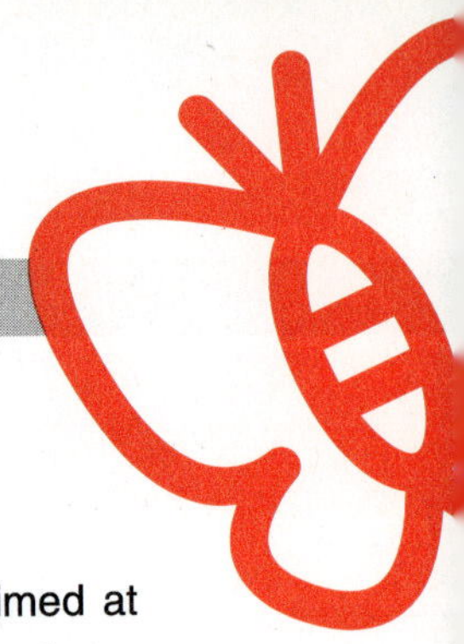

11. North Korea proposed to South Korea that the third round of Red Cross talks aimed at discussing the reunion of families separated by the Korean War ___________ this month.
(a) hold
(b) be held
(c) to hold
(d) to be held

Part III. Identify the option that contains an awkward expression or an error in grammar.

12. (a) Excuse me, are you being served?
(b) No. We have been waited for you to come here.
(c) Sorry, sir. May I take your order then?
(d) Sure, two pieces of chocolate cakes and two cups of milk please.

13. (a) Are you good at dealing with machine?
(b) No. Do you have any problem with your computer?
(c) Not my computer but this MP3 player is a troublesome.
(d) You must have it fix to enjoy listening to music.

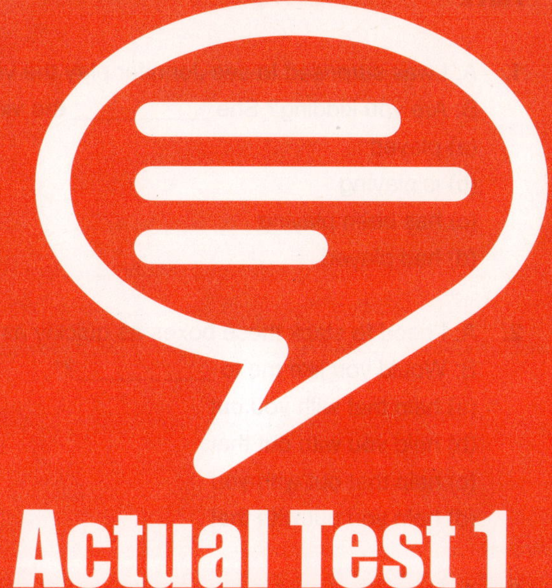

Actual Test 1

Actual Test 1

Part I. Choose the best answer for the blank.

1. A: I was surprised to see Jennifer play the violin so well.
B: Are you kidding? She ___________ the violin since the 3rd grade!
(a) played
(b) is playing
(c) has been playing
(d) had played

[고난이도] **2.** A: I need to stack these boxes as quickly as possible.
B: Would you like me to ___________?
(a) help that with you out
(b) help you with out that
(c) help that out with you
(d) help you out with that

3. A: Have you found any trace of the suspect, detective?
B: No. Neither of the rooms seems to ___________ in.
(a) sleep
(b) have slept
(c) being slept
(d) have been slept

[고난이도] **4.** A: Don't be late for the appointment with the manager.
B: I won't. I know he ___________ on time.
(a) stresses being
(b) stresses to be
(c) stresses
(d) puts stresses

5. I doubt that people will drink less even if the government ___________ a new tax on alcohol.
   (a) is imposing
   (b) will impose
   (c) imposes
   (d) have been imposing

6. We often hear it ___________ that the new missile will solve our defense problems.
   (a) say
   (b) said
   (c) saying
   (d) says

7. I ___________ when I found his work was so sloppy.
   (a) was disappointing
   (b) was disappointed
   (c) am disappointing
   (d) am disappointed

8. If ___________, you will receive full medical insurance and other perks.
   (a) employing
   (b) being employer
   (c) employed
   (d) having employed

Part III. **Identify the option that contains an awkward expression or an error in grammar.**

9. (a) A: Mary looks so fit.
   (b) B: I know. She's working out these days.
   (c) A: Oh? But I thought she hated working out.
   (d) B: Yes, but I convinced her starting.

Part IV. Identify the option that contains an awkward expression or an error in grammar.

10. (a) Christopher Columbus discovered the US Virgin Islands in 1493 on his second voyage to the New World. (b) He so overwhelmed by their beauty that he called them 'The Virgins.' (c) The Danish West India Company purchased and united all three islands under Danish rule. (d) Afterwards they were transformed into one of the major sugar producers in the region.

Chapter 04

조동사

Chapter 04 조동사

[약점 POINT 1] 조동사 + have + p.p.

> - 조동사를 이용한 지난 일에 대한 판단은 조동사 자체의 현재형 · 과거형과 상관없이 조동사의 뒤를 완료시제(have + p.p.)로 나타낸다.
>
> - 중요 표현
>   would have p.p.: ~했을 것이다
>   may(might) have p.p.: ~했을지도 모른다
>   could have p.p.: ~했을 수도 있다
>   must have p.p.: ~했음이 틀림없다
>   cannot have p.p.: …했을리가 없다
>   should(ought to, had better) have p.p.: ~했어야 했다(그런데 안 했다)
>   would rather have p.p.: ~하는 편이 나았을 것이다(그러나 안 했다)
>   need not have p.p.: ~할 필요가 없었다(그런데 했다)

1. Jack must have attended the meeting last weekend, but he didn't. (○, ×)
   (잭은 지난 주말에 회의에 참석했어야만 했는데 그러지 않았다.)

2. A: Why did you get angry with her?
   (왜 그녀에게 화를 냈니?)
   B: I don't know. I should. (○, ×)
   (나도 모르겠어. 그럴 필요는 없었는데.)

3. Jack would rather have to marry Jill. (○, ×)
   (잭은 질과 결혼하는 편이 나았을 것이다.)

[약점 POINT 2] used to의 용법

- **used to** + 동사원형
  과거의 불규칙적인 습관은 **would**로, 과거의 규칙적인 습관은 '**used to** + 동사원형' 으로 나타낸다.

  There used to be a tall tree beside our house.
  (예전에 우리 집 옆에 큰 나무 한 그루가 있었다.)

  I used to get up early. (나는 일찍 일어나곤 했었다.)
  = I was in the habit of getting up early.
  = I made it a rule to get up early.
  = I made a point of getting up early.
  = I made it a point to get up early.

- **be used to** + 명사, 동명사
  be used to 다음에 반드시 명사 또는 동명사가 오며 '~에 익숙하다' 의 뜻을 갖는다. 그러나 **be accustomed to** 다음에는 동사원형 또는 명사나 동명사가 모두 쓰인다.

  He is used to Japanese food. (그는 일본 음식에 익숙하다.)
  He is used to driving a car. (그는 차를 운전하는 것에 익숙하다.)
  = He is accustomed to drive a car.
  = He is accustomed to driving a car.

1. I used to going to the zoo when I was young. (○ , ×)
(나는 어릴 때 동물원에 가곤 했다.)

2. I am used to learn new things. (○ , ×)
(나는 새로운 것들을 배우는 것에 익숙하다.)

Answer

P1 1. X (must have attended →should have attended) 2. X (should →need not have gotten) 3. X
(have to marry →have married)

P2 1. X(going →go) 2. X(learn →learning)

- **used to**는 과거의 규칙적 습관 또는 현재와 다른 과거의 사실을, **would**는 흔히 '빈도부사'와 함께 과거의 불규칙적인 습관을, **will**은 주어의 불변적 습관 또는 성향을 나타낸다.

- **would like to(=want to)**는 사용하나, **would want to**는 사용하지 않는다.

- **would rather(=sooner) leave than stay**
  = **would as soon leave as stay**
  = **prefer to leave rather than (to) stay**
  = **prefer leaving to staying**
  = **may(might) as well leave as stay**

- '**would rather + (that)절**'의 구문에서 **that**절의 동사는 가정법으로 나타낸다.

- **Would you mind if I smoked?**
  = **Do you mind if I smoke?**

1. I would want to spend Christmas at home this year. (○ , ×)
(나는 올해 집에서 크리스마스를 보내고 싶다.)

2. You would rather help people than to cheat them. (○ , ×)
(너는 사람들을 속이기보다 도울 것이다.)

3. Would you mind as I open the window? (○ , ×)
(내가 창문을 연다면 꺼려 하시겠습니까?)

[약점 POINT 4] 주어 + 명령 · 주장 · 강조 · 요구동사 + that + 주어 + (should) 동사원형 + ~

- 동사의 뜻이 제안(**propose, suggest**), 주장 · 요구(**insist, urge, require, request, demand**), 명령 (**command, order**), 조언 · 추천(**advise, recommend**), 동의 · 재청(**move, second**), 조건 · 규정 (**condition, stipulate**)의 타동사이어야 한다.—시제 관계없음
- 목적어 자리에 **that** (명사절)이 와야 한다.
- 목적어 **that** (명사절)의 내용이 주어의 주관적인 판단이나 주장이어야 한다. (객관적인 사실일 경우 해당되지 않음)

1. They strongly suggested that the store improves its service. (○, ×)
(그들은 그 상점이 서비스를 개선해야만 한다고 강력하게 제안했다.)

2. Jack demanded that the newspaper print a full apology. (○, ×)
(잭은 그 신문이 사과문을 실을 것을 요구했다.)

3. Jill insisted that Tom to go with her for shopping. (○, ×)
(질은 톰에게 자기와 함께 쇼핑 가자고 고집했다.)

- **had better** + 동사원형 : ~하는 게 낫겠다
  권유의 **should**와 의미는 비슷하나 **had better**는 약간 경고의 뉘앙스를 지닌다.
  You'd better not go to school now. (지금 학교에 가지 않는 것이 낫겠다.)
  had better를 덩어리로 하나의 조동사처럼 여기기 때문에 not이 뒤에 위치한다.

- **would rather A than B** : B 보다 차라리 A하다 = **would like to** 동사원형
  I would rather die than live in dishonor. (불명예스럽게 사느니 죽겠다.)
  I would rather have a big lunch than a big dinner.
  (저는 푸짐한 저녁 식사보다 푸짐한 점심 식사가 더 좋아요.)

- **may(might) as well A as B** : B 보다 A 하는 게 낫겠다 = **had better**
  I might as well walk as drive. (차를 타고 갈 바엔 차라리 걸어가겠다.)
  cf. 실현 가능성이 있을 때는 may를 사용하고 실현 불가능한 일일 경우는 might를 사용한다.

- **may well** + 동사원형 : ~하는 것이 당연하다
  cf. 과거 : **may well have** + p.p.
  He may well say so.
  (그가 그렇게 말하는 것이 당연하다.)

- **He may well not say so.**
  (그가 그렇게 말하지 않는 것이 당연하다.)

- **cannot(couldn't) but** + 동사원형 : ~하지 않을 수 없다
  = **cannot help -ing**
  = **have no choice but to** 부정사
  I cannot but laugh. (나는 웃지 않을 수 없다.)
  = **I cannot help laughing.**

- **cannot ~ too** : 아무리 ~해도 지나치지 않다
  You cannot be too careful when it comes to driving a car.
  (차를 운전하는 것에 대해서는 네가 아무리 조심해도 지나치지 않다.)

1. You'd better go to school now. (○ , ×)
  (지금 학교에 가는 것이 낫겠다.)

2. I would rather be an optimist than a pessimist. (○ , ×)
(저는 염세주의자가 되기보다는 오히려 낙천주의자가 되겠습니다.)

3. You may well not knowing a thing at all as know it imperfectly. (○ , ×)
(그것을 불완전하게 아느니, 차라리 전혀 모르는 것이 낫다.)

4. Housewives may as well complain about their daily routine. (○ , ×)
(주부들이 틀에 박힌 그들의 일상에 대해 불평하는 것은 당연하다.)

5. The Administration cannot but looking for alternative sources of revenue. (○ , ×)
(정부는 다른 세입원을 구할 수밖에 없다.)

[약점 POINT 6] 유의해야 할 조동사 특징

- had better not, would rather not, ought not to, used not to(=didn't used to) 등의 조동사구
  에서 not의 위치에 유의한다.
- Have some more, won't you?(권유문), Wait for me downstairs, will you?(명령문), Let's go
  for a drive, shall we?(제안문)의 부가의문문의 형태에 유의한다.

Brian used to have his own office. ○ 예전엔 ~하곤 했었다, 과거엔 ~이었다
(브라이언은 과거에 그의 개인 소유의 사무실을 가지고 있었다.)

Jack is not used to asking a favor of people. ○ ~에 익숙하다
(잭은 사람들에게 부탁을 하는 것에 익숙하지 않다.)

Dictionaries are used to look up unfamiliar words. ○ ~에 사용된다
(사전은 친숙하지 않은 단어들을 찾는 데에 사용된다.)

1. Jill had not better ask her father for the car key. (○ , ×)
(질은 그녀의 아버지에게 차 열쇠를 요구하지 않는 것이 낫겠다.)

2. Jack used not to smoke before, but nowadays he does. (○ , ×)
(잭은 전에 담배를 피우지 않았지만, 지금은 담배를 피운다.)

3. Let's stop about here and take a short break, will we? (○ , ×)
(여기에서 멈춰서 잠시 휴식을 취하자, 그렇게 할 거지?)

Answer

P5 1. ○ 2. ○ 3. X (may well not → may as well not know) 4. X (may as well → may well) 5. X
(looking → look)

P6 1. X (had not better → had better not) 2. X (used not to → didn't use to) 3. X (will we → shall we)

[약점 POINT 7] 조동사 can의 활용법

- cannot...without~ : …할 때마다 ~하다, …하려면 ~해야 한다
- cannot...too much(to excess, enough, fully) : 아무리 …해도 지나치지 않는다

1. I cannot see this picture without thinking of her. (○, ×)
(나는 이 사진을 보면 그녀를 생각하게 된다.)

2. These pills can rarely be efficacious without being taken everyday. (○, ×)
(이 알약들은 매일 섭취하지 않으면 거의 효능이 없을 수 있다.)

3. You cannot praise your secretary for her savvy any much. (○, ×)
(당신은 비서의 재치를 아무리 칭찬해도 지나치지 않아요.)

[약점 POINT 8] 조동사 need의 활용법

- 의문문과 부정문에서는 조동사로 사용되나, 그 외에는 일반동사로 사용된다.
- 부정문(not 앞에)과 의문문(문두)에 쓰이는 조동사 need는 수와 시제가 존재하지 않으며, 원형동사가 연결된다.
- 긍정문의 본동사 need는 수(needs)와 시제(needed)가 있고, to + 동사원형을 목적어로 취한다.

1. Jill doesn't need apologize. (○, ×)
(질은 사과할 필요가 없다.)

2. Needs he attend the meeting? (○, ×)
(그가 회의에 참여할 필요가 있나요?)

[약점 POINT 9] 부정문, 의문문에서의 조동사 need / dare

need와 dare는 조동사로 쓰일 수 있다는 공통점이 있다. 긍정의 평서문에서는 둘 다 본동사로 쓰이며 본동사로 쓰일 경우 to 부정사를 목적어로 취한다(조동사로 쓰이는 경우에는 동사원형을 목적어로 취한다). 의문문이나 부정문으로 쓰이는 경우에는 본동사냐, 조동사냐에 따라서 형식이 달라진다.

- need
  He needs your help. ○ 긍정문 - 본동사
  (그는 너의 도움을 필요로 한다.)

He need not go there. ○ 부정문 - 조동사
= He does not need to go there. ○ 본동사
(그는 거기에 갈 필요가 없다.)
Need I go there? ○ 의문문 - 조동사
(내가 거기에 갈 필요가 있니?)
cf. need not have + p.p. : ~할 필요가 없어서 ~했다
    did not need to ~ : ~할 필요가 없었다

He need not have written to her again. ○ 조동사
(그는 그녀에게 편지를 다시 쓸 필요가 없었는데 ― 그런데도 썼다.)

He did not need to write to her again. ○ 본동사
(그는 그녀에게 편지를 다시 쓸 필요가 없었다. ― 썼는지의 여부는 모름)

- dare : 부정문, 의문문에서 조동사로 쓰여 '감히 ~하다'
  I dare not go there.
  (나는 감히 거기에 갈 수가 없다.)

  How dare you say such a thing to my face?
  (내 면전에서 네가 감히 그런 말을 할 수 있는가?)

- dare to do : 본동사로서 '감히 ~하다'
  dare say = probably = perhaps = maybe : 아마

  He does not dare to tell us.
  (그는 감히 우리에게 말을 할 수가 없다.)

Part I. Choose the best answer for the blank.

1. A: Do you smoke?
B: No, but I ___________.
(a) must not
(b) used to
(c) do
(d) dare to

Part II. Choose the best answer for the blank.

2. The damage from the accident was so severe that I ___________ as well buy a new car.
(a) do
(b) was
(c) might
(d) shall

3. He must ___________ that he was supposed to pick me up at lunch time.
(a) have forgotten
(b) forgotten
(c) forget
(d) had forgotten

4. Tom often wore a heavy coat because he was not ___________ in such a cold climate.
(a) used living
(b) used to live
(c) used to living
(d) accustomed to live

5. The broken window has caused a lot of accidents. It ___________ repaired a long time ago.
(a) must be
(b) should have
(c) must have been
(d) should have been

6. You ____________ your visa extended before it expires.
    (a) had better get
    (b) had to get better
    (c) had better to get
    (d) had better got

7. It is hard to escape the conclusion that this project ____________.
    (a) should ever been started
    (b) never should been begun
    (c) has never have been begun
    (d) shouldn't have been begun

8. My tomb________________ in a spot where the north wind may scatter the roses over it.
    (a) will be
    (b) shall be
    (c) would be
    (d) was

Part III. **Identify the option that contains an awkward expression or an error in grammar.**

9. (a) A: You have a bruise on your right cheek. What happened?
    (b) B: I walked into the bathroom door.
    (c) A: Oh no! That must have hurt.
    (d) B: Yeah. They have.

Chapter 05

가정법

Chapter 05 가정법

[약점 POINT 1] 가정법과 직설법의 혼용

- 한 절 속에 가정과 직설이 섞여 있는 경우에도 가정법 형태는 그대로 쓰인다.
- 한 절은 가정, 한 절은 직설로 나타낸 구문에서 시제와 접속사에 유의한다.

1. If she (knew, had known) that you were ill, she would have visited you.
(그녀는 네가 아픈 걸 알았더라면, 너를 방문했을 것이다.)

2. I didn't know your number then, (if, so, but, or) I would have called you.
(나는 그때 너의 번호를 알지 못했다. 그렇지 않았으면 너에게 전화했을 것이다.)

3. He took a taxi to the airport last night; otherwise he would (miss, have missed) his flight.
(그는 어젯밤 택시를 타고 공항에 갔다; 그렇지 않았으면 그는 그의 비행기를 놓쳤을 것이다.)

[약점 POINT 2] If 생략 시 도치

if가 생략되면 주어 동사(조동사)는 도치가 된다.

1. Be it not for his injury, Jack could play in the field. (○, ×)
(그의 부상이 아니었다면, 잭은 경기에서 뛸 수 있었을 것이다.)

2. Were a fire to break out, we would jump down.(○, ×)
(화재가 발생하면, 우리는 뛰어내릴 것이다.)

[약점 POINT 3] 가정법의 기본 형태

- 가정법 과거 (현재사실 반대)
  If + 주어 + 과거동사, 주어 + 과거조동사 + 동사원형
  It is (about, high, the right, the very) time + 주어 + 과거동사(=should + 동사원형)
  I wish (that) 주어 + 과거동사

- 가정법 과거완료 (과거사실 반대)
  If + 주어 + **had** 과거분사, 주어 + 과거조동사 + **have** 과거분사
  I wish (that) 주어 + **had** 과거분사

- 혼합가정법 (조건절-가정법 과거완료시제, 주절-가정법 과거시제)

  If + 주어 + **had** + 과거분사, 주어 + 과거조동사 + 동사원형

- 가정법 미래

  If + 주어 + **should** + 동사원형, 주어 + 과거조동사(현재조동사) + 동사원형

  If + 주어 + **were to** + 동사원형, 주어 + 과거조동사 + 동사원형

  If + 주어 + **would** + 동사원형, 주어 + 과거(현재)조동사 + 동사원형

1. If you had four kids to take care of, how could you manage it? (○ , ×)
(만약 네가 돌보아야 할 4명의 아이가 있었다면, 너는 어떻게 했을 것 같니?)

2. If things had changed, we might make a bigger profit. (○ , ×)
(사정이 달라졌더라면, 우리는 더 큰 이윤을 얻을 수 있었을 텐데.)

3. I wish I will take their offer at that time. (○ , ×)
(내가 그때 그들의 제안을 받아들였다면 좋았을 텐데.)

4. If the war had not happened, he would live on the farm now. (○ , ×)
(만약 전쟁이 발발하지 않았더라면, 그는 지금쯤 농장에 살고 있을 것이다.)

5. If you were to speak Chinese, you should have enjoyed more opportunities. (○ , ×)
(네가 중국어를 말한다면, 너는 더 많은 기회를 누릴 것이다.)

6. Jack thinks it's about time we will think carefully before making any decision. (○ , ×)
(잭은 우리가 결정을 내리기 전에 신중하게 생각해야 할 때라고 생각했다.)

Answer

P1   1. had known 2. or 3. have missed
P2   1. X (Be →Were) 2. O
P3   1. O 2. O 3. X (will take →had taken) 4. O 5. X (have enjoyed →enjoy) 6. X (will think → thought or should think)

[약점 POINT 4] 가정법을 사용하는 다양한 구문

- I wish + 주어 + 동사의 과거형, had + p.p.
- as if (though) + 동사의 과거형, had + p.p.
- It is (high) time + 동사의 과거형 (should + 동사원형) : ~해야 할 때이다
- would rather + 동사의 과거형 (had + p.p.) : ~한다면 좋을 텐데, ~했더라면 좋았을 텐데
- If it were not for = But for = Without (현재) : ~가 없다면
  If it had not been for (과거) : ~가 없었더라면

1. I wish you come back to me. (○ , ×)
(나는 당신이 내게 돌아왔으면 좋겠다.)

2. It is time that you went to school. (○ , ×)
(네가 학교에 가야 할 때이다.)

3. I would rather take a trip to India although my parents were strongly opposed to it. (○ , ×)
(비록 내 부모님이 강하게 반대하시지만, 나는 인도로 여행을 가는 게 낫겠다.)

4. If it were not for my cold, we could take a trip together. (○ , ×)
(내 감기가 아니었더라면, 우리는 함께 여행할 수 있었을 텐데.)

5. You pretend to be ok as if you were Superman or something. (○ , ×)
(당신은 슈퍼맨이나 되는 것처럼 괜찮은 척하는군요.)

Answer

P4　1. X (come back →had come back or came)　2. O　3. X (take →took or had taken)　4. O　5. O

Part I. Choose the best answer for the blank.

[고난이도] **1.** A: How did Catherine respond to her boss's questions?
B: She didn't flinch. She responded as if she ___________ the upper hand.
(a) has had
(b) had
(c) had had
(d) did have

2. A: You didn't bring your umbrella? It's pouring outside.
B: I would have, if I ___________ the weather was going to be like this.
(a) had known
(b) knew
(c) could know
(d) have known

3. A: The party was just awful.
B: Well, it ___________ worse.
(a) could be
(b) must have been
(c) could have been
(d) had been

[고난이도] **4.** A: ___________ anything unexpected happen, just let me know.
B: I sure will. Thanks.
(a) Would
(b) Should
(c) Could
(d) Might

5. A: Did you finish your homework, Sally?
B: I would have if ___________.
(a) I were enough time
(b) I have enough time
(c) I don't have enough time
(d) I'd had enough time

6. A: Cox injured her back while she was using the parallel bars.

    B: That's too bad. She __________ more careful.

    (a) should have been

    (b) shouldn't have been

    (c) must have been

    (d) need not have been

Part III. Choose the best answer for the blank.

7. I wish that my sponsored child __________ live happily ever after.

    (a) will

    (b) would

    (c) being

    (d) were

8. I would rather __________ things I could not have than had things I was not able to appreciate.

    (a) have appreciated

    (b) appreciate

    (c) appreciated

    (d) had appreciated

9. But for my help, you would __________ after all.

    (a) have failed

    (b) had failed

    (c) failed

    (d) fail

10. He looked at her as if he __________ her before.

    (a) saw

    (b) didn't see

    (c) had never seen

    (d) have never seen

11. It is about time you ___________ virtual reality technology to express our computer program.
    (a) use
    (b) have used
    (c) used
    (d) had used

12. ___________ been blocked completely, the patient would have died.
    (a) The cell were to
    (b) Had the cell
    (c) If the cell
    (d) The cell is

13. ___________ resigned, the committee would have been forced to sack him.
    (a) Had he not
    (b) Have he not
    (c) He had not
    (d) He not had

Part IV. Identify the option that contains an awkward expression or an error in grammar.

14. (a) My friend told me that I was ready to ski down from the top of the mountain. (b) I told him I wasn't confident enough, but he kept persuading me to go to the top with him. (c) So, in the end, I agreed, but on the way down I lost control and ended up breaking my leg. (d) If I hadn't listened to him, I wouldn't have been in this situation.

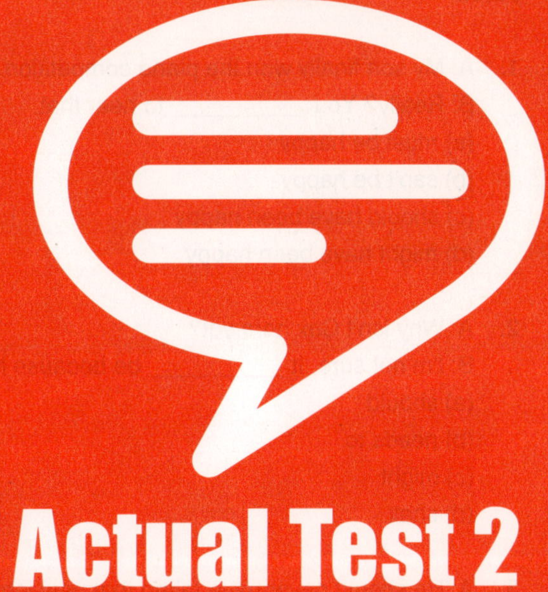

Actual Test 2

Part I. **Choose the best answer for the blank.**

1. A: My son finally won the piano competition.
B: Really? You ___________ to hear that.
(a) must be happy
(b) can't be happy
(c) should have been happy
(d) might have been happy

2. A: Why isn't Cox here yet?
B: I'm not sure. It ___________ be because his mother is ill again.
(a) should
(b) needs to
(c) might
(d) shall

3. A: He should never have taken that new job.
B: If only he ___________ to his wife's advice.
(a) had listened
(b) has listened
(c) listens
(d) is listening

[고난이도] **4.** A: We've decided to stage a play for a foundation day.
B: ___________ to decide which play will be performed?
(a) Whose will be
(b) Whose
(c) Who will be
(d) Who is

Part II. Choose the best answer for the blank.

5. If Mr. Cox is promoted, as I sincerely hope he __________, he will have to move to Chicago.
    (a) could
    (b) will be
    (c) should
    (d) should be

6. The woman __________ anything to have the painting she saw at the gallery.
    (a) had given
    (b) gives
    (c) should give
    (d) would have given

7. The widespread use of petroleum to make chemicals __________ in the early 20th century.
    (a) had begun
    (b) has begun
    (c) began
    (d) begun

8. The vacation starts next Friday. We __________ to class until mid-September.
    (a) need to not go
    (b) need to go
    (c) don't need to go
    (d) not need to go

Part III. Identify the option that contains an awkward expression or an error in grammar.

9. (a) A: What did you do at the weekend?
    (b) B: I visited the university where my father graduated from.
    (c) A: Is it located nearby?
    (d) B: No, it's not. It's 40 miles away from here.

Part IV. Identify the option that contains an awkward expression or an error in grammar.

10. (a) Whenever I made a mistake, no matter how small, my father would had punished me severely. (b) He had huge expectations that I had to live up to, and he would never change his attitude. (c) Even after I entered college, my father still tried to run my life. (d) He just wouldn't let me decide for myself.

Chapter 06

부정사

Chapter 06 부정사

[약점 POINT 1] 준동사의 동사적 성질 : 의미상 주어

- to부정사의 의미상 주어는 일반적으로 그 앞에 'for + 명사'
- 사람의 성질·성격에 대한 칭찬 및 비난을 나타내는 형용사(kind, thoughtful, considerate, generous, nice, clever, foolish, stupid, rude, cruel)가 오면 'of + 명사'

1. It's kind of you helping me. (○, ×)
(저를 도와주시다니 친절하시군요.)

2. To get a habit of waking up early in the morning is quite hard for me. (○, ×)
(아침에 일찍 일어나는 습관을 갖는 것은 내게 무척 어렵다.)

[약점 POINT 2] to부정사를 목적어로 가지는 타동사

want, expect, hope, wish, care, desire, long, plan, design, prepare, decide, determine, resolve, choose, arrange, promise, swear, agree, assent, consent, afford, tend, pretend, refuse, threaten, seek, struggle, strive, dare + to부정사

1. I was just wondering how he dared to say that to me. (○, ×)
(나는 어떻게 그가 감히 내게 그러한 말을 했는지 궁금했다.)

2. The House resolved taking up the bill. (○, ×)
(의회는 법안을 채택하기로 결의했다.)

[약점 POINT 3] be + to부정사 용법

to부정사는 시간적으로 미래를 나타내므로 'be + to부정사'의 형식, 즉 상태동사 be와 결합하여 다음과 같은 의미를 나타내게 된다.

We were to leave yesterday. ○ 예정
(우리는 어제 떠날 예정이었다.)

You are to finish it by seven. ○ '의무'를 나타낸다.
(당신은 일곱 시까지 그것을 끝내야 합니다.)

Study hard if you are to pass the exam. ○ '의도·소망'을 나타낸다.
(시험에 합격하려면 열심히 공부해라.)

The car is not to be bought with this money. ❍가능성을 나타낸다.
(그 차는 이 돈으로는 살 수 없다.)

He was never to see his native country again. ❍운명을 나타낸다.
(그는 자신의 조국을 다시는 못 볼 운명이었다.)

1. I am to climbing Mt. Halla this summer vacation. (○ , ×)
(나는 이번 여름방학에 한라산에 오를 예정이다.)

2. I am to meet him at my hometown someday. (○ , ×)
(나는 언젠가 그를 나의 고향에서 만날 것이다.)

Answer

P1 1. X (helping →to help) 2. O
P2 1. O 2. X (taking →to take)
P3 1. X (climbing → climb) 2. O

[약점 POINT 4] 독립부정사

독립부정사란 주절과 문법적으로 독립된 관계(보통 주절의 주어와 부정사의 의미상의 주어가 다르다)에 있는 부정사로, 문장 전체를 수식하는 부사구로서의 역할을 하는 부정사를 말한다.

To tell the truth, I don't believe it.
(솔직히 말하면 나는 그것을 믿지 않는다.)
He is, so to speak, a walking dictionary.
(말하자면 그는 걸어다니는 사전이다.)
She is charming, to be sure.
(확실히 그녀는 매력적이다.)

독립부정사는 문두에 오는 것이 일반적이지만, 문장 중간이나 문미에도 올 수 있다. 이외에 자주 쓰이는 독립부정사는 다음과 같다.
to begin with (우선, 첫째로)
to make matters worse (설상가상으로)
to be brief (간단히 말하면)
to make a long story short (간단히 말하면)
to tell the truth (진실을 말하면)
to be frank with you (솔직히 말하면)

1. (To tell the truth/Telling the truth), she is not fair.
(솔직히 말해서 그녀는 아름다운 것은 아니다.)

2. She is, (so/as) to speak, like a flower.
(그녀는 말하자면 꽃과 같은 존재이다.)

[약점 POINT 5] 준동사의 명사적 용법 : 일반 주의사항

- 명사적 용법에서 의문사와 함께 쓰이는 것은 to부정사이다.
- 명사적 용법에서 전치사의 목적어 역할을 하는 것은 동명사이지만, 전치사 뒤에 (to) 동사원형이 결합되는 구문에도 유의한다.
- look forward to -ing, get used(accustomed) to -ing, what do you say to -ing, when it comes to -ing, with a view to -ing, lead to -ing, come near (to) -ing, be addicted to -ing, devote oneself to -ing, object to -ing, see to -ing, take to -ing, a solution(secret, key, answer, approach) to -ing 같은 'to + -ing' 구문을 'to+동사원형' 구문과 혼동하지 않도록 유의한다.

1. Could you explain to me (how filling in, how to fill in) this tax form?
(이 세금 양식을 작성하는 법을 설명해주시겠어요?)

2. He does nothing but (complain, to complain) about his work.
(그는 자기 일에 대해 불평하는 것 외엔 아무것도 안 한다.)

3. As there was no hot water for coffee, he couldn't but (boil, to boil) the water.
(커피를 끓이기 위한 뜨거운 물이 없었으므로, 그는 물을 끓일 수밖에 없었다.)

4. We bought the house with a view to (settle, settling) down there after retirement.
(우리는 퇴직 후에 그곳에 정착할 생각으로 그 집을 구입했다.)

5. I look forward to meeting you at your earliest convenience. (○ , ×)
(나는 되도록 빨리 당신을 만나기를 고대합니다.)

6. The new regulations will lead to (improve, improving) our water supply.
(새로운 규정은 우리들의 급수 시설을 향상시킬 것이다.)

[약점 POINT 6] to부정사의 명사적 용법

문장의 주어, 목적어, 보어, 역할을 하는데 주로 타동사의 목적어 역할을 한다.

1. I've agreed (teaching, to teach) Sarah to drive this weekend.
(나는 이번 주말에 사라에게 운전을 가르쳐 주기로 동의했다.)

2. I intend trying windsurfing when summer comes. (○ , ×)
(나는 여름이 오면 윈드서핑을 해볼 생각이다.)

Answer
P4   1. To tell the truth 2. so
P5   1. how to fill in 2. complain 3. boil 4. settling 5. O 6. improving
P6   1. to teach 2. X (intend trying →intend to try)

주로 주격보어 또는 목적격보어로 사용되거나 명사를 후치 수식한다.

- someone to depend on, a house to live in, nothing to be afraid of, a pen to write with, a company to invest in 등의 to부정사의 후치 수식용법에서 전치사가 누락되면 틀린다.
- '…하기로 되어 있다(예정, 의무, 가능, 의도, 운명)'를 뜻하는 be + to부정사 구문에서는 to부정사의 태가 능동인지 수동인지를 파악한다.
- seem(appear), prove(turn out), grow(get, come), manage(fail), happen(chance) + to부정사
- the only, the next, the first, the tallest + 명사 + to부정사

1. In Canada, $20,000 a year is hardly enough money living. (○ , ×)
(캐나다에서 1년에 2만 달러는 생계를 유지하기에 충분한 돈이 아니다.)

2. They failed to provide solid security for us. (○ , ×)
(그들은 우리에게 견고한 보안을 제공하는 데 실패했다.)

3. Jill is the last lady telling a lie. (○ , ×)
(질은 거짓말을 할 여자가 아니다.)

4. If you are to bring your car into the city, you (are to pay, are to be paid) extra money. And your seatbelt (is to fasten, is to be fastened) without fail.
(만약 당신이 이 도시에 차를 가지고 오려면, 당신은 별도의 비용을 내야 합니다. 그리고 당신의 안전벨트는 반드시 매어져 있어야 합니다.)

5. She managed fighting off her attacker. (○ , ×)
(그녀는 그녀를 공격하는 사람들을 어떻게든 물리쳤다.)

- 부정사 구문 : to be honest(to speak roughly)
  The novel is easy to read(=to be read).
  There is nothing to do(=to be done).
  Who is to blame(=to be blamed)?
  This is a house to let(=to be let).

1. She herself is to blame for the breakup of their marriage. (○ , ×)
(그녀 자신이 그들의 파경에 대해 책임이 있다.)

2. Bobby deserves (to praise, to be praised) for his modesty.
(바비는 겸손한 태도 때문에 칭찬받을 만하다.)

[약점 POINT 9] 준동사의 동사적 성질 : 태

먼저 해당 준동사의 의미상 주어를 파악한 후, 그 의미상 주어와 준동사의 태 관계를 따져본다. 특히 분사구문에서의 태 관계에 유의한다.

1. The food was so cold that he required it (to take away, to be taken away).
(그 음식은 너무 차가워서 그는 그것을 치우도록 요구했다.)

2. She resents (blaming, being blamed) for something she didn't do.
(그녀는 자기가 하지 않은 일에 대해 욕 먹는 것에 화를 낸다.)

3. (Taking, Taken) everyday, this medicine will work right away.
(매일 섭취하면, 이 약은 즉시 효과가 있을 것이다.)

4. (Comparing, Compared) with his novel itself, he remained relatively unknown.
(그의 소설과 비교해보면, 그는 비교적 잘 알려져 있지 않다.)

5. (Considering, Considered) one of the most advanced civilizations, the Mayans are credited with architectural development.
(가장 진보된 문명 중 하나로 여겨지는 마야 문명은 건축의 발전으로 높이 평가되고 있다.)

Answer

P7 1. X (living → to live) 2. O 3. X (telling → to tell) 4. are to pay, is to be fastened 5. X (fighting → to fight)

P8 1. O 2. to be praised (deserve는 의미상 주어의 불일치가 허용되지 않음)

P9 1. to be taken away 2. being blamed 3. Taken 4. Compared 5. Considered

[약점 POINT 10] 문두 준동사구의 이해 : 준동사구, 절(S + V)

절(S + V) 앞에 위치하는 문두의 to부정사구는 목적의 의미를 나타낸다.

1. To lower production costs, (the number of the employees was cut, they cut the number of the employees) to a minimum.
(생산비를 낮추기 위해, 직원의 수가 최소한의 수준으로 감소되었다.)

2. (Understanding, Having understood, Understood, To understand, To have understood) how film reacts to light, you'll have to study the chemicals in the film.
(영화가 빛에 반응하는 방식을 이해하기 위해, 너는 영화에서의 화학물질에 대해 공부해야만 할 것이다.)

3. Seeing his parents off, he went to the airport just ago. (○ , ×)
(그는 부모님을 배웅하기 위해, 방금 전에 공항에 갔다.)

4. He did his homework to watch TV and play computer games . (○ , ×)
(그는 텔레비전을 보고 컴퓨터 게임을 하기 위해 숙제를 했다.)

Answer
P10 1. the number of the employees was cut 2. To understand 3. X (Seeing →To see) 4. O

Part I. Choose the best answer for the blank.

1. A: Can you children please stop making so much noise!
   B: Cox, you should ___________ it upset you so much.
   (a) not try to let
   (b) try not to let
   (c) not try let
   (d) try to let not

2. A: We must finish this work as soon as possible.
   B: But I really ___________ a break now.
   (a) need taking
   (b) need to have taken
   (c) need take
   (d) need to take

Part II. Choose the best answer for the blank.

3. You can use a turnstile ___________ the building.
   (a) entering
   (b) to enter
   (c) entered
   (d) enter

4. There is only one week ___________ before the final exam.
   (a) to going
   (b) going
   (c) gone
   (d) to go

5. I strongly object ___________ him into the office of mayor.
   (a) to inducting
   (b) to induct
   (c) inducting
   (d) with inducting

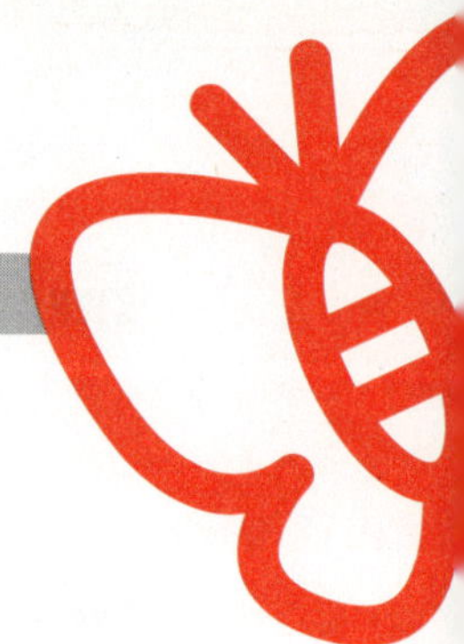

6. She told us that she ____________ other people.
   (a) was used to helping
   (b) was used to help
   (c) used to helping
   (d) used to being helped

7. Mr. Miller does not like to ____________ to perform before a large audience.
   (a) asked
   (b) have asked
   (c) asking
   (d) be asked

8. Green grocers would bring the prices down in the last half-hour ______________ get rid of everything before they close.
   (a) as to so
   (b) as so to
   (c) so as to
   (d) such as to

9. The garage was just about big enough for two cars ____________ in.
   (a) fit
   (b) fitting
   (c) to fit
   (d) to be fitted

Part III. Identify the option that contains an awkward expression or an error in grammar.

10. (a) A: So, how's life been treating you?
   (b) B: Quite well, thank you. I'm actually thinking to retire sometime this year.
   (c) A: Really? I guess it's quite early to retire at your age.
   (d) B: True, but I want to enjoy the rest of my life with my wife taking a trip.

Chapter 07

동명사

Chapter 07 동명사

[약점 POINT 1] 동명사의 관용표현

- be busy -ing : ~하느라 바쁘다
  We are busy preparing for the English grammar test.
  (우리는 영문법 시험을 준비하느라 바쁘다.)

- go -ing : ~하러 가다
  The weather is fine. Why don't we go boating at the river?
  (날씨 좋네. 강에 보트 타러 가는 것이 어때?)

- There is no -ing : ~하는 것은 불가능하다
  There is no knowing when earthquakes will occur.
  (언제 지진이 일어날지를 아는 것은 불가능하다.)

- be worth -ing : ~할 가치가 있다
  The play is worth seeing together.
  (그 연극은 함께 볼 만한 가치가 있다.)

- feel like -ing : ~하고 싶은 생각이 나다
  I don't feel like reading the book today.
  (나는 오늘 그 책을 읽고 싶은 생각이 없다.)

- on -ing : ~ 하자마자(=as soon as ~)
  On hearing the news, she called her mother.
  (그 소식을 듣자마자, 그녀는 어머니께 전화했다.)

- How[What] about -ing : ~하는 것이 어떻겠는가?
  How about going to the concert?
  (콘서트에 가는 것이 어떤가요?)

- prevent[keep] + 목적어 + from -ing: (목적어)가 ~ 하는 것을 못하게 하다
  The rain prevented us from going to the concert.
  (우리는 비 때문에 콘서트에 가지 못했다.)

- It is no use[good] -ing : ~해도 소용없다
  It is no use regretting his rash action.
  (그의 경거망동한 행동을 후회해도 소용없다.)
  = It is (of) no use to regret his rash action.
  = It is useless to regret his rash action.

- cannot help -ing : ~하지 않을 수 없다(= cannot but + 동사원형)
  I can't help falling in love with you.
  (나는 당신을 사랑할 수밖에 없습니다.)

1. There is no knowing what will happen in the future. (○, ×)
(미래에 어떤 일이 발생하는지 아는 것은 불가능하다.)

2. How about go to the cinema with me? (○, ×)
(저와 함께 영화관에 가는 건 어때요?)

3. I cannot but leaving school now. (○, ×)
(나는 지금 학교를 떠날 수밖에 없다.)

[약점 POINT 2] 일반 · 관용적인 전치사 to+동명사(-ing) 형태

be addicted to -ing : 중독 · 습관화되다
devote oneself to -ing : 헌신하다
object to -ing : 반대하다
see to -ing : 지켜보다
take to -ing : 빠지다, 의지하다
look forward to -ing : 기대하다
get used[accustomed] to -ing : 익숙해지다
What do you say to -ing? : 하는 게 어떠니?
when it comes to -ing : ~에 관해서라면
with a view to -ing : 입장 · 관점에서
lead to -ing : 야기시키다
come near (to) -ing : 근접하다
a solution[secret, key, answer, approach] to -ing : ~에 대한 해결책

1. Could you explain to me how to fill in this tax form? (○, ×)
(이 세금신고서 작성하는 방법을 설명해 줄 수 있나요?)

2. He does nothing but complain about his work. (○, ×)
(그는 자기 일에 대해서 불평밖에 하지 않는다.)

Answer
P1 1. ○ 2. X (go →going) 3. X (leaving →leave)
P2 1. ○ 2. ○

[약점 POINT 3] 문두 동명사구의 이해 : 동명사구, 절(S + V)

절(S + V) 앞에 위치한 문두 동명사구는 '전치사 + -ing' 의 형태를 취한다. by -ing, on -ing, in -ing, besides -ing, instead of -ing, far from -ing

1. Besides to think of everything concerned about my sister's wedding, I have to deal with my project of the company. (○ , ×)
(여동생의 결혼식에 관한 문제 말고도 나는 회사의 프로젝트에도 신경을 써야 한다.)

2. Far from studying hard, he didn't even read the book yet. (○ , ×)
(그는 공부를 열심히 하기는커녕 책을 읽어 보지도 않았다.)

[약점 POINT 4] 동명사의 명사적 용법

타동사의 목적어로 주로 쓰인다.
- 완료(finish, quit, abandon), 연기 · 회피(delay, postpone, avoid, escape, miss, resist), 시인 · 부인(admit, deny), 숙고 · 회상 · 후회(consider, recollect, repent), 선호(enjoy, mind), 기타(resent, suggest, anticipate, stand, risk, practice) + -ing
- begin, start, continue, cease, attempt, intend, like, love, hate, prefer + to 동사원형/-ing
- remember, forget, regret, recall + to부정사(미래)/-ing(과거)
- mean, stop, try + to부정사(~을 의도하다, ~하기 위해 멈추다, ~하려 하다)/-ing

1. The government will delay (making, to make) any announcement temporarily.
(정부는 어떠한 발표도 잠정적으로 보류할 것이다.)

2. They continued (to quarrel, quarreling) over who was right.
(그들은 누가 옳았는지를 놓고 계속 언쟁을 했다.)

3. Missing the bus means (to wait, waiting) for another hour; so I mean (to leave, leaving) right now.
(버스를 놓친다는 것은 한 시간을 더 기다리는 것을 의미한다. 그래서 난 지금 떠나야 한다.)

[약점 POINT 5] 동명사의 의미상 주어

동명사의 의미상 주어는 그 앞에 소유격 또는 목적격으로 표시해 준다.

1. Jack attempted a couple of jokes to the guests to break the ice. (○ , ×)
(잭은 어색한 분위기를 깨기 위해서 손님들에게 몇 가지 농담을 했다.)

2. It was stupid of her to trust Jack. (○ , ×)
(그녀가 잭을 믿은 것은 바보 같은 행동이었다.)

3. We really appreciate your giving us so much of your time. (○ , ×)
(당신이 시간을 많이 내주셔서 정말 감사합니다.)

4. There is a good chance of him coming. (○ , ×)
(그가 올 확률은 꽤 높다.)

[약점 POINT 6] 준동사의 동사적 성질: 시제(tense)와 태(voice)

준동사(부정사 · 동명사 · 분사)도 동사에서 근원한 것이기에 동사의 기본 성질인 시제와 태를 그대로 유지한다.

1. The food was so cold that Jill required it to take away. (○ , ×)
(음식이 너무 식어서 질은 그것을 치워야 했다.)

2. Jill resents blaming for something she didn't do. (○ , ×)
(질은 자신이 하지 않은 일에 대해서 책임을 지게 돼서 화났다.)

3. Taking everyday, this medicine will work right away. (○ , ×)
(매일 복용한다면 이 약은 바로 효과가 나타날 것이다.)

4. Jack is said to have been injured in the war. (○ , ×)
(사람들은 잭이 전쟁에서 부상을 입었다고 말했다.)

5. He admits having given the false information. (○ , ×)
(그는 잘못된 정보를 준 것을 시인했다.)

6. Not having met him before, I don't know him well. (○ , ×)
(그를 만나본 적이 없어서, 난 그를 잘 모른다.)

준동사(부정사 · 동명사 · 분사)의 바로 앞에 부정의 의미를 나타내는 부사가 쓰일 수 있다.

1. Jack advised me to not believe the report. (○ , ×)
(잭은 나에게 그 보고서를 믿지 말라고 충고했다.)

2. Jill seems not to have noticed me at a glance. (○ , ×)
(질은 첫눈에 나를 알아보지 못한 것 같다.)

3. They are used to not using the programs. (○ , ×)
(그들은 그 프로그램을 사용하지 않는 데 익숙해져 있다.)

4. Not having heard from her for a long time, Jack misses her. (○ , ×)
(그녀에게서 오랫동안 연락을 받지 못해, 잭은 그녀를 그리워한다.)

Answer

P7   1. X (to not → not to) 2. ○ 3. ○ 4. ○

Part I. Choose the best answer for the blank.

1. A: Have you seen the latest sequel to *Star Wars*?
    B: Not yet. But I'm really looking forward __________ it.
    (a) to seeing
    (b) to be seeing
    (c) seeing
    (d) to see

[고난이도] 2. A: Hey, why don't you join us for a drink?
    B: I'd like to, but I'm already late for my next class. I'm afraid I have to get __________.
    (a) gone
    (b) go
    (c) going
    (d) to go

Part II. Choose the best answer for the blank.

3. Poets devote themselves to __________ their inspiration into words.
    (a) transforming
    (b) transform
    (c) being transformed
    (d) be transformed

4. The government will delay __________ any announcement for the moment.
    (a) to making
    (b) to have made
    (c) making
    (d) to make

5. I was on the verge __________ into tears when you came back to me.
    (a) of being broken down
    (b) to be broken down
    (c) to break down
    (d) of breaking down

6. He does nothing but __________ about his work.
   (a) complain
   (b) to complain
   (c) complaining
   (d) to complaining

7. I watched the Vampire movie the other night and I was afraid __________ the bloody things.
   (a) of seeing
   (b) to see
   (c) to seeing
   (d) to be seen

Part III. Identify the option that contains an awkward expression or an error in grammar.

8. (a) A: Are you aware of where Jill is at the moment?
   (b) B: Yes, he may have a meal in the cafeteria downstair. What's up?
   (c) A: Well, I forgot talking to Jill before, but I remember to meet Jill tonight.
   (d) B: I'll let her know as I see her.

[고난이도] **9.** (a) A: You look quite excited. What happened to you?
   (b) B: Well, I have a big news for all of us.
   (c) A: Is it about our company's interest or something?
   (d) B: Yes. The new regulations will lead to improve an increase of our exports.

Part IV. Identify the option that contains an awkward expression or an error in grammar.

10. (a) Vegetarians who eat no meat or dairy foods may need a supplement. (b) But they should be cautious before take vitamins. (c) Very large doses of vitamins have been linked to many side effects. (d) In other words, you should check with your doctor first.

Chapter 08

분사

Chapter 08 분사

[약점 POINT 1] 비인칭 독립분사구문

- 판단: considering all things, taking all things into consideration, given all things, seeing all things, judging from all things
- 양보: admitting, admitted, granting, granted, allowing
- 의견: strictly speaking, speaking of politics
- 조건·가정: providing, provided, supposing, suppose

1. Jack deserves to praise for his modesty. (○ , ×)
(Jack의 겸손함은 칭찬받을 만하다.)

2. Considered all things, we made the right decision. (○ , ×)
(모든 것을 고려했을 때, 우리는 옳은 결정을 했다.)

3. Man, (biologically considering, biologically considered), is the feeblest of all things.
(인간은 생물학적으로 봤을 때 가장 약한 생물이다.)

[약점 POINT 2] 문장 앞의 분사구문

절(S + V) 앞에 위치한 분사구문은 시간, 조건, 이유, 양보, 부대상황을 나타낸다.

1. Having been deceived by him before, (she doesn't believe him, he is untrustworthy).
(전에 그에게 속은 적이 있었기 때문에 그녀는 그를 믿지 않는다.)

2. (Making, You to make, For you to make, By your making) a simple telephone call, a cheque can be stopped.
(간단하게 전화 한 통만 하면 수표를 무효화할 수 있다.)

3. (To use, To be used, Using, Used) economically, this fuel can last at least two weeks.
(경제적으로 활용한다면, 이 연료는 적어도 2주 동안 사용할 수 있다.)

[약점 POINT 3] 분사의 형용사적 용법

- 분사는 동사가 형용사처럼 한정·서술적으로 명사 수식 또는 보어에 사용되는 것이다.
  현재분사(동사원형 -ing) : 능동, 진행
  과거분사(동사원형 -ed) : 수동, 완료

- 감정상태 분사

  현재분사(동사원형 **-ing**) : 사물 수식

  과거분사(동사원형 **-ed**) : 사람 수식

> - 타동사의 현재분사(**interesting, boring**)는 '능동 사실' 을, 타동사의 과거분사(**interested, bored**)는 '수동 사실' 을, 자동사의 현재분사(**living, growing, remaining**)는 '진행 또는 상태' 를, 변형자동사의 과거분사(**fallen, retired, grown**)는 '결과적 상태' 를 나타낸다.
> - **concerning(=regarding), according to(=depending on), excepting, including, coupled with(=accompanied by / with)** 등의 분사형 전치사의 형태에 유의한다.
> - 명사 + 분사(**time-consuming, thought-provoking, mouth-watering, self-made**), 부사+분사 (**long-cherished, long-standing, hard-working, half-baked**), 분사+전치사(**waited-for, sought-after, unlooked-for**), 형용사+명사(=의사분사)(**blue-eyed, kind-hearted, strong-willed, thirteen-storied**) 등의 복합형 분사의 형태에 유의한다.

1. We have noticed grown support for the poor wanting more food. (○ , ×)

(우리는 음식이 더 필요한 가난한 사람들에 대한 지원이 증가한 것을 느꼈다.)

2. Jack longed to go home for he had had a very tired that day. And when he finally got home exhausting, he turned in straight away. (○ , ×)

(Jack은 그날 아주 피곤했기 때문에 몹시 집에 가고 싶었다. 그리고 지친 몸을 이끌고 집에 도착하자마자 바로 잠이 들었다.)

3. Jill wrote me a touching letter of thanks. (○ , ×)

(Jill은 나에게 감동적인 감사의 편지를 보냈다.)

4. I've never felt so (humiliating, humiliated) in my whole life.

(나는 내 인생에서 그렇게 굴욕적인 감정을 느낀 적이 없었다.)

Answer

P1 1. X (praise →be praised)   2. X (Considered all things →Considering all things)   3. biologically considered

P2 1. she doesn't believe him   2. By your making   3. Used

P3 1. X (grown →growing)   2. X (exhausting →exhausted)   3. O   4. humiliated

Part I. Choose the best answer for the blank.

1. A: Honey, Look at our lovely kids sleeping.
B: Be quiet, darling. We should come out ___________ not to wake them up.
(a) unnotice
(b) unnoticing
(c) unnoticed
(d) to be unnoticed

2. A: Let's give Kathy a surprise party for her birthday.
B: Great idea! But make sure not to get ___________ planning it.
(a) a catch
(b) to catch
(c) be caught
(d) caught

Part II. Choose the best answer for the blank.

3. ___________ in a humorous tone, the story instantly catched the reader's attention.
(a) Having written
(b) Written
(c) To be written
(d) Writing

4. ___________ the next president's inauguration speech, there is going to be a break for 20 minutes.
(a) Followed
(b) Following
(c) Being Followed
(c) To follow

5. Famous actress Nicole's driver had the car ___________ for her next schedule in advance.
(a) to be waiting
(b) to be waited
(c) waited
(d) waiting

6. __________ on a date, she was very pleased and sang for joy.

   (a) Being asked out

   (b) Asking out

   (c) Having asked out

   (d) Asked out

7. __________ your skiing skills is continuous practice.

   (a) To improve

   (b) That improves

   (c) What improves

   (d) Improving

[고난이도] **8.** __________ close to extinction, the rhino is once again common in this area.

   (a) Hunting

   (b) Being hunted

   (c) Having hunted

   (d) Having been hunted

9. It's __________ disappointing to know that he lied to me.

   (a) very

   (b) much

   (c) very much

   (d) so much

Part III. Identify the option that contains an awkward expression or an error in grammar.

10. (a) A: Excuse me, sir. There will be a penalty charging.

   (b) B: Please, you don't say. I didn't do anything wrong.

   (c) A: You were overspeeding. Here is a traffic ticket for fast driving.

   (d) B: Please overlook my fault this time, officer.

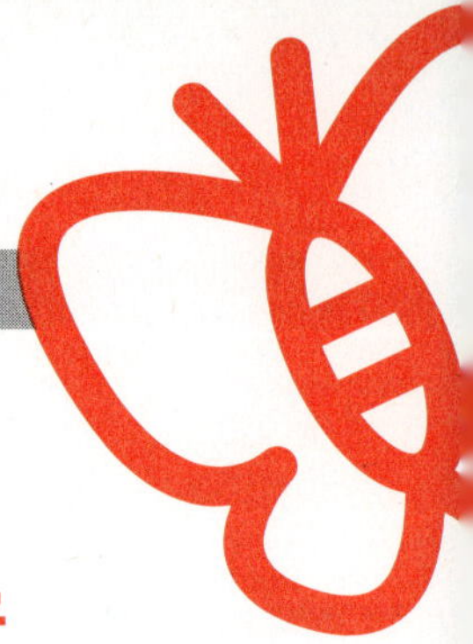

11. (a) The new premises we plan to occupy in Camford are now being built. (b) The outskirts of this city are an ideal site for a company like ours. (c) Some of our staff in the U.S. are being asked to relocate, and eventually around ten percent of our U.S. workforce is to move to Britain. (d) However, the majority of our new employees is to recruit locally, and we think that the local community are going to benefit enormously from this development.

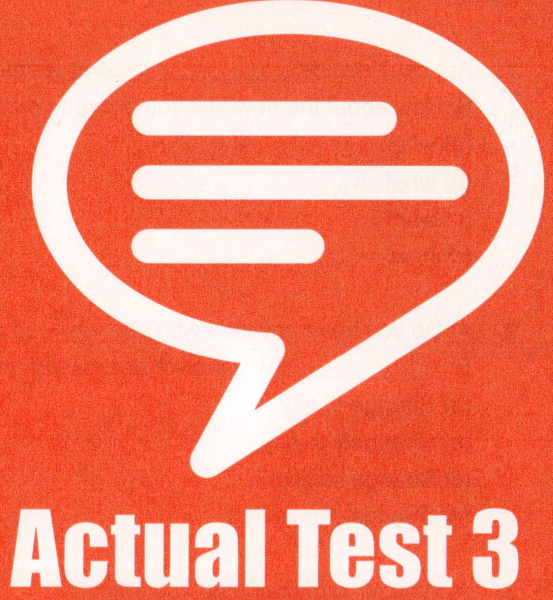

Actual Test 3

Part I. **Choose the best answer for the blank.**

1. A: I can't decide __________ to wear for the party.
    B: How about the new suit you bought yesterday?
    (a) when
    (b) what
    (c) where
    (d) how

2. A: Do you have any idea why she looks so upset today?
    B: __________, she got quite depressed after accepting the offer.
    (a) Strange to say
    (b) Strangely to say
    (c) Strange saying
    (d) Strangely to saying

3. A: What kind of sports do you enjoy?
    B: I like __________.
    (a) skiing and scuba diving
    (b) skiing and to scuba dive
    (c) to ski and scuba diving
    (d) ski and to scuba dive

4. A: I'm going to keep dieting until I lose at least another 20 kilos.
    B: Well, it's going to __________ at this rate.
    (a) take a while to you
    (b) take a while of you
    (c) take you for a while
    (d) take you a while

5. ___________, he muttered a few words to himself.
   (a) Don't know what to say
   (b) Not knowing what to say
   (c) Knowing not that to say
   (d) Doesn't know that to say

6. She seems __________ the piano really hard this semester.
   (a) to have practiced
   (b) to practice
   (c) practicing
   (d) as if practicing

7. The cave __________ Mammoth Cave is famous for its unique structure.
   (a) known as
   (b) it is known to be
   (c) is known as
   (d) to be known

8. The new computer system __________ next month.
   (a) is be installed
   (b) is to be installed
   (c) is to install
   (d) is been installed

Part III. **Identify the option that contains an awkward expression or an error in grammar.**

9. (a) A: There are two young ladies outside asked for you.
   (b) B: Did they tell you what they wanted?
   (c) A: They said they've brought dinner over for you.
   (d) B: It must be my sister and her friend.

Part IV. Identify the option that contains an awkward expression or an error in grammar.

10. (a) Bill had a tendency pulling pranks on people. (b) One day, he made a crank call to the police to reporting a burglary in the neighborhood. (c) When he came back home, he found his own house was broken into. (d) After the incident, he never did it again.

Chapter 09

접속사, 관계사, 전치사

STEP 1 약점 포인트

[약점 POINT 1] 부사절을 유도하는 종속접속사

- '시간, 조건, 양보' 의 부사절 속에서 미래시제는 현재시제로, 미래완료는 현재완료로 대체된다.
- '…이래로' 를 뜻하는 **since** 구문에서 주절은 현재완료시제로, 종속절은 과거시제로 나타낸다.
- **now** (that)은 (이전까지와는 다른) 현재의 이유의 절을 유도한다.
- **as**는 시간, 이유, 양태 (…하듯이, …이듯이, …함에 따라), 비교(원급)의 절을 유도하며, '형용사 · 분사 · 부사 · 명사(무관사) + **as** + 주어 + 동사' 의 도치 양보절을 유도한다.
- 시간을 나타내는 부사절

  when, while, before, after, as soon as, since, whenever, once, until, as, as(so) long as
- 원인 · 이유를 나타내는 부사절

  because, since, as, now that
- 조건을 나타내는 부사절

  if, unless, in case (that), as, provided (that), providing (that), on condition that, so long as, as(so) far as
- 목적을 나타내는 부사절

  that/so that/in order that + 주어 + may(can, will) 동사원형 ~ : ~하기 위해서

  lest + 주어 + should 동사원형 ~ : ~하지 않도록 하기 위해서
- 결과를 나타내는 부사절

  so + 형용사 · 부사 + that + 주어 + 동사 ~

  such + 명사 + that + 주어 + 동사 ~

  so that 주어 + 조동사 + 동사원형 ~ ⊙ 목적 부사절
- 양보를 나타내는 부사절

  though, although, even though, even if, while, if

1. Jack played tennis until he was exhausted. (○, ×)

(Jack은 지칠 때까지 테니스를 쳤다.)

2. Once your mother arrives, we will eat dinner. (○, ×)

(일단 네 어머니가 오시면 저녁을 먹을 것이다.)

3. Jill arrived at the office as we finished the meeting. (○, ×)

(Jill은 우리가 미팅을 끝낼 때쯤 사무실에 도착했다.)

4. I can remember seeing Jill somewhere in that you mention it. (○, ×)

(네가 그 얘기를 하니 나도 어디선가 Jill을 본 것이 기억난다.)

5. Let's go on a picnic this Sunday so long as the weather will be nice. (○ , ×)
(날씨가 괜찮다면 이번 일요일에 소풍을 가자.)

6. we will be late unless we will hurry. (○ , ×)
(서두르지 않으면 우리는 늦을 것이다.)

7. The team will go breaking even if they will get benefits from the film. (○ , ×)
(그 팀은 영화에서 수익을 얻더라도 수지가 엇비슷해질 것이다.)

8. Strange (because, since, as, if) it may sound, I quite enjoy living alone.
(이상하게 들리겠지만 나는 혼자 사는 것을 즐긴다.)

9. (Granting that, Except that, So that, Now that, Would that) the weather is warm enough, we can play tennis outside.
(밖에 날씨가 따뜻하다면 밖에서 테니스를 칠 수 있다.)

[약점 POINT 2] 등위접속사

- 등위접속사 and, or, but, than 등의 앞·뒤는 병렬(동등한 품사)구조여야 한다.
- nothing but(=only), anything but(=never), all but(=almost, all except)
- 명령문, and ~. (~해라, 그러면 ~ 될 것이다)
- 명령문, or (=otherwise)~. (~해라, 그렇지 않으면 ~ 될 것이다)
- 문장과 문장 사이의 접속사 for는 because의 뜻이지만, 문두에는 오지 않는다.
- for는 대등접속사이고, because는 종속접속사이다.
- nor + V + S = and neither + V + S = and…not, either

1. Make haste, so we will get there on time. (○ , ×)
(서둘러라, 그러면 우리는 거기에 제시간에 도착할 것이다.)

2. Jack doesn't smoke, and he doesn't drink, too. (○ , ×)
(Jack은 담배도 안 피우고 술도 마시지 않는다.)

3. For he worked hard, Jack must be tired. (○ , ×)
(Jack은 열심히 일했으므로 피곤할 것이다.)

Answer

P1 1. ○ 2. ○ 3. ○ 4. X (in that →now that) 5. X (will be →is) 6. X (unless we will hurry →unless we hurry) 7. X (even if they will get → even if they get) 8. as 9. Now that

P2 1. X (so →and) 2. X (too →either) 3. X (For →Because)

- both A and B(=at once A and B, A and B alike), between A and B
- not A but B(=B not A, not A rather B), not only A but (also) B(=not only A but B as well), B as well as A, B in addition to A, not that절 but that절(=not because절 but because절)
- both … alike, both … as well, both … as well as 등은 사용되지 않는다.
- either A or B, neither A nor B
- 대등 접속사구가 주어일 때, 동사와의 수일치는 동사와 가까이 있는 것에 맞춘다.
  (단, '명사 as well as 명사'는 예외적으로 앞의 명사에 맞춘다.)

1. Our vacation was a disaster: not only was the food terrible, but the weather was awful in addition. (○ , ×)

(우리의 휴가는 대실패였다 : 음식도 맛이 없었지만 날씨는 더 안 좋았다.)

2. Jill has both the originality as well as the beauty. (○ , ×)

(Jill은 미모와 독창성을 겸비하고 있다.)

3. Schools normally do not allow either wearing jeans or to dye hair. (○ , ×)

(대부분의 학교들은 염색이나 청바지 입는 것을 금지한다.)

4. Jack neither smokes or drinks. (○ , ×)

(Jack은 술도 안 마시고 담배도 안 피운다.)

[약점 POINT 4] 관계대명사 what

- 관계대명사 what(명사절), 관계대명사 which(형용사절), 단순 사실을 유도하는 that(명사절)의 차이를 이해한다.
- what is worse(better, more), what is called(=what they call, so called), reading is to the mind what(=as) exercise is to the body, what one is is more important than what one has or what one does. 등의 what의 관용구문에 유의한다.
- what(the thing 선행사 + 주격 관계대명사) + 동사 + ~.
- what(the thing 선행사 + 목적격 관계대명사) + 주어 + 동사 -불완전문장

1. Jill will throw away all these things, so you can take what you like. (○ , ×)

(Jill은 이 물건들을 다 버릴 것이므로 원하면 가져가도 좋다.)

2. Jill heard a story what made her sad. (○ , ×)

(Jill은 그녀를 슬프게 만드는 이야기를 들었다.)

3. That made me leave the neighborhood was its constant crimes. (○ , ×)

(내가 그 동네를 떠난 이유는 끊임없이 일어나는 범죄 때문이었다.)

4. Which hundreds of people are sleeping on the streets of New York with no possibility of finding a home doesn't sound real.

(뉴욕이라는 도시에서 수백 명의 사람들이 집이 없어 길거리에서 잔다는 사실은 믿겨지지가 않는다.)

[약점 POINT 5] It be … that의 강조

She wants to meet him in the office.

(그녀는 사무실에서 그를 만나기를 원한다.)

→ **It is** she **that**(=who) wants to meet him in the office.

(사무실에서 그를 만나기를 원한 사람은 바로 그녀이다.)

It is him **that**(=whom) she wants to meet in the office.
It is in the office **that**(=where) she wants to meet him.

특히 강조하는 것이 주어일 때 **that**절속의 동사의 수에 유의한다.

1. (Novels, In novels, It is in novels) that wolves are described as dangerous, but they actually prefer to avoid human beings.

(소설에서는 늑대가 위험한 동물로 묘사되지만 사실 그들은 인간을 회피하려고 한다.)

2. It was the winter of 1940 that are said to have been the worst winter of their lives. (○ , ×)

(1940년의 겨울은 그들 인생에서 최악의 겨울이었다고 한다.)

Answer

P3 1. O 2. X (as well as →and) 3. X (to dye →dying) 4. X (or →nor)
P4 1. O 2. X (what →that) 3. X (That →What) 4. X (Which →That)
P5 1. It is in novels 2. X (are said →is said)

- **that** 단순사실 절 : '…라는 사실(=the fact that)' 이라는 완전한 사실절을 유도한다. 전치사 뒤에 절(S + V)이 연결되어 있으면 틀린다. **in that**(…라는 사실에 있어서)과 **except that**(…라는 사실을 빼놓곤) 구문 이외에 **that** 앞에 전치사가 위치하면 틀린다. 선행사를 포함한 관계대명사 **what**절과의 차이를 이해한다.

- 정보명사 + **that** 동격절 : the fact(truth, idea, plan, opinion, notion, belief, evidence, proof, conviction, criticism, news, possibility, rumor, statement) + **that** 동격절

- **whether vs. if** 선택절 : whether(whether or not, whether A or B) 선택절은 모든 명사절에 쓰이는 반면, if 선택절은 타동사(know, ask, doubt, wonder)의 목적절로만 쓰이며 **or not**과 결합하면 틀린다.

- 간접의문 : 의문사절(wh-)이 명사절의 역할을 하는 것을 말하며, 평서문(S + V)의 어순을 취한다. 특히 **Do you know who he is?**와 **Who do you think he is?**의 차이를 이해한다.

① that/if(~인지 아닌지=whether) + S + V ~.
② 의문사 + S + V ~. (간접의문문)
③ 동격의 **that** 절 (앞에 선행사 역할을 하는 정보명사 **the fact**, **the rumor** 등이 필요함)
④ what + V + ~.
⑤ what + S + V [→ 목적어 또는 목적이 생략된 불완전한 문장]

1. The magazine is facing a criticism that it is not colorful enough. (○ , ×)
(그 잡지는 충분히 화려하지 않다는 비판에 직면해 있다.)

2. I'm wondering what you can help us or not. (○ , ×)
(난 네가 우리를 도와 줄 수 있는지 없는지 궁금하다.)

3. Nobody knows what he is at home or at the office. (○ , ×)
(아무도 그가 집에 있는지 사무실에 있는지 모른다.)

4. Jack is not interested in that kind of job he is looking for. (○ , ×)
(Jack은 어떤 직업을 구할지에 대해서 별로 관심이 없다.)

5. Who do you think broke the window? (○ , ×)
(누가 창문을 깼다고 생각하니?)

[약점 POINT 7] 부정접속사: 중복 부정은 인정되지 않는다

- but(if ··· not, that ··· not) : 중복부정×
  Not a day passes **but** I think of her.
  (하루도 내가 그녀를 생각하지 않은 적이 없었다.)
  It never rains **but** it pours.
  (비가 오기만 하면 퍼붓는다.)
  No man is so old **but** he may learn.
  (사람은 늙었어도 배울 수 있다.)
  cf. There is no rule but has some exceptions.
  (예외 없는 규칙은 없다.)

- unless(if ··· not) : 중복부정×, 미래시제는 현재시제로 사용한다.

- lest(=so that ··· may not, for fear that) : 중복 부정×, 동사는 (should) + 동사원형으로 사용한다.

- nor(=and neither, and ··· not ··· either) : 중복 부정×, 무조건 도치, 대동사의 선택에 유의하다.

1. I didn't turn on the light lest I should not wake the baby. (○ , ×)
(아기를 깨우기 싫어서 나는 불을 켜지 않았다.)

2. Unless the weather doesn't improve, we'll have to call off the game. (○ , ×)
(날씨가 좋아지지 않는다면 우리는 경기를 취소해야 할 것이다.)

3. It never rains but it doesn't pour. (○ , ×)
(비가 오기만 하면 퍼붓는다.)

4. The workers are unhappy but will not complain (lest that, lest, so that, unless) they might not lose their jobs.
(노동자들은 불만이 있지만 해고당할까 봐 불평하지 못할 것이다.)

Answer

P6   1. O 2. X (what → whether) 3. X (what → if) 4. X (that → what) 5. O
P7   1. X (should not 삭제) 2. X (doesn't improve → improves) 3. X (doesn't pour → pours) 4. so that

[약점 POINT 8] 부사절에서 주어가 대명사일 경우, be동사는 함께 생략한다.

주절의 주어와 부사절의 주어가 같을 때, 부사절의 대명사는 be동사와 함께 생략할 수 있다. 시험은 주로 생략된 이후에 남는 형태가 -ing인지, -ed인지를 묻는다.
cf. if (it is) necessary, if (it is) possible, when (it is) convenient

1. Milk quickly turns sour, unless refrigerated. (○, ×)
   (우유는 냉동 보관하지 않으면 빨리 쉬어 버린다.)

2. These pills, is taking everyday, can be really curative. (○, ×)
   (이 약을 매일 먹는다면 치료 효과가 뛰어나다.)

3. He experienced all those things when (live, is living, living, lived) abroad.
   (그는 외국에 살 때 그런 일들을 모두 경험했다.)

4. You can use the computer whenever (you are necessary, it is necessary).
   (컴퓨터가 필요하면 언제든지 써도 된다.)

[약점 POINT 9] 의사 관계대명사

Such data as he has is really informative.
(그가 가진 그러한 데이터는 정말 유익하다.)
This is the same car as I had before.
(이것은 내가 가졌던 것과 같은 차이다.)
I need as much money as he has.
(나는 그가 가진 것만큼의 돈이 필요하다.)
We have more guests than were expected.
(우리가 예상했던 것보다 더 많은 손님이 왔다.)
There is no rule but has exceptions.
(예외 없는 규칙은 없다.)

1. The result of the tests can vary according to such faculties (that, which, as) are influenced by sex or age.
   (그 실험의 결과는 성별 또는 연령에 의해 영향을 받는 그러한 집단에 따라 달라질 수 있다.)

2. He is late again, as is often the case with him. (○, ×)
   (그가 또 늦었는데, 그것은 그에게 종종 있는 일이다.)

- 복합관계대명사(whoever, whichever, whatever) : 격이 출제의 초점이며, 그 격은 관계사절 속에서 담당하는 역할에 따라 결정된다. 주로 명사절 또는 부사절을 유도한다.
  Jill gives this ticket to whoever wants it. You can take whichever you want.
  (Jill은 원하는 모든 사람에게 이 티켓을 준다. 당신은 원하는 모든 것을 가질 수 있다.)

- 복합관계형용사(whichever, whatever) : 명사절 또는 부사절을 유도한다.
  You can take whichever thing you want.
  (당신은 원하는 모든 것을 가질 수 있다.)
  Jack may have whatever little money I have.
  (Jack은 비록 적지만 내가 가진 모든 돈을 갖고 있다.)

- 복합관계부사(whenever, wherever, however) : however절과 how절의 구분이 중요하다. however 절은 부사절을 유도한다.
  However stupid Jill is, she won't believe it. - 부사절
  (Jill이 아무리 멍청하더라도, 그것을 믿지 않을 것이다.)
  They don't know how stupid Jill is. - 명사절
  (그들은 Jill이 얼마나 멍청한지 모른다.)

1. Jack always smiles at whomever come to ask him for advice. (○ , ×)
(Jack은 자신에게 조언을 구하러 오는 사람 누구에게나 미소를 짓는다.)

2. I'll give this ticket to whoever you recommend. (○ , ×)
(네가 추천하는 사람에게 이 티켓을 주겠다.)

3. I will appreciate whatever help you can give me. (○ , ×)
(당신이 도와준다면 정말 감사히 여기겠습니다.)

4. He gave whoever came to the door an attractive smile (○ , ×)
(그는 자기 집에 오는 누구에게나 매력적인 미소를 지었다.)

5. (How hard you try, How you try hard, However you try hard, However hard you try), you can't change anything.
(네가 아무리 노력해도 아무것도 바꿀 수 없다.)

Answer
P8 1. ○ 2. X (is taking →taken) 3. living 4. it is necessary
P9 1. as 2. ○
P10 1. X (whomever →whoever) 2. X (whoever →whomever) 3. ○ 4. X (whoever →whomever)
  5. However hard you try

[약점 POINT 11] 관계대명사에서 주의해야 할 사항

- 주격 관계대명사절의 동사의 수일치는 선행사에 일치시킨다.
- 소유격 관계대명사 **whose**는 선행사가 사물인 경우에 'the 명사 + of which' 또는 'of which + the 명사' 로 바꿔 쓸 수 있다. 이 때 **the**가 빠지면 틀린다.
- 관계대명사절 속에 삽입절이 들어 있는 경우 관계대명사의 격에 유의한다.
- 관계대명사 **that**은 제한적 용법의 모든 주격 및 목적격 관계대명사를 대신할 수 있다. 그러나 **comma** 뒤, **whose** 대신, 전치사 뒤에는 주격 · 목적격 **that**을 사용할 수 없다.

1. You should put plants in your fish tank because they produce oxygen which dissolves in the water and keeps the fish alive. (○ , ×)
   (수족관에 식물을 넣어 두어야 한다. 왜냐하면 식물들이 물에 녹아서 물고기를 살게 하는 산소를 만들기 때문이다.

2. The computer programmes which has recently been introduced seem to be constantly creating new problems. (○ , ×)
   (새로 나온 컴퓨터 프로그램이 계속 문제를 일으키고 있는 것 같다.)

3. Jack asked me a question which the answer was meaningless. (○ , ×)
   (Jack은 답할 가치가 없는 질문을 했다.)

[약점 POINT 12] 전치사와 목적격 관계대명사와의 관계

- 앞에 전치사가 위치한 경우 관계대명사는 생략하거나 **that**으로 대신할 수 없다.
- 전치사는 목적격 관계대명사 앞으로 갈 수 있다. (단, **that** 앞에는 불가하다.)
- 목적격 관계대명사에 밑줄이 있는 경우는 '전치사의 누락 여부' 또는 '정확한 선택 여부' 를 묻는 것이며, 이는 선행사를 관계사절 속에 집어넣어 봄으로써 확인한다.
- 목적격 관계대명사가 생략되었을 경우에는 다시 문장의 뒤에 위치한다.
- 'some, most, all, each, many, much + of + which(whom)' 등의 부정대명사에 연결된 관계대명사절을 이해한다. 특히 관계대명사절 속의 동사의 수에 유의한다.

1. This is the house in she lives. (○ , ×)
   (이것이 그녀가 사는 집이다.)

2. Jill has offered a new procedure to which no one readily agrees. (○ , ×)
   (Jill은 아무도 동의하지 않는 새 절차를 제안했다.)

3. He is attempting to renew the project which I have been engaged for years. (○ , ×)

(그는 내가 몇 년 동안 일궈 놓은 프로젝트를 재개하려고 하고 있다.)

4. He has lots of books, (most of them, some of which, each of which) are very old.

(그는 많은 책을 갖고 있는데, 그 중 일부는 매우 낡았다.)

[약점 POINT 13] 관계부사

> 선행사(명사) 에 따라서,
>
> - 방법: the way, how, the way in which, the way that 등으로 나타내며, the way how나 the way in that은 사용하지 않는다.
> - 이유: the reason why, the reason for which, the reason that

1. I don't understand the way that Jill solved the problem. (○ , ×)

(나는 Jill이 그 문제를 푼 방식을 이해하지 못한다.)

2. Do you know any ways by which we can contact Jack? (○ , ×)

(Jack에게 연락할 수 있는 방법을 아니?)

3. Jill used to get depressed, which is the reason she committed suicide. (○ , ×)

(Jill은 자주 우울증을 겪었고, 그것이 그녀가 자살한 이유이다.)

[약점 POINT 14] 장소 · 방향의 전치사 관련 주의사항

> - 선 · 면에의 접촉 : on the + floor, wall, window, ceiling, desk, stove, lake, farm
> - 출발점을 기준으로 한 방향 : leave, start, depart, head, make + for
>   *cf.* go, come, return, rush, bring + 사람, take 사람 + to

1. Cattle are raised in that farm. (○ , ×)

(소떼가 그 농장에서 자라고 있다.)

2. The train will leave the platform to Athens. (○ , ×)

(그 기차는 정거장을 떠나 아테네를 향해 갈 것이다.)

Answer

P11 1. O 2. X (which has → which have) 3. X (which → of which)
P12 1. X (in she → in which she) 2. O 3. X (which → in which) 4. some of which
P13 1. O 2. X (by which → in which) 3. O
P14 1. X (in → on) 2. X (to → for)

[약점 POINT 15] 시간 전치사 관련 주의사항

- **in the morning, at night**과 **on Monday morning, on the night of July**의 구분
  원래 아침 점심 저녁을 나타내는 것은 **at**을 쓴다. 그러나, 정관사 **the**와 결합이 되어서 **in the morning**으로 쓰는 경우도 있다. 또한 특정의 아침을 나타낼 때는 **on Monday morning**이나 **on the night of July**처럼 **on**을 사용한다.

- **for**는 기간 정보(얼마 동안)를 나타내며 불특정 수치적 기간과 결합한다.
  for + days, months, ages, three days, five years, ever, a long time

- **during**은 때 정보(언제)를 나타내며 특정 시점을 알려주는 한정사와 결합한다.
  during + the night, his childhood, that time, this period, which time
  He has been on the phone for the last two hours.
  (그는 지난 2시간 동안 통화중이었다.)
  cf. **He has had three calls during the last two hours.**
  (그는 지난 2시간 동안 3통의 전화를 했다.)

- 과거의 특정 시점 : **since + the accident, April 4th, last weekend, she married**

---

1. Nobody in his right mind would not go out (at, in, on) night like this.
(제 정신을 가진 사람이라면 아무도 이 밤에 밖에 나가지 않을 것이다.)

2. They left early (in, on) the morning of Dec. 14 on the honeymoon.
(그들은 12월 14일 아침에 신혼여행을 떠났다.)

3. I stayed in Japan (for, during) two months, and (for, during) that time I met her. But I haven't seen her (during, in) years since then.
(나는 일본에서 2달 동안 지냈고, 그 기간에 그녀를 만났다. 하지만 그 후 그녀를 본 적이 없다.)

4. The students have been studying in the library (for, during) the last three months.
(그 학생들은 도서관에서 지난 3달 동안 공부해왔다.)

5. (For, During, Since) more than 10 years of political turmoil, (for, during) which Russians have gone to the polls five times, democracy is far from established.
(지난 10년 이상의 정치적 혼돈 속에 러시아는 5번의 선거를 치렀다. 민주주의가 발들일 틈이 없었다.)

- 능가, 제압, 지배, 우위 : control, command, influence, dominance, rule, victory, triumph, advantage + over

  cf. under the + control, influence, guidance, command, rule
- 비유적인 정도·한도 : beyond + description(words), comparison, dispute, belief, doubt, praise, measure, one's power, one's ability

  cf. He is above telling lies.

  (그는 거짓말에 능숙하다.)
- between(둘 사이에)과 among(셋 이상의 사이에)
- 결과, 정도·한도 : be starved to death, to my joy, be bored to death, to some extent, to no purpose(avail), to the full, to the bone
- 차이, 기준·척도, 배분의 단위 : miss a flight by a minute, increase by 60%, by a narrow margin(escape), by a hair's breadth, judge 사람, by appearances, be known by

  beside(…의 곁에; …을 벗어나)와 besides(…이외에도; 게다가)의 구분

1. Financial support from the government gives these firms an unfair advantage (to, about, over, with) us.

(이 기업들에 대한 정부의 금융지원은 우리보다 우월한 입장에 서게 하는 아주 불공평한 정책이다.)

2. That the reports were stolen is (beside, above, beyond, behind) dispute; what we need to know is who took them.

(리포트가 도둑맞았다는 것은 확실하다. 우리가 알아야 할 것은 누가 훔쳤느냐다.)

3. She seated herself down among the two competitors. (○, ×)

(그녀는 두 경쟁자 사이에 앉았다.)

4. (At, To, By) the best of my knowledge, he is the last man to deceive us.

(내가 알기로 그는 절대 우리를 속일 사람이 아니다.)

5. The number of road accidents has increased (at, for, in, by, with) fifty percent during the last five years.

(교통사고 건수가 지난 5년간 50퍼센트나 증가했다.)

6. Besides his age, he is still too unexperienced. (○, ×)

(그의 나이 말고도 그는 너무 경험이 없다.)

Answer

P15 1. at 2. in 3. for, during, in 4. for 5. for, during

P16 1. over 2. beyond 3. X (among → between) 4. To 5. by 6. O

[약점 POINT 17] 그 밖의 주의해야 할 전치사 II

- blame him for the failure = blame the failure on him
  cf. depend on you for help = depend for help on you
- pray, ask, call, send, hope, hunt + for (행위의 목적, 기대, 획득)
  chase, seek, run, take, name + after (추구, 쫓음, 따라감)
  on + business, leave, a picnic, a journey, an errand (용무, 용건)
  aim, laugh, look, make an attempt + at (겨냥, 목표)
  come to her rescue, go to their aid
- 양보의 전치사 : in spite of, despite, for all, with all, notwithstanding
- by + bus, plane, air, sea, land, letter, mail, fax (방법적 수단: …에 의해서),
  with + a pen, a knife, my eyes, his right hand (도구적 수단: …을 써서)

1. Whenever children behave badly, people always try to blame the teachers (on, for) it.
   (아이들의 행동이 불량하면 사람들은 항상 선생님 탓만 한다.)

2. If you send him (on, for) an errand, he runs away before he has heard everything you want him to do.
   (그에게 심부름을 시키면 그는 다 듣지도 않고 서둘러 나가버린다.)

3. (In spite, Despite) her friends' warnings, Amy is determined to travel alone.
   (친구들의 만류에도 불구하고 Amy는 혼자 여행하려고 결심했다.)

   cf. Despite he is young, he is very considerate. (○, ×)

4. (Nevertheless, For all, Due to, By way of) violent opposition, they managed to pass anti-slavery laws.
   (격렬한 반대에도 불구하고 그들은 노예폐지법을 통과시켰다.)

5. They have always chosen to travel (by, on) a train since the accident.
   (그들은 그 사고 이후 항상 기차로만 여행해왔다.)

[약점 POINT 18] 전치사 관련 주의사항

- **in** + 날씨, 계절, 년도, 세기, 월
- **on** + 날짜, 요일, 특정한 날
- **in>on>at** (위치)
- **in** (위치상: ~ 안에), (시간상: ~ 이후에) / **within** (시간상: ~ 이내에)
- 동안에
  - 웹 **for** + 숫자 + 시간명사
  - 웹 **during** + 특정기간 명사
  - 웹 **while** + S + V ~

1. Everyone who really wants Jack to play a game in this coming Sunday will be expected to watch the game. (○ , ×)
(Jack이 이번 일요일에 경기할 것을 원하는 모든 사람들은 그 경기를 볼 것으로 예상된다.)

2. All students required to attend the field trip will be going to stay here during two days for the orientation. (○ , ×)
(현장학습에 참여할 것을 요구받은 모든 학생들은 오리엔테이션을 받기 위해 여기서 이틀간 머무를 것이다.)

3. Since Jill left her hometown to go to college, her mother, Jessica has been in hospital during the winter. (○ , ×)
(Jill이 대학에 진학하기 위해서 고향을 떠난 이후, 그녀의 어머니 제시카는 겨울동안 병원에 입원했다.)

4. Most of the onlookers were disappointed then after watching Jack's playing manners on the game. (○ , ×)
(대부분의 관중은 경기 동안 잭의 경기 매너를 보면서 실망을 했다.)

5. Lisbon that is the metropolis of the Republic of Portugal is located on the west of Spain. (○ , ×)
(포르투갈의 수도인 리스본은 스페인의 서쪽에 위치해 있다.)

Part I. Choose the best answer for the blank.

1. A: What's been eating you lately? Don't you realize how rude and irritable you've become?
   B: I'm really sorry for ___________ these days.
   (a) I've been acting that way
   (b) that I've been acting that way
   (c) the way I've been acting
   (d) my acting the way

2. A: How about this townhouse?
   B: It's exactly ___________ I've been looking for.
   (a) that
   (b) in that
   (c) which
   (d) what

3. A: We've been working on this report for two hours. How about getting something to eat?
   B: ___________ you mention it, I am kind of hungry.
   (a) Because
   (b) If
   (c) Although
   (d) Now that

4. A: Can we have a look around the house?
   B: Of course. Go ___________.
   (a) wherever
   (b) wherever you're wanted
   (c) wherever you want to
   (d) wherever you want to do

5. A: Do you know when Jane will visit us?
   B: Yes, she's coming ___________.
   (a) next week
   (b) for next week
   (c) in next week
   (d) till next week

6. Last weekend we went to see ___________ everybody calls masterpiece and were disappointed by it.
(a) of which
(b) that
(c) what
(d) which

7. You might be happy to have such a boyfriend ___________ always love you.
(a) who will
(b) that will
(c) of will
(d) as will

8. Our company has been on the brink of bankruptcy and what ___________ my house became out of repair because of natural disaster.
(a) make the matter worse
(b) makes the matter worse
(c) the matter is made worse
(d) the matter makes worse

9. We need a procedure ___________ the session is extended and the representatives get together in one place to reach an agreement.
(a) in which
(b) of which
(c) what
(d) that

10. Someone's birthday is ___________ one is celebrated with joy and happiness of the birth to life.
(a) when
(b) time
(c) to which
(d) for which

11. No sooner __________ the movies than she burst into tears.
(a) she has watched
(b) had she watched
(c) has she watched
(d) she had watched

12. Jennifer talked to me in whispers __________ he should be heard.
(a) for fear that
(b) so that
(c) in order that
(d) no lest that

13. It won't be long __________ your scandal comes to light.
(a) that
(b) before
(c) after
(d) when

14. __________ this problem occurs so frequently in the summer, people should bring along something to protect their skin.
(a) Because
(b) For
(c) If
(d) So that

15. You should be in the airport __________ an hour to catch the flight.
(a) after
(b) before
(c) in
(d) by

16. Shane needs to update new materials __________ a regular basis to keep up with the speedy technology and information.
(a) in
(b) on
(c) to
(d) for

17. Jack keeps asking me for money, _____________ makes me sick of him.
    (a) that
    (b) which
    (c) what
    (d) of which

Part III. Identify the option that contains an awkward expression or an error in grammar.

18. (a) A: I'd better leave right away.
    (b) B: What's the rush?
    (c) A: I should meet my advisor at ten.
    (d) B: That's out of question. It's already ten thirty!

Part IV. Identify the option that contains an awkward expression or an error in grammar.

19. (a) Luck is often associated with gambling. (b) But most of the professional gamblers would be out of business even they relied solely on 'luck.' (c) They know their game, inside and out. (d) Even so, they always seem to depend on it.

Chapter 10

형용사, 부사, 비교

Chapter 10 형용사, 부사, 비교

[약점 POINT 1] 원급 및 비교급을 이용한 최상급 의미 표현

- He is the politest manager in the company. ◑최상급
  (그는 그 회사에서 가장 예의바른 매니저이다.)

- No manager in the company is so polite as he. ◑원급
  (회사의 어떤 매니저도 그만큼 예의바르지 않다.)

- He is as polite as any in the company.
  (그는 그 회사의 어느 누구보다도 예의바르다.)

- No manager in the company is politer than he. ◑비교급
  (그 회사의 어떤 매니저도 그보다 더 예의바르지 않다.)
  = He is politer than any other manager in the company.
  = He is politer than (all) the other managers in the company.

1. No language is so widely spoken as English in the world. (○ , ×)
(영어처럼 널리 쓰이는 언어는 없다.)

2. Jack is taller than any others boy in the class. (○ , ×)
(Jack은 자기 반에서 제일 크다.)

[약점 POINT 2] 비교구문 일반 주의사항

- 형용사나 부사를 비교급·최상급으로 쓸 때 〈-er, -est〉의 형태와 〈more, most〉의 형태를 이중으로 겹쳐 쓰면 틀린다.
  cf. the impatientest student (×)

- 집단한정 비교(…중에서) : 비교 틀의 선택에 유의하고, the를 생략하지 않는다.
  비교급 : He is the politer of the two. (of the twins, of the ears, between the two)
  (그는 둘 중에 더 친절하다.)
  최상급 : He is the politest of the three. (of all, among them, in the company)
  (그는 3명 중 가장 친절하다.) ◑동일 인물 비교
  원급 : He is as tall as (tall) can be.
  (그는 가장 키가 크다.)
  He acted as wisely as possible.(=as…as one can)
  (그는 가능한 한 가장 현명하게 행동했다.)
  비교급 : He is more polite than shy. (=rather…than)
  (그는 수줍기보다는 친절하다.)

1. That is one of (the longest, the most longest) rivers in our country.
(그것은 우리나라에서 가장 긴 강 중의 하나이다.)

He is less polite than she is. (○, ×)
(그는 그녀보다는 덜 친절하다.)

2. Among the managers, he is (the politer, the politest).
(매니저들 중에 그가 제일 친절하다.)

3. This is the least dangerous method of the two. (○, ×)
(이것이 둘 중에서 그나마 덜 위험한 방법이다.)

Answer

P1　1. ○　2. X (others → other)
P2　1. the longest, ○　2. the politest　3. X (the least → the less)

He is **as** bright **as any**.
(그는 누구보다도 밝다.)
He is **as** polite **as ever**.
(그는 어느 때보다도 친절하다.)

- **not so much** a father **as** a dictator = **not** a father **so much as** a dictator = **less** a father **than** a dictator = **more** a dictator **than** a father = **rather** a dictator **than** a father = a dictator **rather than** a father

  He has **as many as** five kids.
  (그는 아이가 다섯 명이나 된다.)
  He has gained **as much as** 10 pounds.
  (그는 10파운드나 벌었다.)

- 이미 비교급 형태인 superior, senior, preferable 등의 라틴계 비교급은 그 앞에 **more**, **very**가 오면 틀린다. 또한 뒤에도 **than**이 아닌 **to**를 이용하여 비교 대상을 취한다.

- 이중 원급 및 비교급 중 어느 한 틀이 누락되지 않도록 유의한다.
  He is **as** clever **as** or possibly **cleverer than** she is.
  (그는 그녀만큼, 어쩌면 그녀보다 더 현명하다.)

- 동일인물 최상급 비교, 소유격 뒤의 최상급, 부사의 최상급은 **the**를 붙이지 않는다.

1. He is not so much a manager (as, than) a tyrant. Right! He is (more, less) a manager than a tyrant.
("그는 매니저가 아니라 독재자야!" "그래! 그는 매니저가 아니라 독재자야!")

2. The new president is (more, very, much, far) superior to the old one. And for him, retraining the existing employees is (more, rather) preferable to hiring new ones.
(새로운 사장은 예전 사장보다 훨씬 낫다. 그리고 그는 새로운 사람들을 뽑는 것보다 지금 일하고 있는 사람들을 품고 가는 것을 지향한다.)

3. He is as clever as, if not cleverer, she is. (○ , ×)
(그는 최소한 그녀만큼 똑똑하다.)

4. At that time China was the world's (most, the most) powerful country.
(그 시절에 중국은 세계에서 제일 강대한 국가였다.)

[약점 POINT 4] 원급 및 비교급 구문에서의 비교 대상의 병치

- 원급 및 비교급 구문에서 비교가 되는 대상은 가능한 한 동일한 문법적 구조나 형태로 나타내준다. (형태적 병치, 내용적 일치)

- A is different from B, A is similar to B, A is like B, A outgrow(excel, exceed, surpass, top) B 등의 구문도 일종의 비교구문임에 유의한다.

1. To answer quickly is more important than answering accurately. (○ , ×)
(빨리 대답하는 것이 정확하게 대답하는 것보다 더 중요하다.)

2. We should donate some money as well as working some extra hours. (○ , ×)
(우리는 추가 근무를 하면서 약간의 기부금도 내야 한다.)

3. His idea is more practical than you. (○ , ×)
(그의 아이디어는 네 것보다 더 실용적이다.)

4. It is just as important to submit the report in time as (do, to do, doing) it neatly.
(리포트를 제시간에 제출하는 것만큼 깔끔하게 마무리하는 것도 중요하다.)

Answer
P3 1. as, less 2. far, rather 3. X (cleverer → cleverer than) 4. most
P4 1. X (answering → to answer) 2. X (working → work) 3. X (you → yours) 4. to do

[약점 POINT 5] 형태는 같으나 형용사와 부사로 나눠져 사용되는 경우

close 가까이 — **closely** 긴밀히	**deep** 깊숙이 — **deeply** 매우
dear 비싸게; 소중히 — **dearly** 매우	**hard** 열심히; 단단히; 심하게 — **hardly** 거의 … 않다
high 높게; 비싸게 — **highly** 매우	**near** 가까이 — **nearly** 거의
pretty 매우 — **prettily** 예쁘게	**fair** 공정한; 공정히 — **fairly** 공정히; 매우
most 대부분의; 대부분; 가장 — **almost** 거의 — **mostly** 대체로	
bad 나쁜; 매우 — **badly** 나쁘게; 매우	

1. The wind was blowing so hard that I could hardly walk any more. (○ , ×)
(바람이 너무 세게 불어서 걸을 수가 없었다.)

2. It is high unlikely that they will meet each other halfway. (○ , ×)
(그들이 중간 지점에서 만날 확률은 거의 없다.)

3. The book was written so badly that I didn't get further than the first chapter. (○ , ×)
(그 책은 엉망이어서 1장 뒤로 읽지 않았다.)

- **It is** + 감정형용사(glad, happy, sorry, grateful)의 형태는 쓰지 않는다.
- 난이형용사(difficult, hard, easy, (im)possible, (un)necessary, (un)important, (in)convenient)는 사람을 주어로 쓰지 않는다.
- **It is** + 판단형용사(necessary, required, essential, urgent, important, advisable, desirable, natural, right) + **that** + 주어 + (should) + 동사원형

1. It is sorry that you are sick. (○ , ×)
(아프다니 안됐네.)

2. He thinks that (he is impossible, it is impossible) to attend the conference.
(그는 컨퍼런스에 참가하는 건 불가능하다고 생각한다.)

3. She is difficult to do the task. (○ , ×)
(그녀가 그 일을 하기는 힘들다.)

4. He is hard to please. (○ , ×)
(그는 비위 맞추기가 힘들다.)

5. You can write me back whenever (you are convenient, it is convenient to you).
(네가 형편이 될 때 답변해주면 된다.)

6. It is important that she (will read, reads, read) this instructions with care.
(그녀가 이 지침서를 주의 깊게 읽는 것은 중요하다.)

7. It is necessary that every window (close, closes, is closed, be closed).
(모든 창문을 닫을 필요가 있다.)

Answer

P5 1. O 2. X (high → highly) 3. X (badly → bad)

P6 1. X (It is → I'm) 2. it is impossible 3. X (She is difficult → It is difficult for her) 4. O (It is hard to please him도 가능) 5. it is convenient to you 6. read 7. be closed

> considerable 상당한 — considerate 신중한, 친절한
> respectable 훌륭한 — respectful 공손한 — respective 저마다의
> imaginable 상상할 수 있는 — imaginary 상상의, 가상의 — imaginative 상상력이 풍부한
> literary 문학의 — literal 글자의 — literate 글을 읽고 쓸 줄 아는 — illiterate 문맹의
> industrial 산업의 — industrious 근면한
> broke 파산한 — broken 부서진

1. He spent (considerable, considerate) time and money on the project.
(그는 그 프로젝트에 꽤 많은 시간과 돈을 투자했다.)

2. If children were taught to be more (respectable, respectful, respective) towards their elders, all those crimes would not happen so often.
(아이들에게 노인들을 더욱 공경하라고 가르쳤다면 이런 범죄들이 그렇게 자주 일어나진 않을 것이다.)

[약점 POINT 8] 주의해야 할 형용사의 용법

> • 한정용법: 명사 앞 · 뒤에서 명사 수식
>   서술용법: 보어 자리에서 주어 또는 목적어 수식
> • -thing/-body 명사에서 형용사는 반드시 명사 뒤에 위치
> • 서술형용사(alive, asleep, alike, afraid, alone, ashamed, awake, aware)는 한정용법에서 명사의 뒤에 위치 (명사 앞에 위치하면 틀린다.)
>   This book is **worth** reading. (○)
>   This is a **worth** book. (×)
>   (이 책은 읽을 가치가 있다.)
>
> • an able man, be able to + 동사원형, be unable to + 동사원형
>   *cf.* an unable man (×)
>   This room is **able** to hold twenty people. (×)
>   (이 방은 20명을 수용할 수 있다.)
>   I am certain(sure) that~ , It is certain that~ *cf.* It is sure that… (×)
>   She was pleasant to hear the news. (×)
>   (그녀는 그 뉴스를 듣고 기분이 좋았다.)

1. Be careful not to wake up the sleeping baby. (○ , ×)
(잠자는 아기를 깨우지 않도록 조심해라.)

2. We should pay more attention to all the animals alive. (○ , ×)
(우리는 살아 있는 모든 동물들에게 더 많은 관심을 보여야 한다.)

3. There seems to be something strange about her behaviour. (○ , ×)
(그녀의 행동이 뭔가가 이상하다.)

4. We picked up very worth information unexpectedly. (○ , ×)
(우리는 아주 귀중한 정보를 우연히 얻었다.)

[약점 POINT 9] 수량형용사 : 수사 관련 주의사항

- 수량이나 부정 수량형용사(few, several, many)의 수식을 받는 '수 단위'는 five hundred, several thousand처럼 단수로 나타낸다. 하지만 막연한 범위의 수는 hundreds of, thousands of처럼 복수로 나타낸다.
- 표현은 복수일지라도, 하나의 단위 · 범위로 묶은 경우에는 단수 취급한다.
- 분자는 기수, 분모는 서수로 사용한다. 분자가 복수일 때에는, 분모는 복수서수를 사용한다.
- '기수 + 측정 단위'가 결합하여 명사를 수식할 때, 그 측정 단위는 a twenty-dollar bill, a six-year-old boy처럼 단수로 나타낸다. (복합 수량형용사)

1. A few hundred is supposed to stage a large-scale demonstration. (○ , ×)
(수백 명은 대규모 시위를 벌일 수 있다.)

2. Three quarters of the participants were current teachers. (○ , ×)
(참가자 중 3/4은 현직 교사들이었다.)

Answer
P7 1. considerable 2. respectful
P8 1. ○ 2. ○ 3. ○ 4. X (worth → worthy)
P9 1. ○ 2. ○

- very + 형용사 · 부사 / 원급 / ···ing / the very same / the very tallest / very late
- much + 동사, 비교급 / 최상급 / ···ed / much the same / much the tallest / much too late
- too는 긍정 동의에, either는 부정 동의에 쓰인다.
- hardly, scarcely, rarely, barely, seldom, neither : 중복 부정×, 문두 강조시 무조건 도치
- A rather than B는 'B라기보다는 오히려 A인' 의 뜻이고, A other than B는 'B가 아니라 A인(=except)' 의 뜻이다.

1. This is (the very same, very the same) church where we were married, and it looks (very, much) the same as years ago.
(여긴 바로 우리가 결혼한 교회인데 몇 년 전이랑 똑같은 모습이다.)

2. He is always (too much, much too) late for an appointment.
(그는 항상 약속에 많이 늦는다.)

3. You won't need a passport, and you hardly need a visa, either. (○ , ×)
(여권이나 비자는 필요 없다.)

4. The thief had not (even, scarcely) gone a mile when he got caught. Hardly do the police (ever, never) miss a lawbreaker nowadays.
(도둑은 1마일도 채 가지 못해서 잡혔다. 요즘 경찰들은 좀처럼 범법자들을 놓치지 않는다.)

5. His hair covers his eyes, so that you cannot hardly see his face. (○ , ×)
(그의 머리카락이 그의 얼굴을 가려서 얼굴 보기가 힘들다.)

6. Being a scholar doesn't mean being a boring person with no interests (rather than, other than) science. Scholars are unsociable (rather than, other than) boring.
(학자는 과학 이외에는 관심도 없는 지겨운 사람이란 뜻은 아니다. 학자들은 지루하기보다는 사교성이 없다.)

[약점 POINT 11] 부정 수량형용사

- 부정 수량형용사 : many, a number of, not a few(=quite a few), a few, few, several, a couple of + 복수 가산명사
- 부정 수량형용사 : much, a good deal of, a large amount of, not a little, a little, little + 불가산명사
- 부정 수량공통 형용사 : a lot of, lots of, plenty of, all, most, more, enough, some, any, no + (복수) 가산명사 · 불가산명사

1. It will take you many hours to get there because there is much traffic on the road. (○, ×)
(거기에 가려면 차가 막히기 때문에 많은 시간이 걸릴 것이다.)

2. It is difficult for retailers to either buy or stock large amounts of the products. (○, ×)
(소매업자들이 물품을 대규모로 구입하거나 재고로 두는 것은 어렵다.)

Answer

P10 1. the very same, much 2. much too 3. ○ 4. even, ever 5. X (cannot hardly → cannot or can hardly) 6. other than, rather than
P11 1. ○ 2. X

[약점 POINT 12] 형용사와 한정사 어순

- 형용사는 대명형용사(소유격 인칭대명사, 지시형용사, 부정형용사) + 수량형용사(수사, 부정수량형용사) + 형용사(일반 형용사)의 순서로 쓴다.
- 대명형용사에 관사를 더해 한정사라 하며, 이들은 어느 두 개를 나란히 쓰지 않는다.
  his this book (×), a my friend (×), most the firms (×)
- all, both, 배수사(half, double, twice)를 전치한정사라 하며, 이들은 예외적으로 한정사 앞에 위치할 수 있다.
  all those cars, both his bright sons, buy it at twice(half) the price
- 서수가 기수 앞에 위치한다.
  the first two chapters, the last four runners
- 부정대명사(some, any, all, many, most) 또는 부분표시어(half, part, the rest, two thirds, 20%) + of + (명사) 구문에서 명사는 특정 집단이나 대명사로 표시한다.

1. Have you ever seen his three pretty pets? (○ , ×)
(그의 귀여운 세 마리의 애완동물을 본 적 있니?)

2. We'll be moving into either of these two offices next month. (○ , ×)
(우리는 다음 달에 이 두 사무실 중 하나로 이사한다.)

3. We won't be able to read those all books in a month. (○ , ×)
(우리는 저 모든 책들을 한 달 만에 읽을 수 없을 것이다.)

4. Almost of attempts to export their goods proved a failure. (○ , ×)
(자기네 상품을 수출하려는 시도들은 거의 다 실패했다.)

[약점 POINT 13] 수량의 정도 표시에 주의해야 할 경우

- 집합 의미의 명사(population, family, audience)는 large나 small로 정도를 표시하며, 이미 수치 개념이 포함된 단어(price, age)는 high나 low로 그 정도를 표시한다.
- 또한 이들 명사는 How much(many) …? 대신 What …?(또는 How large …?, How high …?)을 이용해 그 정도를 묻는다.

1. He has a (many, large) family and lives in the house of which the price is very (much, expensive, dear, high).
(그는 대가족과 함께 아주 비싼 집에서 산다.)

2. (How much, How many, How high, What) is the population of the Philippines?

(필리핀의 인구는 어느 정도 되나?)

3. How much is the price of that? (○ , ×)

(저거 얼마야?)

[약점 POINT 14] 부사의 중요 위치

- 긍정문과 의문문에선 **still**, **yet** 어느 것이나 쓸 수 있다. 단, 부정문에선 **still**은 부정어 앞에, **yet**은 부정어 뒤에 위치한다.
- 형용사 **enough**(명사 수식)는 명사의 전·후 어디에나 위치할 수 있지만, 부사 **enough**(형용사, 부사, 동사 수식)는 명사의 뒤에서 수식한다.
- 부사가 형용사·부사를 수식할 때는 바로 앞에서 수식한다.
- '타동사 + 부사(전치사 형태)'의 타동사구는 목적어가 대명사인 경우는 **check it out**처럼 타동사와 부사의 사이에 위치하며, 일반명사인 경우는 **check the report out** 또는 **check out the report**처럼 어느 쪽에나 위치할 수 있다.

1. Jack yet hasn't finished cleaning up the house. (○ , ×)

(Jack은 아직 집안 청소를 끝내지 못했다.)

2. We got to the airport enough early since there was little traffic on the road. (○ , ×)

(우리는 차가 막히지 않아서 공항에 충분히 일찍 도착했다.)

Answer

P12 1. ○ 2. ○ 3. X (those all → all those) 4. X (almost → most)
P13 1. large, high 2. What 3. X (How much → What)
P14 1. X (yet hasn't → hasn't yet) 2. X (enough early → early enough)

- 2형식의 주격보어 또는 5형식의 목적격보어의 자리에 부사(-ly)가 오면 틀린다.
- 명사 앞의 수식어구가 '부사 + 형용사 + 명사(a completely free lunch)' 의 구조인지, '형용사 + 형용사 + 명사(a big free lunch)' 의 구조인지 유의한다.
- 원급, 비교급 구문에서 비교되는 품사가 형용사인지 부사인지에 유의한다.

1. This medicine may prove poisonously if taken in large quantities. (○ , ×)
(이 약은 많이 먹으면 독극물이나 다를 게 없다.)

2. The food smelled so deliciously that I couldn't keep my mouth from watering. (○ , ×)
(음식 냄새가 너무 좋아서 나는 계속 침을 흘리지 않을 수 없었다.)

3. It is always an (extreme, extremely) difficult job to get your first novel published.
(첫 번째 소설을 출간한다는 것은 언제나 극도로 힘든 작업이다.)

4. The heavy soil of the Delta produces (exceptionally, exceptional) high-yields of rice and wheat.
(Delta 지대의 흙은 질 좋은 쌀과 밀을 재배시킨다.)

5. The older we grow, the more (cautious, cautiously) we become. But some people behave as (indiscriminate, indiscriminately) as ever.
(우리는 나이가 들수록 더 조심스러워진다. 하지만 몇몇 사람들 여전히 무분별한 행동을 보인다.)

- He is almost(nearly, just, exactly, half, twice, not) as bright as she.
  (그는 거의 그녀만큼 총명하다.)
- He is much(even, still, far, by far, a lot, a little, twice, not) brighter than she.
  (그는 그녀보다 훨씬 더 총명하다.)
- He is much(far, by far, not) the brightest boy in the class. (=the very brightest boy)
  (그는 그 교실에서 가장 총명한 소년이다.)

1. In Spain football is (many times as popular, as many times popular) as bullfighting.
(스페인에서 축구는 투우보다 몇 배 인기가 많다.)

2. Car prices in Britain are (very higher, much higher) than those in other countries.
(영국에서는 다른 나라보다 자동차 가격이 훨씬 비싸다.)

3. He is (much the, the much, very the, the very) cleverest man I ever know.
(그는 내가 아는 가장 똑똑한 사람이다.)

Part I. Choose the best answer for the blank.

1. A: May I help you?
B: I'm looking for a copy of the *New York Times*. Can I ___________ here?
(a) pick up it
(b) pick it up
(c) pick up them
(d) pick them up

2. A: ___________ your new history teacher?
B: She's terrific, isn't she?
(a) Do you think how is
(b) How do you think
(c) Do you think what is
(d) What do you think of

3. A: Why do you prefer walking to driving?
B: It's because walking is ___________ driving.
(a) more invigorating than
(b) more invigorating as
(c) as invigorating than
(d) much invigorating than

Part II. Choose the best answer for the blank.

4. The house was ___________ but not luxurious.
(a) comfortable enough
(b) comfortable enough to
(c) enough comfortable
(d) enough to comfortable

5. There are many stores on ___________ sides of Newbury Street.
(a) either
(b) both
(c) all
(d) other

6. A: What's the biggest difference between Japan and China these days?

B: China's economy is growing more rapidly than ___________.

(a) Japan

(b) that of Japan

(c) the one of Japan

(d) those of Japan

7. The closer it gets to Christmas, ___________ most children become.

(a) to be happier

(b) they get happier

(c) the happier

(d) they are happier

8. It was quite difficult for Jason ___________ a risk instead of Jack.

(a) taking

(b) to take

(c) to be taken

(d) to be taking

9. I'm going to succeed to my uncle's estate and become rich ___________ long.

(a) after

(b) for

(c) before

(d) in

10. I don't understand why you keep ordering ___________ to me.

(a) the ridiculous

(b) ridiculous

(c) being ridiculous

(d) being the ridiculous

11. (a) A: Hey, isn't there anything else worth to watch?
    (b) B: There's a documentary on channel 11.
    (c) A: Well, I'd rather watch a football game.
    (d) B: All right then.

Chapter 11

명사, 관사, 대명사

Chapter 11 명사, 관사, 대명사

[약점 POINT 1] 불가산명사

- 절대 불가산명사 : information, news, evidence, advice, knowledge, fun, leisure, luck, progress, traffic, weather, health, 집합적 물질명사
- 불가산명사와 가산명사의 뜻이 다른 명사 :
  company 동료, 친구 – a company 일행, hair 머리 – a hair 한올
  room 여지 – a room 방, have time 시간 – have a good(hard) time 때, 경험
  authority 권위, 권한 – an authority 권위자 – authorities 당국
  office 직무 – an office 사무실, work 일 – a work of art 미술 작품 – works 공장, 공사

1. This book gives useful informations on how to repair cars. (○ , ×)
(이 책은 자동차 정비에 관한 실용적인 정보를 담고 있다.)

2. They put together the evidences to form one coherent explanation. (○ , ×)
(그들은 증거들을 합쳐서 하나의 논리적인 이론을 만들었다.)

3. We had a hard time finding our way to his house. (○ , ×)
(우리는 그의 집으로 찾아가는데 고생을 했다.)

4. She has a black hair. (○ , ×)
(그녀는 검은 머리를 가졌다.)

[약점 POINT 2] 명사의 전용 : 불가산명사의 가산명사화(=보통명사화)

- 물질명사 : a fire, a rain, an iron, a bronze, a precious stone, glasses
- 추상명사 : a beauty, a democracy, a favor, an invention, an authority, a pity, a success, a failure, a great experience, a great pleasure
- 고유명사 : three Picassos, an Edison, a Mr. Smith, the Browns, a Ford, an Apple

1. Everything she does is a tremendous success. (○ , ×)
(그녀가 하는 일은 모두 엄청난 성공이다.)

2. Doctors have been trying to find a cure for cancer for many years. (○ , ×)
(의사들은 오랫동안 암 치료법을 찾기 위해 노력해왔다.)

- 단 · 복수 동형의 명사 : means, species, series, Japanese, Chinese, sheep, deer, aircraft
- 단수 취급하는(-s) 명사 : measles, billiards, news, the United Nations, 학문 명
- 단 · 복수의 뜻이 다른 분화명사 : good 선, 득 - goods 상품, a manner 방법 - manners 예의, water 물 - waters 바다, cloth 천 - clothes 옷, regard 관계 - regards 안부, respect 존경 - respects 문안, a spectacle 광경 - spectacles 안경, arm 팔 - arms 무기, a letter 편지 - letters 문학
- 상호복수명사 : shake hands with, make friends with, change cars, be on good terms with, take turns (at) -ing

1. There are a lot of means of learning the truth. (○ , ×)
(진리를 배우는 방법은 많다.)

2. The news of the events has become part of the cultural debate. (○ , ×)
(이벤트에 대한 뉴스는 문화 토론의 주제 중 하나가 되었다.)

3. In the market they were busy selling their good. (○ , ×)
(시장에서 그들은 자기네 물건들을 팔기에 바빴다.)

4. We can take turn driving on the way. (○ , ×)
(우리는 교대로 운전하면 돼.)

Answer

P1 1. X (informations → information) 2. X (evidences → evidence) 3. O 4. X (a black hair → black hair)

P2 1. O 2. O

P3 1. O 2. O 3. X (good → goods) 4. X (turn → turns)

[약점 POINT 4] 집합명사의 수

- 일반 집합명사 : 일반 집합명사(family, committee, audience, team)는 집합체 자체(껍데기)를 의미하면 단수(=단순 집합 명사적 용법), 구성원들(알맹이)을 의미하면 복수(=군집 명사적 용법) 취급한다.
- 군집명사 : 항상 구성원들을 의미하는 집합명사를 말하며 복수 취급한다. the를 붙여 쓰는 the police, the jury, the clergy류와, the 없이 쓰는 people, cattle류가 있다.
- 단순집합명사(=집합적 물질명사) : 항상 집합체 자체를 의미하는 equipment, merchandise, clothing, baggage, machinery(jewelry, scenery, weaponry, stationery, poetry, pottery) 등을 말하며 단수 취급한다. 또한 이들은 불가산명사이다.

1. His family (is, are) very large, and his family (has, have) all got red hair.
(그의 가족은 대가족이고, 그의 가족들은 전부 빨간 머리이다.)

2. The cattle which (was, were) raised on that farm have been stolen, and the police (is, are) looking into this case.
(그 농장에서 키우던 소들을 도난당했고 경찰이 수사를 진행하고 있다.)

3. A lot of merchandise (has, have) been loaded into the truck.
(많은 물품이 트럭에 실렸다.)

[약점 POINT 5] 그 밖의 명사 관련 주의사항

- an angel of a wife, a palace of a house
- 불가산명사인 물질 · 추상 명사는 부정 수량 형용사(much, little), 부정 수량공통 형용사(some, a lot of), 조수사를 이용해 정도나 양을 표시한다.
  a cup of(two cups of) **water**, a piece of(many pieces of) **advice**
- of + 추상명사 = 형용사 : of + use, ability, value, help, importance, industry
- She is **beauty itself**. = She is **all beauty**. = She is very beautiful. = She is **a beauty**.
- the table's legs (×), the car's door (×)

1. It is of no use talking about the thing happened in the past. (○, ×)
(과거에 벌어진 일에 대해 말해봐야 소용없다.)

2. There are lots of the table's legs which are broken. (○, ×)
(부러진 책상 다리가 많이 있다.)

- 보어로 쓰인 관직·지위·신분, 자격의 **as** 뒤 : They elected him mayor. (그들은 그를 시장으로 선출했다.)
- 본래의 용도로 쓰인 건물·장소·가구 : go to bed(court, hospital), in church(class, bed, at table(school)
- 계절·식사·운동·학과명 : like summer, have dinner, play baseball, hate math
- 중병 : die of cancer, suffer from pneumonia   cf) have a cold(a fever, a headache)
- **by** + 교통·통신수단 : by bus(plane, train, air), by letter(mail, fax)
- **as** 도치 양보절의 문두 명사

1. The president appointed her as a minister. (○ , ×)
(대통령은 그녀를 장관으로 임명했다.)

2. A little boy as he was, he was very considerate. (○ , ×)
(비록 작은 소년이지만 그는 매우 사려 깊었다.)

Answer

P4 1. is, have 2. were, are 3. has
P5 1. O 2. X (table's → table)
P6 1. X (a 삭제) 2. X (A 삭제)

- They are selling shoes for $20 a pair. (=per)
- of **a** mind, of **an** age, of **a** height (=the same)
- 한정 의미 강조 : **the** tallest boy, **the** first chapter, **the** only way, **the** same means, **the** very thing, **the** late Mr. Gore, **the** English language, **the** Seoul city
- 악기명 : Do you play the piano?
- 신체 부위 : pull sb by **the** hand, stare sb in **the** face, pat sb on **the** shoulder
- 배분의 단위 : be sold by **the** pound, be paid by **the** day
- 후치 한정어구의 수식을 받는 명사 : **the** Edison of Korea, **the** water in this bottle
- the + 형용사 = 복수 보통명사 : **the** young, **the** dying, **the** injured, **the** unemployed

1. Birds of feather flock together. (○, ×)
(유유상종(끼리끼리 어울리다))

2. Jack used to play the guitar when he was in bad mood. (○, ×)
(Jack은 기분 나쁠 때마다 기타를 치곤 했다.)

3. The wounded were carried to the nearest hospital by ambulance. (○, ×)
(부상자는 앰뷸런스에 의해 가까운 병원으로 이송되었다.)

4. Jack had kindness to show me the way. (○, ×)
(Jack은 나에게 길을 가르쳐 줄 만큼 친절하다.)

[약점 POINT 8] 부정대명사 관련 주의사항

- one(=a + 명사)은 불가산명사 대신 사용할 수 있다.
- One should do **one's(his)** best to make oneself(himself) worthwhile.
(자신을 가치 있게 하려면 최선을 다해야 한다.)
- one (처음 하나 · 한 명), another (또 다른 하나 · 한 명 – 나머지 있음 전제), the other (나머지 하나 · 한 명), others (또 다른 것들 · 사람들; 타인), the others (나머지 모두)
- Every man and woman **has** donated **his** blood. (=his or her)
(모든 남녀는 자신의 피를 기증했다.)
every two **weeks** = every second **week** = every other **week** = on alternate **weeks**
- either와 neither는 2를 전제로 하며 항상 단수로 취급한다.

None of the students **know** about it.
(학생 중 누구도 그것에 대해 알지 못한다.)
None of the information **is** revealed.
(어떤 정보도 새나가지 않는다.)
Anyone can **not** solve the problem. (×)
(어느 누구도 그 문제를 풀 수 없다.)

1. Jill prefers white wine to red one. (○ , ×)
(Jill은 레드 와인보다 화이트 와인을 더 좋아한다.)

2. No one can blame him for doing his duty. (○ , ×)
(아무도 그가 자신의 임무를 수행한 것에 대해서 비난할 수 없다.)

3. To know is one thing and to explain it to others is other. (○ , ×)
(아는 것과 설명하는 것은 다르다.)

4. Jack is so careless that our advice goes in one ear and out the other. (○ , ×)
(Jack은 너무 덜렁대어 조언을 해줘봤자 한 귀로 듣고 한 귀로 흘린다.)

5. Each and every employee have expressed their anger. (○ , ×)
(모든 근로자들이 그들의 분노를 표시했다.)

6. They take away garbage every three days. (○ , ×)
(그들은 3일마다 쓰레기를 버린다.)

7. Do either of you want a part-time or a full-time job? (○ , ×)
(둘 중 아무 분이나 파트타임이나 풀타임 직업을 원하세요?)

8. I'm afraid we don't seem to have coffee; there are none left. (○ , ×)
(우리 이제 커피가 없어요; 재고가 없습니다.)

Answer

P7　1. X (feather → a feather) 2. X (bad mood → a bad mood) 3. O 4. X (kindness → the kindness)
P8　1. O 2. O 3. X (other → another) 4. O 5. X (have → has) 6. O 7. O 8. X (are → is)

- 일반적인 경우 : a very polite person
- such, many, what + a(n) + 형용사 + 명사
  such a fine day, such fine days, such fine weather
- so, as, too, how, however + 형용사 + a(n) + 명사
  so fine a day(○), so fine days (×), so fine weather (×)
  so + many, few, much, little + 명사

1. It was so a cold day that I decided to stay indoors. (○, ×)
(너무 추워서 집에 있기로 결정했다.)

2. It was such cold weather that I decided to stay indoors. (○, ×)
(날씨가 너무 추웠기 때문에 집안에 있기로 결정했다.)

- 아이(baby, infant, kid, child, newborn, fetus)나 동물은 성별이 미확인된 경우 중성인 it으로 받는다.
- 동격에 쓰이는 인칭대명사의 격에 유의한다.
- 주어와 목적어가 같을 경우, 목적어는 인칭대명사가 아니라 재귀대명사로 쓴다.
- 재귀대명사의 관용적 용법 : in spite of oneself (무의식적으로, 자신도 어쩔 수 없이), beside oneself (제 정신이 아닌, 미친), for oneself (혼자 힘으로), by oneself (홀로), to oneself (독점하여, 혼자만), in itself (본질적으로, 그 자체로서), of itself (저절로), between ourselves (우리끼리 이야기지만)

1. That child is a torment to its parents. (○, ×)
(그 아이는 부모에게 고통을 안겨다 준다.)

2. The gray squirrel jumped to the roof of the porch to escape (his, its) enemy.
(회색 다람쥐가 적을 피하기 위해서 현관 지붕으로 뛰었다.)

3. He specifically told them, Bob and he, to get ready. (○, ×)
(그는 구체적으로 Bob과 그에게 준비하라고 말했다.)

4. When our body is ill, it tries to regain strength by cooling (it, itself).
(몸이 아프면 우리 몸은 스스로 열을 내려서 기력을 회복하려 한다.)

5. The accident forced (him, himself) to quit his job, so he had to find another job.
(그 사고로 그는 직장을 그만둘 수밖에 없었고 따라서, 다른 직장을 구해야 했다.)

[약점 POINT 11] 지시대명사 관련 주의사항

- 후치 한정어구의 수식을 받는 (the + 명사)는 **that** 또는 **those**로 나타낼 수 있으며, 이때 수에 유의한다.

- He has **such a great ability** that everyone envies him. (=so great an ability)
  = His ability is **such** that everyone envies him. (=His ability is so great that...)
  = **Such** is his ability that everyone envies him. (=So great is his ability that...)
  (그는 모든 사람들이 시기할 만큼 대단한 능력을 갖고 있다.)

- 긍정문, and so + 동사 + 주어 : 무조건 도치, 대동사 선택에 유의

- **the** same, **the** same ⋯ as, **the** same ⋯ that, much **the** same, **the** very same

---

1. The wages in our company are almost similar to (that, those) in your company.
(우리 회사의 봉급은 당신 회사의 봉급과 거의 비슷하다.)

2. He is just a new employee and should be treated (such as, as such).
(그는 신입 사원일 뿐이고 그에 걸맞게 대우해 주어야 한다.)

3. (Such great, So great) was her kindness that we wrote her a thank-you letter.
(그녀가 너무나 친절하였기 때문에 우리는 감사의 편지를 보냈다.)

4. He has changed a lot, and so (is, was, does, has) she.
(그는 많이 바뀌었고, 그녀도 그랬다.)

5. This is the same car as I used to drive. (○, ×)
(이것은 내가 예전에 몰던 것과 똑같은 차이다.)

[약점 POINT 12] 의문대명사 관련 주의사항

- 〈정도·방법〉은 **how**로 묻지만, 〈의견〉은 **what**으로 묻는다.

- 목적격 **whom**의 자리에 주격 **who**가 대신할 수 있다.
  Who are you waiting for? (○)
  (당신은 누구를 기다립니까?)

- **How is the weather? = What is the weather like?**
  (날씨 어때요?)

---

1. (How, What) do you think of his plan?
(그의 계획에 대해서 어떻게 생각해?)

2. For who are you waiting? (○ , ×)
(누구를 기다리는 겁니까?)

Answer
P12 1. What 2. O

Part I. **Choose the best answer for the blank.**

1. A: Is the Socialist Party offering anything new in its latest statement?
   B: No, ___________.
   (a) it would not appear
   (b) it would appear not
   (c) it not would appear
   (d) not it would appear

2. A: Why were you teasing Cox about her new hairdo?
   B: I didn't mean to offend her. I was simply saying that it was too elaborate ___________.
   (a) to a girl of her age
   (b) to an aged girl
   (c) for a girl of her age
   (d) for an aged girl

Part II. **Choose the best answer for the blank.**

3. People know the first ___________ lasts a long time sometimes by their experiences.
   (a) impress
   (b) impressively
   (c) impressive
   (d) impression

4. It's hard to read ___________ since its printing type is quite small.
   (a) paper
   (b) a paper
   (c) papers
   (d) a page of paper

5. According to custom of our company, we have paid a worker ___________ not the hour.
   (a) by the piece
   (b) by piece
   (c) by pieces
   (d) by the pieces

6. San Diego's new 16-mile trolley line ____________ with the Mexican border city of Tijuana.

(a) will link up San Diego city

(b) will link San Diego

(c) shall be linking

(d) links it

7. Not many children realize ____________ parents play in their lives.

(a) how significant role

(b) how a significant role

(c) how significant a role

(d) how a role significant

Part III. Identify the option that contains an awkward expression or an error in grammar.

8. (a) A: Mom, is there anything I can do for you?

(b) B: Would you help me wash fresh vegetables and fruits?

(c) A: Ok, I will. What should I do after that?

(d) B: Then, clean the floor and help me do the laundries.

9. (a) A: Dinner is ready! Please come and help yourself!

(b) B: Hmm, it smells so yummy and every food looks so wonderful.

(c) A: How does this cake taste of?

(d) B: It tastes like heaven.

10. (a) A: Why don't you try some of this carrot cake?

(b) B: No thanks. You know I don't have a sweet tooth.

(c) A: But I baked it just for yours.

(d) B: Well, I'll have one piece then.

11. (a) A : How are the tablets and the cream for?

(b) B : The tablets should reduce the swelling, and the cream should clear up the rash.

(c) A : How long will it be before the rash clears up?

(d) B : If it doesn't go away in two weeks, come back again.

12. (a) Here's tonight's weather in the Midwest. (b) Scattered showers and thunderstorms will continue through night. (c) Watch for lightning, large hail and possible tornadoes. (d) This system will also affect the surrounding areas.

Chapter 12

일치 · 특수구문

Chapter 12 일치 · 특수구문

[약점 POINT 1] 병렬 구조

- 대등접속사의 앞 · 뒤

  He enjoys **fresh air**, **sunshine**, and **to take long walks**. (×)

  (그는 신선한 공기, 햇볕 그리고 긴 산책을 하는 것을 좋아한다.)

  Her duties are **to receive** visitors, **to check** mails and **typing** letters. (×)

  (그녀의 임무는 방문객을 맞고, 우편물을 확인하며 편지를 타이핑하는 것이다.)

  cf. **To teach** is to learn.

  (가르치는 것이 배우는 것이다.)

  To know is one thing and to teach is another.

  (아는 것과 가르치는 것은 별개의 것이다.)

- 대등 상관접속사구의 A, B

  The regulations are neither **so simple** nor **obvious**. (×)

  (그 규칙은 단순하지도 분명하지도 않다.)

  I waited not only **for** you but **your sister**. (×)

  (나는 너뿐 아니라 너의 누이도 기다렸다.)

  This is not **to help** the employers but **provide** work for the newly employed. (×)

  (이것은 고용주를 돕기 위한 것이 아니라 새로운 직원에게 일을 주기 위한 것이다.)

  Research continues both **home** and **abroad**. (×)

  (연구는 국내외에서 계속되었다.)

  I object to war not **because** it drains the economy but **that** it seems inhuman. (×)

  (나는 전쟁이 경제를 소모해서가 아니라 비인간적으로 보이기 때문에 반대한다.)

1. He is not only famous in the United States, but also abroad. (○, ×)

(그는 미국에서뿐만 아니라 외국에서도 유명하다.)

2. He died at the age of 70, friendless and no money. (○, ×)

(그는 친구도 돈도 없이 70살의 나이로 죽었다.)

[약점 POINT 2] 주어와 동사의 수 일치

- A accompanied by B, A coupled with B, A as well as B, A along with B, A together with B, A with B, there are[have]~

  There have been a lot of changes happening lately.

  (최근 많은 변화가 일어났다.)

  His parents as well as his sister, are supposed to get here.

  (그의 부모와 그의 누이도 여기 오기로 되어 있다.)

- neither A nor B, either A or B, A or B, not A but B, not only A but also B

  Neither you nor she is responsible for the failure.
  (너 또는 그녀도 그 실패에 책임이 없다.)

- A number of cars are parked in the neighborhood on weekends.
  (많은 차들이 주말에는 이 부근에 주차된다.)

  The number of cars visiting here is on the steady increase.
  (이곳을 방문하는 차들의 수는 점진적으로 증가 추세에 있다.)

- Many people have come here to enjoy the holiday.
  (많은 사람들이 휴일을 즐기러 이곳에 온다.)

  Many a person has come here to enjoy the holiday.
  (많은 사람들이 휴일을 즐기러 이곳에 온다.)

- One of the factories that produce cars wants to relocate here.
  (차를 생산하는 공장 중 한 곳이 이곳으로 이전하기를 원한다.)

  The only one of the factories that produce cars wants to relocate here.
  (차를 생산하는 공장 중 단 한 곳이 이곳으로 이전하기를 원한다.)

- All work and no play has left him friendless.
  (일만 하고 놀지 않으면 친구가 없다.)

  – slow and steady, a needle and thread, a watch and chain, curry and rice

- Five months have passed since I came here.
  (내가 이곳에 온지 5개월이 지났다.)

  Five months is too short for us to finish the task.
  (5개월은 우리에게 너무 짧아서 그 일을 끝낼 수 없다.)

- Whether he will join us or not doesn't matter at all.
  (그가 합류하든지 말든지 전혀 문제되지 않는다.)

- His shoes are old, so a new pair of shoes is perfect for this birthday.
  (그의 신발이 낡아서, 새로운 신발 한 켤레는 이번 그의 생일 선물로 완벽하다.)

  – a pair(set, pack) of, a group of, a series of

1. There was only seventeen cents left with us. (○ , ×)
(우리는 17센트밖에 남지 않았다.)

2. Neither her appearance nor her manners was satisfactory. (○ , ×)
(그녀의 겉모습이나 태도는 불만족스러웠다.)

3. Either the landlord or his wife were not telling the truth. (○ , ×)
(지주와 그의 아내는 진실을 말하고 있지 않았다.)

4. The total number of houses under water amounts to 1500. (○ , ×)
(물에 잠긴 가구는 총 1500 가구 정도 된다.)

5. That is the only one of those watches that require no winding. (○ , ×)

(저 시계는 태엽을 감지 않아도 되는 시계 중 유일한 것이다.)

6. Bread and butter was all we had. (○ , ×)

(우리는 가진 것이 별로 없었다.(우리는 빵과 버터밖에 없었다.))

7. A series of meetings was held recently regarding the crisis. (○ , ×)

(최근 이번 위기와 관련하여 미팅이 자주 열렸었다.)

[약점 POINT 3] 도치 : 조동사 · be동사는 직접 주어 앞으로, 일반동사는 do동사로 대신해서 주어 앞으로 이동된다.

● 부정어구를 문두에 강조할 때

Never have I dreamed of such a weird thing before.

(나는 전에 그렇게 기묘한 것을 꿈도 꾸지 못했다.)

Not only was he disappointed but he got angry.

(그는 실망했을 뿐 아니라 화도 났다.)

Little does he realize the importance of this project.

(그는 이 프로젝트의 중요성을 거의 인식하지 못한다.)

Hardly had I got into the building when it began to rain.

(그 건물에 들어가자마자 비가 내리기 시작했다.)

● 한정어구를 문두에 강조할 때

Only then could I recognize her.

(그제서야 나는 그녀를 알아볼 수 있었다.)

Only when he called my name did I turn back and see him.

(그가 나의 이름을 불렀을 때만 나는 뒤로 돌아 그를 봤다.)

● 정도 강조어를 문두에 강조할 때

So great is her ability that they praise her.

(그녀의 능력은 너무 대단해서 그들은 그녀를 칭찬한다.)

● 긍정 동의 및 부정 동의

He is greedy and **so** is his wife.

(그는 욕심이 많은데 그의 부인도 그러하다.)

He doesn't enjoy sea food, **nor(=and neither)** does his wife.

(그는 해산물을 좋아하지 않는데, 그의 부인도 그러하다.)

1. Rarely you will meet a character exactly like yourself in fiction. (○ , ×)
(소설에서 정확히 너와 똑같은 인물을 찾는 것은 어려울 것이다.)

2. Not until the Enlightenment societies seriously question the state's power to kill. (○ , ×)
(계몽 운동 후 여러 사회에서는 국가의 사형 집행권에 대해서 심각하게 문제를 제기했다.)

3. Not only they ignore the protest, but they also lied to the press. (○ , ×)
(그들은 항의를 무시했을 뿐만 아니라 언론에 거짓말도 했다.)

4. Only now are we beginning to come to terms with getting the final decisions. (○ , ×)
(이제서야 우리는 최종 결정에 대한 합의를 보기 시작했다.)

5. So great was the force coming out of the Chinese monk's hands that it was known to lift a grownup man from the seat. (○ , ×)
(그 중국 승려의 손에서 나오는 기운은 너무 강력해서 앉아 있는 어른이 들린다고 알려졌다.)

[약점 POINT 4] 부가의문문 : 주어 + 동사, 동사 not + 주어?

- 긍정 → 부정, 부정 → 긍정, 조동사 · be동사 → 조동사 · be동사, 일반동사 → do동사

- 부가의문문의 주어는 인칭대명사가 원칙이며, 단 there 구문은 there로 일치시킨다.

- had better → hadn't, would rather → wouldn't, used to → didn't, ought to → shouldn't, have to → don't

- 복문은 There is no one here that you want, is there?처럼 주절에 일치시키지만, 판단동사 I think (believe, guess, imagine, suppose, presume) that… 구문은 종속절(=목적절)에 일치시킨다.

1. You have to wear the seatbelt in your country, (haven't, don't) you?
(너희 나라에서는 안전벨트 매야 하지, 그렇지?)

2. I don't think the girl over there is pretty, is she? (○ , ×)
(저기 있는 여자는 안 예쁜 거 같아, 그렇지?)

3. I don't think he is smart, do I? (○ , ×)
(나는 그가 똑똑하다고 생각하지 않아, 그렇지?)

Answer

P1 1. O 2. X (no money → moneyless)
P2 1. X (was → were) 2. X (was → were) 3. X (were → was) 4. O 5. X (require → requires) 6. O
  7. O
P3 1. X (you will → will you) 2. X (societies → did societies) 3. O 4. O 5. O
P4 1. don't 2. X (is she → isn't she) 3. X (do I → isn't he)

[약점 POINT 5] There 구문의 수 일치와 도치

1. There (is, are) supposed to be a coffee machine somewhere around here.
   (이 주위에 커피 자판기가 있을 텐데.)

2. There (have, has) been a few misunderstandings over the terms of the contract.
   (계약 조건에 대해서 오해가 많았다.)

3. There seem to be something wrong with him. (○, ×)
   (그에게 무슨 문제가 있는 거 같다.)

[약점 POINT 6] 수량 부정대명사와 부분 표시어의 수

1. One fourth of a worker's income are paid in taxes and social security. (○, ×)
   (노동자의 수입 중 1/4은 세금과 사회보장료로 지불된다.)

2. Two thirds of the surface of the earth are water. (○, ×)
   (지구 표면의 2/3는 물로 이루어져 있다.)

3. I really like his novels, some of which (is, are) on my bookshelf.
   (나는 그의 소설을 정말 좋아해. 그 중 몇 개는 내 책꽂이에 있다.)

4. When two thirds of the ship (was, were) under water, half of the passengers (was, were) already drowned.
   (배의 2/3가 물에 잠겼을 때 절반 정도의 승객들이 이미 익사했다.)

[약점 POINT 7] 명사와 대명사의 수 일치

대명사는 앞에 나온 명사를 받는 것이므로 앞에 나온 명사의 단·복수에 일치해야 한다.

1. Very few colleges these days refuse (its, their) admission on grounds of age alone.
(요즘 단지 나이 때문에 입학을 거부하는 대학은 몇 군데 안 된다.)

2. Few husbands are willing to give a hand to (his, their) wives.
(자신의 와이프를 기꺼이 도와주려는 남편은 거의 없다.)

3. Many a man is afraid of losing (his, their) jobs.
(많은 사람들이 직장을 잃을까 두려워한다.)

4. We must know that the regulations are neither simple nor obvious as we expected (it, them) to be.
(그 규칙들이 우리가 예상하는 것처럼 단순하지도 분명하지도 않다는 것을 우리는 알아야 한다.)

Answer

P5   1. is 2. have 3. X (seem → seems)
P6   1. X (are → is) 2. X (are → is) 3. are 4. was, were
P7   1. their 2. their 3. his 4. them

- Normally, my father usually keeps early hours. (×)
  (일반적으로, 아버지는 일찍 일어나신다.)

- Of nearly approximately 5,000 stars, only several hundred have proper names. (×)
  (거의 5,000개의 별 중에, 오직 수백 개의 별만이 적절한 이름을 갖고 있다.)

- This is a wordy and redundant article. (×)
  (이것은 장황하며 중복이 되는 글이다.)

- The reason she lost the key was because she was careless. (×)
  (그녀가 열쇠를 잃어버린 이유는 부주의하기 때문이다.)

- Whenever she is in trouble, she always asks me for help. (×)
  (곤란에 처할 때마다, 그녀는 항상 나에게 도움을 청한다.)

- Don't overwork yourself too much. (×)
  (너무 과로하지 마라.)

- repeat ~ again, proceed(advance) ~ forward, return ~ back, join ~ together (×)

- visible to the eyes, audible to the ears, The sound sounded like ~ (×)
  cf. visible to the naked eyes, visible to one eye (○)

1. Diamonds they are the most precious of all stones. (○ , ×)
(다이아몬드는 모든 돌 중에서 가장 가치가 있는 것이다.)

2. Strangely, that it turned out that way. (○ , ×)
(이상하게도 그것은 결국 그런 식으로 드러났다.)

3. Though he was exhausted, but he helped us. (○ , ×)
(그는 지쳤음에도 불구하고 우리를 도왔다.)

4. Because he was so excited that he didn't hear his name called.(○ , ×)
(그는 너무 흥분했기 때문에 자신의 이름이 불리는 것을 듣지 못했다.)

Answer

P8　1. X (they 삭제)　2. X (that 삭제)　3. X (but 삭제)　4. X (that 삭제)

Part I. Choose the best answer for the blank.

1. A: ____________ to come to the reception tomorrow?
    B: I'm afraid I can't.
    (a) Are you possible
    (b) Is it able you
    (c) Is it capable of you
    (d) Is it possible for you

Part II. Choose the best answer for the blank.

2. Hardly ____________ the building when it began to rain.
    (a) I had got into
    (b) had got into I
    (c) have I got into
    (d) had I got into

3. She made me go back to college, study hard, and ____________ a degree.
    (a) to attain
    (b) attain
    (c) attaining
    (d) attainment

4. Many a person ____________ inquired concerning a recent message of mine.
    (a) have
    (b) has
    (c) had
    (d) have been

5. It's scheduled to depart at 6:05, but ______________ a delay.
    (a) there will be
    (b) there would be
    (c) there is
    (d) there it will be

6. __________ of the project __________ finished by the team.
(a) One-fourths, was
(b) One-fourth, was
(c) One-fourth, were
(d) One-fourths, were

7. Never before __________ under similar circumstances in the past.
(a) the president resigned
(b) has the president resigned
(c) the president has resigned
(d) has the president resign

8. Susan is good at singing a capella but __________ in playing some instruments.
(a) has no interest
(b) not interesting
(c) is interest
(d) is interestingly

Part III. Identify the option that contains an awkward expression or an error in grammar.

9. (a) A: We spent most of the morning trying to buy tickets.
(b) B: Did you? How long did you have to wait in line?
(c) A: To three hours.
(d) B: That sounds terrible!

10. (a) A: Not only he is lazy but also very selfish.
(b) B: Tell me about it. I'm fed up with working with him.
(c) A: Moreover, little does he realize the importance of this project.
(d) B: And we're on the verge of being exhausted to death.

11. (a) Since the Second World War, the world's economy has grown at an incredible rate. (b) Along with the economy, world trade has also expanded like never before. (c) The expansion of world trade can be attributed to the development of transport technology, telecommunications and the international financial system. (d) It is clear that the increase in world trade have supported this postwar economic growth.

12. (a) It was important for me to get home early as Maggie and Colin were coming over for dinner. (b) But when I got to the station I saw that it was crowded with people waiting for trains delayed because of the bad weather. (c) Just then, a car pulled up and a man inside shouted to me, offer me a lift. (d) My first reaction was to be suspicious of him, but then I realized that it was Maggie's brother.

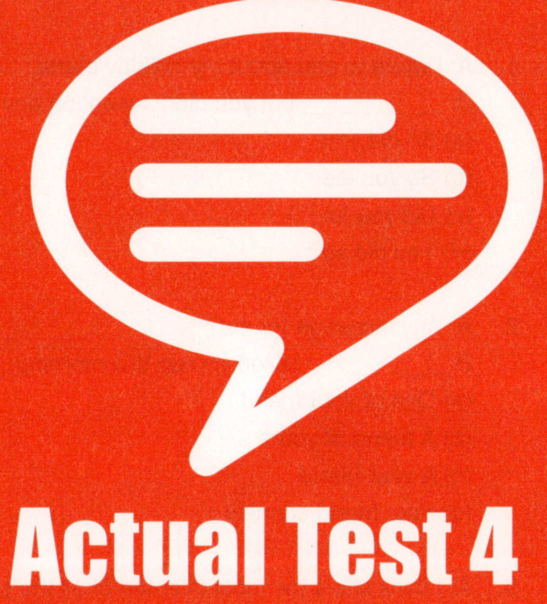

Actual Test 4

Actual Test 4

Part I. Choose the best answer for the blank.

1. A: I wrote to you about my holiday plans.
    B: ____________, but you didn' t mention any dates.
    (a) So did you
    (b) So you did
    (c) Did you so
    (d) You did so

2. A: Any message for me?
    B: ____________ called you up this morning.
    (a) One of your friend
    (b) A friend of yours
    (c) A your friend
    (d) Your friend of one's

3. A: I think she's the most talented of all the students.
    B: ____________. She's a real genius.
    (a) So am I
    (b) So do I
    (c) Neither am I
    (d) Neither do I

[고난이도] 4. A: How are you doing these days?
    B: ____________. I'm really happy with my new job.
    (a) Never been better
    (b) Never better been
    (c) Never being better
    (d) Better never been

Part II. *Choose the best answer for the blank.*

5. The prospective employee asked ___________ medical coverage.
    (a) if she would get
    (b) that she will get
    (c) if she will get
    (d) that she could get

6. In this corner of the region ___________ the world's most beautiful species of butterflies.
    (a) are some of
    (b) some are
    (c) is some
    (d) some of which

7. This rock is four times as ___________ that one.
    (a) bigger than
    (b) big
    (c) the biggest of
    (d) big as

8. Though Mr. Jackson drew up the design for a new kind of airplane, _________ was never completed.
    (a) he invented
    (b) his invention
    (c) to invent
    (d) inventing him

Part III. *Identify the option that contains an awkward expression or an error in grammar.*

9. (a) A: Good morning, sir. May I help you?
    (b) B: I'm here for a city tour.
    (c) A: I'm sorry, but it's been canceled.
    (d) B: Really? That's too bad.

Part IV. Identify the option that contains an awkward expression or an error in grammar.

10. (a) Human activities have increased the amount of carbon dioxide gas in the atmosphere. (b) Scientists expect what this buildup will warm the world over the next few decades. (c) One possible solution may be to soak up the extra carbon dioxide in forests. (d) However, new studies suggest forests can't be a long-term solution to the problem of greenhouse gases.

Final Test

Final Test 1

Part I (1~20) Choose the best answer for the blank.

1. A: Sarah looks really upset. Do you know why?

B: I heard she ___________ this morning.

(a) got her pocket picked

(b) got her pocket picking

(c) had her pocket to pick

(d) had her pocket picking

2. A: Do you know how old our new boss is?

B: I ___________________ 30.

(a) just heard she turned

(b) just heard she turned into

(c) heard she just turned

(d) heard she just turned into

3. A: Excuse me, where should I go to buy a baseball glove?

B: You can find _____________ in the fifth floor.

(a) a range of the sports equipment

(b) a range of sports equipment

(c) a range of the sports equipments

(d) a range of sports equipments

4. A: Oh, no! I forgot ____________ !

B: Don't worry, I did.

(a) that I turn the oven off

(b) turning the oven off

(c) to turn the oven off

(d) to turning the oven off

5. A: That the number of younger workers __________ definitely not a good sign.

B: I don't get it. Please tell me why.

(a) is falling is

(b) are falling is

(c) is falling are

(d) are falling are

6. A: Are you ___________ ?
    B: No. Please bring me the menu.
    (a) served
    (b) serving
    (c) being served
    (d) being serving

7. A: _____________ is the likeliest candidate for the White House?
    B: They say it's McIves, but I think Kingstone will win the election.
    (a) Do you think who
    (b) Who do you think
    (c) Do you think whom
    (d) Whom do you think

8. A: I hate this TV show.
    B: ___________. It's disgusting and no fun at all!
    (a) So do I
    (b) I do, either
    (c) Neither do I
    (d) Nor do I

9. A: Does Jessica go with Paul?
    B: ___________ .
    (a) That I not know
    (b) That I not know of
    (c) Not that I know
    (d) Not that I know of

10. A: If Jason _________ , will you let us know, please?
    B: Only if Jason agrees, sorry.
    (a) come here
    (b) comes here
    (c) came here
    (d) will come here

11. A: When can we meet Joe?

B: She ______________ come here by 3.

(a) supposed to

(b) is supposed to

(c) will suppose to

(d) will be supposed to

12. A: I failed driver's license test again.

B: If you had ever practiced, you _________ that license now.

(a) get

(b) got

(c) will get

(d) would get

13. A: What else should we pack for the trip?

B: A pair of short pants __________, as well.

(a) is needed

(b) are needed

(c) need

(d) needs

14. A: I had a good time ___________ you.

B: So did I. Can we meet again?

(a) to talk

(b) talking

(c) to talk with

(d) talking with

15. A: Mom, please ___________ this homework

B: Sorry, Jacob. It's your job and you need to do it by yourself.

(a) help me do

(b) help me doing

(c) help doing

(d) help I do

16. A: I think this lipstick ____________ your skin color.

B: Then I'll buy that. How much is it?

(a) goes nice with

(b) goes nicely with

(c) goes nice to

(d) goes nicely to

17. A: I was shocked after I heard Mr. Kim's age.

B: Me, too. As he __________, he looks much older than his age.

(a) went bald

(b) went baldly

(c) had gone bald

(d) had gone baldly

18. A: Did you and your brother bury the hatchet?

B: Yes, we did. We are on ________________ each other now.

(a) good terms

(b) good term

(c) good terms with

(d) good term with

19. A: I only earn 200 dollars from this project.

B: Cheer up! 200 dollars _____________ .

(a) is still a lot money

(b) are still a lot money

(c) is still a lot of money

(d) are still a lot of money

20. A: ____________ that anchorman is?

B: It's hard to guess. Well ... maybe 40 to 45?

(a) Do you think how old

(b) Do you how old think

(c) How do you think old

(d) How old do you think

Part II (21~40) **Choose the best answer for the blank.**

21. ______________ in the room alone, he made his testament.
    (a) Be
    (b) Being
    (c) To be
    (d) Having been

22. Foreign intervention, ______________ , invariably leads to "shooting."
    (a) he believes
    (b) he believed
    (c) he believe
    (d) he had believed

23. This program will help you ______________ the most useful computer skills.
    (a) acquaint
    (b) acquaint yourself
    (c) acquaint with
    (d) acquaint yourself with

24. She is wearing the same skirt ______________ .
    (a) as I am
    (b) as I do
    (c) as me
    (d) as mine

25. The number of small businesses and public service workers ______________.
    (a) is increasing
    (b) are increasing
    (c) is increased
    (d) are increased

26. We should delegate everything to an independent research agency ____________ academics with neutrality and expertise.
   (a) consist of
   (b) consists of
   (c) consisting of
   (d) consisted of

27. A series of ____________ revealed later on.
   (a) organized cheating case was
   (b) organized cheating case were
   (c) organized cheating cases was
   (d) organized cheating cases were

28. ______________ his bad temper, I would never have gone out with him.
   (a) Did I know
   (b) Have I known
   (c) Had I known
   (d) Were I know

29. Suppose ____________, whom would you choose?
   (a) you are she
   (b) you are her
   (c) you were she
   (d) you were her

30. This cake ____________ by the time kids arrive.
   (a) have
   (b) have baked
   (c) will have baking
   (d) will have been baked

31. This wine cannot be ______________ .
    (a) highly recommended enough
    (b) highly enough recommended
    (c) recommended highly enough
    (d) recommended enough highly

32. Upon ________ the final score, Jackie and her coach cried for joy.
    (a) hearing
    (b) to hear
    (c) having heard
    (d) Being heard

33. He left a note ____________ the cause of his suicide.
    (a) give
    (b) given
    (c) gave
    (d) giving

34. ____________ bankrupt than she left him.
    (a) No sooner he has gone
    (b) No sooner he had gone
    (c) No sooner has he gone
    (d) No sooner had he gone

35. The ____________ expected to decide in the next three weeks.
    (a) custom
    (b) custom is
    (c) customs is
    (d) customs are

36. Not until his death ______________ his innocence.
  (a) they realized
  (b) did they realize
  (c) they have realized
  (d) have they realized

37. Although she's very old now, she ______________ a beauty when young.
  (a) seems to be
  (b) seems being
  (c) seems to have been
  (d) seemed to have been

38. Group B consists of twelve ______________
  (a) six - year - old
  (b) six - years - old
  (c) six - year - olds
  (d) six - years - olds

39. The title ______ the property was conveyed from them to you.
  (a) of
  (b) for
  (c) to
  (d) on

40. Over 23,000 delinquents filed for bankruptcy ______________ this year.
  (a) in the first nine month
  (b) in the first nine months
  (c) in first nine month
  (d) in first nine months

Part III(41~45) **Identify the option that contains an awkward expression or an error in grammar.**

41. (a) A: I hate being behind on my work.
   (b) B: You couldn't have put it off. What did you do yesterday?
   (c) A: I played computer games all day.
   (d) B: You could enjoy playing games with a peace of mind today if everything had done yesterday.

42. (a) A: Do you think lie detectors as foolproof?
   (b) B: Kind of. Why?
   (c) A: I read an article yesterday, and it said those who minister the test are not necessarily experts.
   (d) B: Then the level of certainty cannot be that high.

43. (a) A: Did you break up with Lucy? What happened?
   (b) B: I want to get married now, but she had a different idea with me.
   (c) A: Why didn't you ask Lucy to marry you?
   (d) B: I made a number of marriage proposal, but she never accepted.

44. (a) A: I think Katie got wind of our plan.
   (b) B: Gee, then her birthday party cannot be a surprise one.
   (c) A: I guess Alex told to her our plan.
   (d) B: I shouldn't have let him know. It's all my fault.

45. (a) A: I'm terribly sorry, but can I postpone our meeting until this Thursday?
   (b) B: Why? Haven't you arrived in Wien yet?
   (c) A: I missed the flight, and the next one is on Wednesday.
   (d) B: It's O.K. for me, but when you arrive, the rest of us will have gone to Paris.

Part IV(46~50) Identify the option that contains an awkward expression or an error in grammar.

46. (a) Tonight, we gather to affirm the greatness of our nation. (b) It's not because of the height of our skyscrapers, or the power of our military, or the size of our economy. (c) Our pride is based on a very simple premise. (d) The premise is sum up in a declaration made over two hundred years ago.

47. (a) I still believe that there is a probability of bullish outcome. (b) The world is having the most severe recession of the postwar era. (c) And the recovery will be sluggish and plagued by inflation. (d) Nevertheless, the doomsday scenario of depression and deflation is farfetched.

48. (a) When I was about 9, my mom started a business photographing women who wanted a glamorous picture of themselves. (b) I held her light meters and her reflectors. (c) My mom would bring me into the darkroom, which was on our back porch, and develop the film. (d) I was fascinated watching the pictures appeared with that red light shining.

49. (a) Modeling is very lonely. (b) Actresses or singers travel with entourages, with their hair and makeup people and tour managers, but models are alone. (c) Even when you're the biggest supermodel in the world, you're alone. (d) So I tried to get to L.A. and hang out with my high-school friends as often as I can.

50. (a) Over 40 years, my experience has been that when everyone is bearish and has acted accordingly, that is invariably right to be gradually buying. (b) The bottom of a stock-market cycle by definition has to be the point of maximum bearishness. (c) The news doesn't have to be good for prices to rally. (d) It just has to be less bad than what has already been factored into the market.

Part I (1~20) Choose the best answer for the blank.

1. A: Hey, why are you here? You're supposed to be on the flight to New York by now, aren't
       you?
    B: Yes I am, but on my way to the airport, I remembered ______ my passport in the office .
    (a) leaving
    (b) to leave
    (c) leave
    (d) left

2. A: If I died today, what would happen to my family's future?
    B: Oh, cut the crap! That's only those ___________ favorite question and you are not
       going to die today anyway.
    (a) life insurance company's
    (b) life insurance companies
    (c) life insurance companies's
    (d) life insurance companies'

3. A: What's exciting about that skater is along with her elegance, she has fire.
    B: Right. We had great expectations and she delivered on ___________!
    (a) every single one of it
    (b) every single one of them
    (c) every single of it
    (d) every single of them

4. A: I cannot remember where I put my cell phone.
    B: Is that ringing one ___________ you are looking for?
    (a) that
    (b) which
    (c) what
    (d) as

5. A: Do you like ice cream?
    B: Sure. Who ___________?
    (a) don't
    (b) doesn't
    (c) isn't
    (d) aren't

6. A: ____________ the National Assembly will endorse the president's choice.

B: I think the Assembly has to re-think the reason for its being.

(a) Chance is that

(b) The chance is that

(c) Chances are that

(d) The chances are that

7. A: It's ________________ .

B: I'm not hungry at all. Can we have it an hour later?

(a) time for a dinner

(b) time for dinner

(c) time to a dinner

(d) time to dinner

8. A: I have to go to pick up Sally at the airport.

B: I'd rather _________ inside than go out in this rainstorm. Sally can come by herself.

(a) stay

(b) stayed

(c) you stay

(d) you stayed

9. A: Did you know that Chris had Mr. Jenkins __________ Amy?

B: Really? Then I guess it's true that Chris is having an affair with him.

(a) fire

(b) to fire

(c) fired

(d) should fire

10. A: Have you read the essay 'poverty with the cheese cake'?

B: No. Who __________ it?

(a) writes

(b) wrote

(c) has written

(d) had written

11. A: If you ___________ tomorrow, how would you spend a day?

B: It's very difficult to answer.

(a) die

(b) died

(c) have died

(d) had died

12. A: I understood ___________ what he said.

B: Same here. He may be a great mathematician, but a failure as a teacher.

(a) a little of

(b) little of

(c) a little

(d) little

13. A: I finally learned that I should never buy shoes on the Internet. What a waste of money!

B: That's all right. A wise person ___________ his mistakes.

(a) profits

(b) profits from

(c) makes profit

(d) makes profit from

14. A: Do successful people have some traits in common?

B: Instead of giving up, the people I interviewed analyzed their failure and figured out what

they ___________ wrong.

(a) do

(b) did

(c) have done

(d) had done

15. A: My wife is _______________.

B: Wow, that's a very unusual case!

(a) senior to me by 9 years

(b) senior than me by 9 years

(c) 9 years senior me

(d) 9 years senior than me

16. A: I heard the pirated version of this book ______________ more than 100,000 copies so far.

    B: Then it definitely is the bestseller of the year.

    (a) sold

    (b) sold itself

    (c) sold themselves

    (d) sell

17. A: ______________ it is!

    B: Yes. The beauty of this place is beyond description.

    (a) What beautiful scenery a

    (b) What beautiful scenery

    (c) What beautiful a scenery

    (d) How beautiful scenery

18. A: Do you think the global economic outlook will ______________ in the latter half of this year?

    B: Sure. Both the stock market and investor mood are very bearish now.

    (a) deteriorate

    (b) be deteriorated

    (c) have deteriorated

    (d) have been deteriorated

19. A: I feel dizzy.

    B: Why don't you go there and ______________ down?

    (a) lay

    (b) laying

    (c) lie

    (d) lying

20. A: This switch has been here since we moved in this house.

    B: Then ______________ it before?

    (a) how come never I saw

    (b) how come I never saw

    (c) how never I saw

    (d) how I never saw

Part II (21~40) Choose the best answer for the blank.

21. The statistics indicates that ____________ on the increase.
   (a) the number of juvenile smokers is
   (b) the number of juvenile smokers are
   (c) a number of juvenile smokers is
   (d) a number of juvenile smokers are

22. Since strict government regulations to curb property speculation were announced, the market ____________ in a slump.
   (a) is mired
   (b) is being mired
   (c) has been mired
   (d) had been mired

23. In spite of serious financial pressure, he ____________ a new brand later this year.
   (a) persisted launching
   (b) persisted in launching
   (c) persisted to launch
   (d) persisted to launching

24. He wrote this classic book ____________.
   (a) behind a bar
   (b) behind bars
   (c) behind the bar
   (d) behind the bars

25. If primitive investors had only remembered 'two plus two still equals four,' then the disaster might ____________.
   (a) avert
   (b) be averted
   (c) have averted
   (d) have been averted

26. ___________ that these young chefs will be fully equipped with high-class skills, self-confidence and, of course, a passion for food, so that they may move forward and carve out their own futures.
(a) It is hoped
(b) It is hoping
(c) It is hopeful
(d) It is hope

27. Our state ___________ thirty counties.
(a) consist of
(b) consists of
(c) is consisted of
(d) is consisting of

28. The faculty of English literature in my university has a very distinguished research and teaching record, ___________ all periods of English Literature.
(a) covers
(b) cover
(c) covered
(d) covering

29. I would like ___________ about your English training course beginning this December.
(a) a information
(b) some information
(c) informations
(d) some informations

30. The price is way above ___________ we can afford.
(a) what
(b) than
(c) where
(d) as

31. He was alleged to ____________ the one carat diamond ring.
    (a) steal
    (b) have stolen
    (c) stole
    (d) had stolen

32. This corporation has also supplied major equipment for two Russian nuclear plants, ____________ an energy company in Canada.
    (a) in alliance with
    (b) in an alliance with
    (c) in the alliance with
    (d) in alliances with

33. Capitalism creates big producers who are constantly in need of larger markets and new countries ____________.
    (a) to sell their product
    (b) to sell their product to
    (c) to sell their products
    (d) to sell their products to

34. The best diet, researchers found, was ____________ calorie intake dramatically.
    (a) one that reduces
    (b) that reduces
    (c) one that reduced
    (d) that reduced

35. The chief director is not ____________ everyone.
    (a) accessible
    (b) accessible to
    (c) accessible for
    (d) access

36. She worked hard so that everything ____________ ready in time.
(a) would be
(b) will be
(c) would have been
(d) will have been

37. The aggregate market value of apartments across the nation rose ____________ nearly $98.4 billion this year.
(a) by
(b) as
(c) for
(d) to

38. The government's intensive efforts to curb the price growth ____________ now.
(a) is working
(b) are working
(c) is worked
(d) are worked

39. The financial panic and the collapse of the world economy took the authories ____________.
(a) by the surprise
(b) to the surprise
(c) by surprise
(d) to surprise

40. There are sycamore trees on ____________.
(a) both side of the street
(b) either side of the street
(c) each sides of the street
(d) every side of the street

Part III(41~45) **Identify the option that contains an awkward expression or an error in grammar.**

41. (a) A: I tried everything I could, and now I get stopping losing my hair is impossible.
(b) B: The more you concern, the more hair you're going to lose. So take it easy.
(c) A: I know. But I hate that I look much older than my age.
(d) B: Accept that going bald is the hereditary condition you will most likely have to live with.

42. (a) A: How come your shop was closed yesterday?
(b) B: My wife and kids were very sick with flu.
(c) A: Sorry to hear that. You should take care of yourself, too. They say that there's a lot of flu going around.
(d) B: Thanks for worrying me.

43. (a) A: Why are you so late? I waited 2 hours!
(b) B: I'm terribly sorry. I remembered forgetting to lock the door on my way here and went home back.
(c) A: But you should give a call at least.
(d) B: I couldn't, because I lost my cell phone yesterday.

44. (a) A: The researchers confirmed what we all knew 'the way to lose weight is to eat less.'
(b) B: Still it matters how you mix and match your carbohydrates, fats and proteins, I heard.
(c) A: The best diet, this article said, was one that reduced calorie intake dramatically.
(d) B: However, no less 1,200 calories everyday.

45. (a) A: How may I help you?
(b) B: I'd like to buy the red jacket in this picture.
(c) A: Sorry, we are out of that. How about other ones? These are the best-sellers in my shop.
(d) B: Well, none of them is in my style.

46. (a) Experts say the quality problems are compounded by poor package instructions. (b) Using the bulbs incorrectly, like screwing low-end bulbs into fixtures which heat is prone to build up, can greatly shorten their lives. (c) Some experts who study the issue blame the government for the quality problems. (d) They say that an intensive federal push to lower the price essentially backfired by encouraging manufacturers to use cheap components.

47. (a) Separate the eggs, putting the whites into one bowl and the yolks into the other. (b) Combine the plain flour, baking powder and milk with the egg yolks and mix until it forms a smooth, thick batter. (c) Whisk the whites with the salt until they form stiff peaks. (d) Fold the whites into the batter — it is now ready to use.

48. (a) The investors' mood is just incredibly depressed. (b) I have never seen anything like it, not even in 1974 when the outlook was very grim indeed. (c) Back then, America had just lost a war in Vietnam and the president nearly impeached. (d) Still, the gloom wasn't at the levels that we are seeing today.

49. (a) We politicians have more works to do. (b) For the workers who are losing their jobs at the plant that's moving to Mexico, and now are having to compete with their own children for jobs that pay 7 dollars an hour. (c) For the father who was losing his job and choking back tears, wondering how he would pay for forty-five hundred dollars a month for the drugs his son needs without the health benefits. (d) For the young woman who has the grades, has the drive, has the will, but doesn't have the money to go to college.

50. (a) Upstairs at Fifteen is the bistro where you can enjoy great food and some fantastic cocktail creations with no reservations required. (b) The atmosphere is relaxed and the service friendly, which making it a great place to meet friends for breakfast, lunch or dinner, or just to chat over a drink. (c) Downstairs in the restaurant, things remain pretty relaxed with the modern design creating the perfect atmosphere for dining with friends or doing business. (d) Visit our website at www.fifteenrestaurant.com.

Final Test 3

1. A: It's _______________ .
    B: I was so busy that I missed the right time.
    (a) time to have lunch
    (b) time we have lunch
    (c) high time we have lunch
    (d) high time we had lunch

2. A: These days, it is not that difficult for a company to lay off or fire employees.
    B: So employees have to work hard lest __________ fired.
    (a) they are
    (b) they are not
    (c) they be
    (d) they be not

3. A: If it _______________ for his quick rescue, I should have died.
    B: We all cannot be more thankful for Mr. Jones, dear.
    (a) wasn't
    (b) weren't
    (c) have not been
    (d) had not been

4. A: My family _______ all vegetarians.
    B: No way. I saw your brother having a ham sandwich a few days ago.
    (a) is
    (b) are
    (c) was
    (d) were

5. A: Joe, how many times do I have to tell you to keep your room tidy!
    B: I _______________ the cleaning!
    (a) was about just to do
    (b) was to do just about
    (c) was just to do about
    (d) was just about to do

6. A: She seems to like Jamie. I don't understand her.

   B: Well, there's no accounting for __________ .

   (a) a taste

   (b) tastes

   (c) the taste

   (d) the tastes

7. A: I cannot wait to play the Rachmaninov Second Piano Concerto.

   B: Don't try to play something that is _______ above your level.

   (a) a lot

   (b) way

   (c) great

   (d) very

8. A: How many libraries do you have?

   B: Five of the libraries are located on campus, with the other two being located

   ______________.

   (a) within walking distance

   (b) within walking distances

   (c) within a walking distance

   (d) within the walking distance

9. A: The earthquake did ____________ damage.

   B: Emergency aid fund and designating as a special disaster zone are needed.

   (a) millions of dollar's worth

   (b) millions of dollars' worth

   (c) worth of millions of dollars

   (d) millions of dollars worth

10. A: He seems ____________ by the task.

    B: I'm so sorry that I can't help him.

    (a) to daunt

    (b) daunting

    (c) to be daunted

    (d) being daunted

11. A: I'm the owner of this building and I'll stay only 10 minutes.

B: _________ car it is, it should be parked appropriately.

(a) Whoever

(b) Whomever

(c) Whatever

(d) Whosever

12. A: Significant changes in industry structure have occurred.

B: Right. For example, sales by local film industry are nearly __________ raised by local shoe manufacturers.

(a) doubling the money

(b) double the money

(c) the double money

(d) double money

13. A: Do you want me to stay with her?

B: No. She prefers _________ alone.

(a) being

(b) be

(c) having been

(d) to have been

14. A: Did you find the cause of death?

B: Not yet, but the police's going to __________ this afternoon.

(a) perform an autopsy

(b) perform the autopsy

(c) perform autopsy

(d) perform autopsies

15. A: Due to the severe weather condition, a delay is needed, I'm afraid.

B: No. I say the project _____________ date in February, Ok?

(a) will meet the completion

(b) will have met the completion

(c) will meet completion

(d) will have met completion

16. A: Is the climate of Sydney milder than _______ of Jeju?

     B: I'm not sure, but I guess they are similar.

     (a) it

     (b) that

     (c) what

     (d) as

17. A: A survey by the National Statistical Office showed consumer sentiment deteriorated in March due to _______________ at home and abroad.

     B: Nobody can deny that we're in an economic recession.

     (a) a range of uncertainty

     (b) a range of the uncertainty

     (c) a range of uncertainties

     (d) a range of the uncertainties

18. A: Actually, I'm considering plastic surgery on my nose.

     B: You'd better leave it __________. It'll make your whole face unbalanced.

     (a) undoable

     (b) to undo

     (c) undone

     (d) undoing

19. A: Disclosure can result in death.

     B: __________ happens, I will keep this secret.

     (a) Whosever

     (b) Whomever

     (c) Whatsoever

     (d) Whichever

20. A: Freesia is ____________ item at my shop, after roses and lilies.

     B: All of them are my favorite.

     (a) the third top-selling

     (b) the top-third selling

     (c) third top-selling

     (d) top-third selling

Part II (21~40) Choose the best answer for the blank.

21. These natural-wax candles burn cleanly without leaving black marks on the glass
__________ inferior candles.
(a) as happen
(b) as happens
(c) as happen with
(d) as happens with

22. They are not in alliance with the working women, __________ through the abolition of
capitalism.
(a) whose needs can only be served
(b) whose only needs can be served
(c) whom only needs can be served
(d) whose needs can only serve

23. After 3 years' war, the whole country is now ________ ruins.
(a) about
(b) beyond
(c) in
(d) at

24. My personal trainer recommended that __________ under 80kg.
(a) I am
(b) I be
(c) I were
(d) should I be

25. __________ the dead body when they closed their eyes.
(a) Scarcely have they seen
(b) Scarcely they have seen
(c) Scarcely had they seen
(d) Scarcely they had seen

26. _____________ have echoed the sentiment.
   (a) A good many others have
   (b) A good many others has
   (c) Many a good others have
   (d) Many a good others has

27. You should come early ____________ of front tickets.
   (a) to assure
   (b) to assure you
   (c) to assure yourself
   (d) for you to assure

28. The fund raised in the stock market ____________ $2,000.
   (a) aggregated
   (b) was aggregated
   (c) was aggregating to
   (d) was aggregated to

29. In a bid to bolster voter turnout, the National Election Commission urged voters to actively ___________ this election.
   (a) be participated
   (b) be participated in
   (c) participate
   (d) participate in

30. The two companies plan to develop a picture-sharing service ____________ online and send them to computers, camera-equipped mobile phones and other devices.
   (a) that allows users to store image files
   (b) users allows image files to store
   (c) that allows image files to store users
   (d) users that allow to store image files

31. She added ___________ debt volume further grows, there may not be need for another separate agency for managing national debt.
(a) whether
(b) while
(c) unless
(d) whereas

32. ___________ that his memory is better than the average.
(a) I need hardly to mention
(b) I need hardly mention
(c) Need I hardly mention
(d) Need I mention hardly

33. The heaviest yellow dust storm this year hit across ___________ yesterday.
(a) Korean Peninsula
(b) korean peninsula
(c) the Korean Peninsula
(d) the korean peninsula

34. It is necessary ___________ late for the interview.
(a) you not be
(b) you are not
(c) you not to be
(d) you not being

35. ___________ very slim that the company will collapse suddenly.
(a) Chance is
(b) The chance is
(c) Chances are
(d) The chances are

36. I am going to urge her _____________ my suggestion.
  (a) taking
  (b) to take
  (c) take
  (d) took

37. _____________ will be reimbursed to those who used the company credit card.
  (a) Every traveling expense
  (b) Every traveling expenses
  (c) All traveling expense
  (d) All traveling expenses

38. There is _____________ chance that the world is facing a long cycle of recession, depression and wealth destruction.
  (a) a 50 percent
  (b) 50 a percent
  (c) 50 percent
  (d) 50 percents

39. These day, too _____________ me crazy!
  (a) many mails make
  (b) many mails makes
  (c) much mail make
  (d) much mail makes

40. Assets of the overseas Chinese business community _____________ to total $2 trillion.
  (a) estimate
  (b) estimates
  (c) is estimated
  (d) are estimated

Part III(41~45) **Identify the option that contains an awkward expression or an error in grammar.**

41. (a) A: How did a housewife become a professional woman makes $40, 000 a year?
    (b) B: She had a severe time training to be a lawyer.
    (c) A: Now the efforts are paying off.
    (d) B: But she lost her family, instead.

42. (a) A: What do you suppose is in the box?
    (b) B: I have no idea. Anyway we were told not to open it.
    (c) A: I'm anxious to know what it is. Don't you?
    (d) B: Actually no.

43. (a) A: What was happened to her?
    (b) B: Her father had a car accident this morning.
    (c) A: That's tragic. So how's she doing now?
    (d) B: She seemed to be out of her senses.

44. (a) A: Written in haste, we cannot deny there are many mistakes in it.
    (b) B: Yes. We all are sorry about it. However, there was no other option.
    (c) A: Anyway it is gratifying to meet the deadline, at least.
    (d) B: We can do better next time.

45. (a) A: I'd like to repaper this room for our new baby.
    (b) B: Good idea. What should we do first?
    (c) A: The measurement of the room is 12 feet by 12 feet.
    (d) B: By the way, how about painting instead of wallpapering?

46. (a) The difference between a typical recession and the severe downturn we are suffering through now is the loss of faith in our economy. (b) We are panicked and, until our fears are quelled, the downturn will rage on. (c) The best measure of investor confidence is the Dow Jones industrial average. (d) This index sometimes goes up but that doesn't signify the end of a recession, and this recession won't end until the Dow will turn up and stay up.

47. (a) Studies show that many men tend to diet for health reasons or health cares, rather than appearance. (b) Women are more likely to diet because of social pressures. (c) We see many big-bellied, 300-pound offensive linemen, all of whom remain happy about their size and the job they earned it. (d) It's less stigmatizing to be overweight if you're a guy.

48. (a) It was just two decades ago that his writing was aimed at the handful of Ph.D. readers. (b) But in the early 1990s, he penned accessible books like "The Age of Diminished Expectations" and "Peddling Prosperity." (c) In 1996 he began writing for a website, and his columns caught the attention of The New York Times, whose publisher decided to add the economist to its op-ed page. (d) As a columnist, however, he hasn't limited him to writing about his specialty: he's spent much of the past eight years criticizing the Bush administration's handling of the war on Iraq and its foreign policy.

49. (a) A mobile phone is, after all, a kind of sensor: every time you send a text message or make a phone call, cellular towers pinpoint your position. (b) With 4 billion handsets in use worldwide, that makes for trillions of data points flowing through the network every month and create digital graphs of our paths. (c) When aggregated, those individual paths convey a picture of a block, a community, a city even a whole society. (d) Our cell phones have become the neurons in the global nervous system.

50. (a) By now the spinach will have cooled down, so squeeze any excess liquid out of it and pour this back into the bowl. (b) Finely chop the spinach and put it back into the bowl. (c) Mix it with the liquid, add the ricotta and a handful amount of Parmesan, and then use a piping bag to squeeze the mixture into the cannelloni. (d) You can make your own piping bag by getting a sandwich bag and putting the spinach mix into the corner of it.

Answers

정답 및 해설

Chapter 01 문장의 형식과 종류

Exercise

1.

해석_ A: 당신이 지원한 자리는 여행을 많이 하는 부서입니다.
B: 괜찮아요. 저는 여행을 좋아합니다.

해설_ apply for (a job)는 '~에 지원하다'라는 의미. post(자리)에 지원하는 것이므로 전치사 for가 같이 와야만 한다. 답은 **(c)**. apply in/to는 '(사물이) 어떤 사람/물건에 적용되다'라는 뜻이다.

정답_ (c)

2.

해석_ A: 그가 서울에 올지 안 올지 아세요?
B: 나도 그것은 잘 모르겠어요.

해설_ 의문사가 없는 일반의문문이 간접의문문의 종속절로 쓰일 때는 'if(whether) + 주어 + 동사'의 어순이 된다.

정답_ (b)

3.

해석_ A: 네 차에 문제가 있는 걸로 생각했는데.
B: 맞아, 그런데 오늘 아침에 고쳤어.

해설_ have는 '목적어+목적보어(원형부정사/p.p.)'와 함께 쓰여 '~을 …하게 하다' 또는 '~이 …되는 것을 당하다'의 뜻으로 사용된다. 여기서는 '차를 수리했다'는 뜻의 표현이 와야 하며, 목적어(it)가 수리를 당하는 입장에 놓이게 되므로 **(b) had it fixed**가 정답이다.

어휘_ fix 수리하다, 고치다

정답_ (b)

4.

해석_ A: 다리가 어찌된 거야?
B: 롤러 블레이드 배우다가 다쳤어.

해설_ '나 자신이 부상을 입은 것'이므로 타동사 hurt의 목적어로 재귀대명사가 와야 한다. 답은 **(c)**. 주어가 I일 경우 목적어로 다시 me를 취하지 않는다.

정답_ (c)

5.

해석_ 영화 제작이야말로 존슨 가족에게 오랫동안 생계 수단이 되어준 것이었다.

해설_ Making films(영화를 제작하는 것)가 문장의 주어이고, 동사는 was이며, was 이하의 what provided … time은 보어가 된다. A was B의 문형으로, what은 주격대명사 역할을 한다.

어휘_ film 영화(movie) living 생계, 생활 수단(livelihood)

정답_ (c)

6.

해석_ 보다 낮은 세율은 사람들이 더 열심히 일하도록 한다.

해설_ encourage A to V : A가 ~하도록 격려하다, 촉구하다

정답_ (b)

7.

해석_ 그들은 정부가 더 많은 여성을 고위직에 임명할 것을 관철하기 위해 노력해 왔다.

해설_ force A to V : A가 ~하도록 강제하다

정답_ (d)

8.

해석_ A: 수잔이 벌써 35살이 되었는지 몰랐어.
B: 그녀가 몇 살이라고 생각했는데?
A: 그녀가 30대보다 훨씬 어릴 거라고 생각했어.
B: 그녀가 실제 나이보다 꽤 어려 보이기는 하지.

해설_ 간접의문문이므로 (b)에서 is she를 she is 로 고쳐야 한다.

정답_ (b)

9.

해석_ (a) 요즘, 많은 유명인사들이 그들의 책을 출판하려는 경향이 있다. (b) 유명한 여배우 신씨와 인기 있는 배우 전씨의 자전적인 소설이 이번 달 출판될 예정이다. (c) 게다가 그 뒤 몇 주 안으로 두 명의 정치가들이 그들의 뒤를 이어 출판 기념회를 열 예정이다. (d) 그들은 정계나 사회에서의 인맥과 영향력을 과시하기 위해 유명인사들을 출판 기념회에 초대할 것으로 보인다.

해설_ 해석상 능동의 의미이므로 'to+동사원형'으로 쓰이는 것이 적절하다. to be demonstrated →to demonstrate

정답_ (d)

Chapter 02 동사의 시제

Exercise

1.

해석_ A: 나는 네가 지난밤에 공부하겠다고 말한 줄로 알았는데.
B: 그러려고 했는데, 엄마가 갑자기 아프셨어.
해설_ 미래시제 대용어구 'be supposed to + 동사원형 : ~할 예정이다'
정답_ (a)

2.

해석_ A: 앤, 왜 이렇게 화가 나 있니?
B: 냉장고가 고장 나서 음식이 모두 상해버렸어.
해설_ 음식이 상해서 지금까지 영향을 미치는 상황이므로 현재완료 시제를 쓴다.
정답_ (c)

3.

해석_ A: 그의 외동딸은 어떻게 됐는지 아세요?
B: 아, 공연 예술가가 됐어요.
해설_ A에서 **what happened**라고 이미 과거임을 전제로 하고 물었기 때문에 정답은 **(c) became**이다.
어휘_ performance 연주, 공연 (작품 등의) 성과
정답_ (c)

4.

해석_ A: 자동판매기 옆에 있는 저 사람 신입사원인가요?
B: 아, 스톤 씨 말인가요? 1990년부터 여기에서 일했는데요.
해설_ 1990년 이래로 이곳에서 계속 일했다는 내용이므로, 계속의 의미를 가진 현재완료가 되어야 한다. 정답은 **(b) has worked**이다.
어휘_ vending machine 자동판매기
정답_ (b)

5.

해석_ A: 제가 먼저 좀 써도 될까요? 아주 급한 전화를 할 일이 있어서요.
B: 어… 예, 그러세요.
해설_ **Would you mind if~**는 '~해도 괜찮을까요(신경 쓰이지 않나요)?'라는 뜻으로 그 다음에는 현재형과 과거형이 다 올 수 있다. 여기서 정답은 **(b)**. 참고로, 과거형(**went**)이 현재형 보다 좀 더 공손한 표현이다.
정답_ (b)

6.

해석_ A: Cox 교수님, 우리 기말고사는 언제인가요?
B: 금요일입니다.
해설_ 명백히 미래의 일을 이야기하고 있는 것이라 해도 정확하게 미

래시제를 나타내는 부사가 함께 올 때는 현재시제의 동사를 쓸 수 있다. 여기서처럼 질문도 현재형으로 묻고 있는 경우 특히 현재형의 동사(**is**)를 써서 대답하는 것이 자연스럽다.
정답_ (b)

7.

해석_ 그 소녀는 이번 토요일에 남자 친구와 영화 보러 갈 예정이다.
해설_ the girl 다음에 **going**이라는 현재분사가 이어지므로 동사가 빠졌음을 알 수 있다. 현재진행형이 '~하려 한다'라는 가까운 미래의 결정된 사실을 나타내는 경우가 있다. 이를 현재진행 시제의 미래 대용이라고 한다. **be going to ~** '~에 가려고 한다'의 구문이 핵심이다. **be going to do**(~하려고 한다, ~할 것이다)의 구문과 혼동하는 일이 없도록 주의해야 한다.
어휘_ go to the movies 영화 보러 가다
정답_ (d)

8.

해석_ 샐리는 아버지에게 언제 이탈리아로 떠나실지 여쭤 보았다.
해설_ 샐리가 묻는 시점이 과거이며, 아버지가 떠나시는 것은 그 시점에서 볼 때 미래이므로, 미래의 조동사 **will**의 과거형 **would**를 써야 한다. 또한, 의문문이 **ask**의 목적어로 쓰인 간접의문문이므로 (주어+동사)의 어순이 되어야 한다. 정답은 **(c) he would**.
어휘_ leave for ~로 떠나다(**go away**), 출발하다
정답_ (c)

9.

해석_ 제이슨이 지금까지 만든 15개 영화 중에서 마지막 것이 제일 나은 것 같다.
해설_ to date(지금까지)라는 표현과 더불어 쓰이고 있으므로 과거부터 현재까지 만들어진, 즉 현재완료 형태의 동사가 와야 한다. **films**와 **Jason** 사이에는 관계사 **which**가 생략되어 있다.
정답_ (c)

10.

해석_ 그런 뒤 선생님은 실험종이를 탁자에 내려놓으셨다.
해설_ 밑줄 친 부분에는 'his experimental paper'를 목적어로 취하는 타동사가 와야 한다. 그런데 **then**(그때)이라는 시간의 부사가 있는 것으로 미루어 시제는 과거시제를 취해야 함을 알 수 있다.
어휘_ lie(lie - lay - lain)는 자동사로 '눕다', **lay(lay - laid - laid)**는 타동사로 '눕히다'
정답_ (c)

11.

해석_ 그 지역 인구 중 약 절반 이상이 영어와 프랑스어를 모두 쓴다.
해설_ 일반적인 사실을 나타내는 현재시제로 사용한다.

정답_ (c)

12.

해석_ 그는 내년까지 5번의 포럼에 참석할 것이다.

해설_ by next year라는 내년까지의 기간 동안 완료됨을 나타내므로 미래완료시제를 사용한다.

정답_ (d)

13.

해석_ 경제상황이 내년에 개선되지 않는다면, 한국에 광범위한 불안감이 있을 것이다.

해설_ 부사절의 **next year**로 보아 미래 시점임을 알 수 있다.

정답_ (d)

14.

해석_ 남자아이가 꽃병을 깨자 그는 잔뜩 화가 났다.

해설_ 시제에 대한 문제이다. 남자가 화난 것은 과거이므로, 아이가 꽃병을 깬 것도 과거에 일어난 일일 것이다. 따라서 정답은 **(b) broke**이다.

어휘_ upset 당황하게 하다, (마음·신경 등을) 뒤흔들다

정답_ (b)

15.

해석_ 자기 전에 **TV** 전원 뽑는 것을 잊지 마세요.

해설_ 미래를 의미하는 내용이라 해도 그것이 부사절로 쓰일 경우는 동사를 현재형으로 대신한다. '네가 자러 가기 전에'라는 내용은 미래를 나타내지만 시간의 부사절로 쓰이고 있으므로 현재형 동사(**go**)를 쓴 **(a)**가 답이 된다.

정답_ (a)

16.

해석_ 완성되면 새 경기장은 5만 명의 관중을 수용할 것이다.

해설_ 여기서 **when**절은 미래의 내용이지만 부사절이므로 현재시제를 쓰고 있다. 그러나 주절에서는 미래의 일임을 나타내는 동사 시제를 써주어야 한다. 답은 **(b)**. 여기서의 **seat**는 타동사로서, '앉히다, 수용하다'라는 의미이다.

정답_ (b)

17.

해석_ A: 한국에 온 지 얼마나 됐니?
B: 9월부터야.
A: 그럼 크리스마스쯤에는 여기 온 지 석 달이 되겠구나.
B: 맞아, 내가 여기 온지도 두 달이 지났어.

해설_ 과거의 **September**부터 시작하여 미래의 **Christmas**가 되면 석 달이 된다고 표현하고자 할 때는 미래완료 시제를 써야 한다. **you will be →you will have been**

정답_ (c)

18.

해석_ A: 한국이 어려운 경제상황에 빠져 있다는 걸 아세요?
B: 예, 그렇습니다. 그러나 번창하는 나라가 경제적 어려움과 접하게 되다니 참 이상한 일입니다.
A: 저도 동감입니다. 하지만, 한국 국민은 교육수준이 높고 굉장한 잠재력을 가진 사람들입니다.
B: 그러니까 모든 어려움이 잘 해결될 거라고 확신하시는군요.

해설_ 문제점들이 미래에 해결된다고 표현하는 것이므로 미래시제를 사용한다. **have → will be**

정답_ (d)

19.

해석_ A: 마이크, 오늘 아침 회의에 왜 안 나왔어요?
B: 죄송해요. 또 늦게 일어났어요.
A: 더 일찍 잠자리에 드는 게 좋을 것 같군요.
B: 저도 그렇게 생각해요.

해설_ 시제 문제이다. 회의에 늦은 것이 과거이므로, 아침에 늦게 일어난 것도 과거의 일이다. 따라서 **(b)**에서 **get**을 과거형 **got**으로 바꿔야 한다.

어휘_ go to bed 잠자리에 들다, 자다

정답_ (b)

20.

해석_ (a) 안데스 산에서 실종된 미국인 등산가 두 명의 안전에 대한 우려가 커지고 있다. **(b)** 그들과 함께 등반했던 세 명의 프랑스인들은 이틀 전 그들이 기지로 돌아오지 않자 놀라 위급함을 알렸다. **(c)** 지난주 눈사태가 그 지역을 여러 번 덮쳤다는 것이 이제 확실해지고 있다. **(d)** 지역 전문가들은 예년에 비해 유달리 따뜻한 날씨가 문제였다고 말한다.

해설_ (a)에서는 과거에 일어난 일에 대한 우려가 계속 커지고 있다고 했으므로 현재완료가 적절하다. 그러나 **(b)**는 과거의 일을 기술하고 있으므로 **when**절 이하도 동사를 과거시제로 써야 하는데 **fail**을 현재형으로 쓰고 있으므로 잘못되었다. **(c)**는 과거의 눈사태와 그 사건이 명확해지는 현재를 섞어 쓰고 있는 것, **(d)**는 지금의 기후조건이 비정상이라는 우려이므로 역시 현재시제가 옳다.

정답_ (b) fail to → failed to

Chapter 03 수동태

Exercise

1.

해석_ A: 또 늦었군요. 무슨 일이에요?

B: 죄송해요. 이번에는 차가 막혀서 꼼짝할 수가 없었어요.

해설_ **stick**은 수동의 형태로 '~에 갇히다, 꼼짝 못하다'라는 의미를 나타낸다. 넘치는 교통량 속에 갇힌 것이므로 전치사는 **in**이 알맞다.

어휘_ **stick** (사람·자동차 등을) 움직이지 못하게 하다

The bus was(got) stuck in heavy traffic.

(버스는 교통 체증으로 움직이지 못했다.)

정답_ (c)

2.

해석_ A: 아내가 죽은 이후 **Cox**은 몰라보게 변해 버렸어.

B: 그래, 요즈음엔 어떤 것에도 신경쓰는 것 같지 않더군.

해설_ **beyond recognition**은 '인식할 수 없을 정도로, (남들이) 알아보지 못할 만큼'이라는 의미. 사람이 너무 많이 변해 그 어떤 일에도 신경을 안 쓴다는 내용으로 답은 **(c)**이다.

정답_ (c)

3.

해석_ 이 레스토랑은 스파게티로 유명하다. (지금까지) 백만 그릇 이상이 팔렸다.

해설_ 과거부터 현재까지의 계속되는 동작을 나타내므로 현재완료시제가 요구되며, 문장의 주어가 **plates**이므로, 수동태가 와야 한다.

어휘_ **plate** (한 접시의) 요리

정답_ (a)

4.

해석_ 1984년 전국을 강타한 태풍에 의해 많은 사람이 죽었다.

해설_ **by the typhoon**으로 보아 수동태가 와야 하는데, **die**는 자동사이므로 수동태가 불가하다.

정답_ (d)

5.

해석_ 그리스에서 유래되어 고대 로마에서도 계속된 고전주의는 우리 삶에서 대개 세속적이라고 여겨지는 측면에 지대한 공헌을 했다.

해설_ **originate**는 자동사로 수동태가 불가능하다.

was originated가 아닌 **originated**가 적절하다.

정답_ (b)

6.

해석_ 죄수가 수감 중 사람들을 만나고 편지와 신문을 받을 권리를 박탈당하는 것이 합의되었다.

해설_ **deprive A of B**: A에게서 B를 박탈하다. **that** 이하의 주어는 **the prisoner**이므로 '권리를 박탈당하는 것이 합의되었다.'를 표현하기 위해 수동태로 나타내야 한다.

정답_ (d)

7.

해석_ 컴퓨터 타이핑과 편집의 장점은 세계의 모든 언어로 이제 확대되고 있다.

해설_ 진행수동형 **be being p.p.**를 묻는 문제이다.

정답_ (a)

8.

해석_ **Cox**는 몇 년간 당뇨로 고생해 왔으며, 이제 **Jill**이 비슷한 문제에 직면해 있다.

해설_ **Cox**는 과거부터 현재까지 당뇨병으로 고생하고 있으므로 현재완료시제를 썼으나 **Jill**의 경우 이제(**now**) 발병한 것을 알았으므로 현재시제로 동사를 선택하여야 한다. **face**는 여기서 동사로 '맞닥뜨리다, 직면하다'라는 의미이다. 따라서 **faces**가 되어야 한다.

정답_ (c)

9.

해석_ 정부는 도심의 배기가스 오염이 심각한 수준에 이른 것을 염려하게 되었다.

해설_ **concern**은 타동사로, 어떤 단체나 사람이 주체인 경우 수동태로 써야 한다는 점에 유의한다. 정부도 근심하고 있는 것이므로 '**be + concerned**'의 형태가 되어야 한다. '점점 근심하게 되었다'는 의미를 더하기 위해 **be**동사 대신에 **become**을 쓴 **(c)**가 정답이다.

정답_ (c)

10.

해석_ 주소에 변화가 있으면 은행으로 연락바랍니다.

해설_ 주소의 변화를 신고하는 주체는 사람이고 주소 변경은 신고되어야 하므로 수동태가 와야 한다. 그리고 '은행으로' 신고되어야 하므로 전치사는 **to**를 써야 한다. 그러므로 정답은 **(b)**이다.

정답_ (b)

11.

해석_ 북한은 한국전쟁으로 헤어진 가족들의 상봉을 논의하기 위한 제 3차 적십자 회담을 이 달에 개최할 것을 남한에 제안했다.

해설_ 주절에 **propose**동사가 왔기 때문에 **that** 이하에 (**should**) + 동사원형이 와야 한다. **should**가 생략되더라도 동사는 원형으로 와야 하며, 이 문장에서 회의가 스스로 열리는 게 아니라 열려짐을 당하는 수동의 대상이므로 수동형으로 와야 한다.

정답_ (b)

12.

해석_ A: 실례합니다, 주문하셨습니까?

B: 아니요, 저희들은 당신이 여기에 오기만을 기다렸어요.

A: 죄송합니다, 손님. 그럼 제가 주문을 받을까요?

B: 그러죠, 초콜릿 케이크 두 개와 우유 두 잔 주세요.

해설_ have been waited → have waited or have been waiting

정답_ (b)

13.

해석_ A: 너 기계를 잘 다루니?

B: 아니, 네 컴퓨터에 무슨 문제 있어?

A: 내 컴퓨터가 아니라 이 **MP**3 플레이어가 지금 문젯거리야.

B: 음악을 즐기고 싶다면 그걸 고쳐야만 하겠구나.

해설_ have it fix → have it fixed : 목적어가 사물이면 수동의 과거분사 **p.p.**를, 목적어가 사람이면 능동의 동사원형을 써준다.

정답_ (d)

Actual Test 1

1.

해석_ A: 제니퍼가 바이올린 연주를 너무나 잘하는 걸 보고 놀랐어.

B: 농담하는 거니? 그 애는 3학년 때부터 바이올린 연주를 했다고.

해설_ since(～이래로)는 과거부터 현재까지 어떤 일이 지속되는 것을 표현할 때 쓰이는 전치사이므로 현재완료 시제와 함께 쓰여야 한다.

어휘_ kid 농담하다 grade 등급, 학년

정답_ (c)

2.

해석_ A: 가능한 한 빨리 이 상자들을 쌓아야 해.

B: 제가 좀 도와드릴까요?

해설_ 박스 쌓는 것을 도와주겠다고 하였으므로, **to**부정사 뒤에는 **help you (with that)**이라는 구문이 와야 한다. 부사 **out**은 **help**를 강조하여 '도와 끝내겠다' 는 의미를 함축하고 있다.

정답_ (d)

3.

해석_ A: 용의자의 흔적을 좀 찾으셨나요, 형사님?

B: 아뇨. 두 방 다 사람이 잔 것 같지 않아요.

해설_ **rooms**가 의미상 주어라는 데 주의해야 한다. 사람이 자는 (**sleep**) 것이지 방이 자는 것이 아니므로 능동이 아니라 수동태가 쓰여야 한다. 누군가가 '이전에' 이 방에서 잔 흔적을 찾는 것이므로 완료부정사가 쓰였다.

어휘_ trace 흔적 suspect 용의자 detective 탐정, 형사

정답_ (d)

4.

해석_ A: 매니저와의 약속에 늦으면 안 돼.

B: 물론이지. 그가 시간 엄수를 강조하는 사람이라는 걸 잘 알아.

해설_ **stress**는 '강조하다' 라는 뜻의 동사로 쓰일 수도 있으며, '강조' 라는 뜻의 명사로 쓰일 수도 있다. 동사로 쓰일 때는 명사나 **that**절을 목적어로 취한다. 명사로 쓰일 때는 **put stresses on** + 명사의 형태를 취한다. 따라서 **puts stresses on time**이 되어야 알맞다. 정답은 **(d)**이다.

어휘_ on time 시간을 엄수하여 stress 강조(역설)하다

He stressed the need for understanding between nations. (그는 국가 간의 이해가 필요하다고 강조했다.)

정답_ (d)

5.

해석_ 정부가 주류에 새로운 세금을 부과한다고 해도 사람들이 술을 덜 마실 거라곤 생각하지 않는다.

해설_ 조건과 시간을 나타내는 부사절, 즉 접속사 **if**나 **when**,

after, **before** 등이 이끄는 부사절에서는 내용상 미래의 일이라도 동사는 현재형을 쓴다. 그러므로 이 문장에서 정부가 새 주세를 부과하는 것은 앞으로 있을 일이라 하더라도 시제는 현재형(**imposes**)이 와야 한다.

어휘 doubt 의심하다, 믿지 않다 **tax** 세금 **alcohol** 알코올, 술 **impose** 부과하다 (on)

정답 (c)

6.

해석 우리는 신종 미사일이 우리의 국방 문제를 해결할 것이라는 얘기를 듣곤 한다.

해설 여기서는 **that** 이하가 말해지는 것을 듣는다는 의미이므로 수동의 과거분사 (b) **said**가 정답이다. **it**은 **that**절 이하를 가리키는 가목적어이다.

어휘 defense 방어, 수비

정답 (b)

7.

해석 나는 그의 작업이 그렇게 날림인 걸 보고 실망했다.

해설 감정을 묘사하는 표현은 대부분 과거분사로 쓰인다. 또한 그의 작업을 본 것이 과거이므로 실망한 것도 과거의 일이다. 따라서 정답은 (b)이다. 능동태로 표현하면 **His sloppy work disappointed me**가 된다.

어휘 sloppy (태도·일이) 부주의한, 조잡한

정답 (b)

8.

해석 만일 채용이 되면, 의료보험의 완전 보장을 비롯해 기타 특전을 받게 됩니다.

해설 분사구문과 수동태를 정확히 이해하는가를 묻는 문제이다. 문맥상 '취업이 된다면' 이라는 뜻이 되도록 빈칸을 채워야 한다. **employ**는 타동사이므로, 수동태로 써야 한다. 그렇다면 **if** 다음에 현재형을 써서 **if you are employed**를 쓰거나, 아니면 분사구문을 활용해 **if employed**라고 써야 적절하다.

어휘 medical insurance 의료보험 **perk**(= **perquisite**)(급료 이외의) 임시 수입, 특전, 부수입

정답 (c)

9.

해석 A: 메리가 아주 건강해 보여.
B: 그래. 그 애가 요즘 운동을 하고 있거든.
A: 정말? 하지만 난 메리가 운동을 싫어하는 줄 알았는데.
B: 그래, 하지만 내가 설득해서 시작하게 됐어.

해설 convince가 '설득하다'는 뜻으로 쓰일 때는 **to**부정사와 함께 쓰인다. 따라서 (d)의 **convinced her starting**을 **convinced her to start**로 써야 옳다.

어휘 fit (몸상태가) 좋은 **work out** (체육관 등에서) 운동을 하다

정답 (d)

10.

해석 (a) 크리스토퍼 콜럼버스는 1493년 두 번째 신세계 항해에서 미국 버진 군도를 발견했다. (b) 그는 군도의 아름다움에 압도되어 '버진(처녀)'이라고 이름 붙였다. (c) 덴마크의 서인도회사가 군도를 사서 세 섬을 통합하여 덴마크의 지배 하에 두었다. (d) 이후 이 섬들은 그 지역의 주된 설탕 생산지 중 하나로 변모했다.

해설 콜럼버스가 군도의 아름다움에 압도된 것이므로 (b)의 **overwhelmed**는 수동태가 되어야 한다.

어휘 be overwhelmed by ~에 압도되다 **unite** 결합하다, 합병하다 **transform** 변형시키다, 바꾸다

정답 (b)

Chapter 04 조동사

Exercise

1.

해석_ A: 담배를 피우십니까?
B: 아닙니다. 하지만 전에는 피웠었지요.

해설_ 맥락에 맞게 알맞은 조동사를 빈칸에 채워 넣는 문제이다. **B**의 (**No, but ~**)이라는 표현으로 보아 지금은 담배를 피우지 않지만, 전에는 피웠다는 사실을 추정할 수 있다. 과거에 일정 기간 지속되다가 중단되어 현재는 지속되지 않는 동작을 나타내려면, 조동사 **used to**를 써야 한다.

어휘_ **smoke** 담배를 피우다 **dare** 감히 ~하다

정답_ (b)

2.

해석_ 사고의 피해가 너무 심해서 차라리 새 차를 사는 게 낫겠다.

해설_ **might as well**은 관용어구로 '차라리 …하는 게 낫다'를 뜻한다. 뒤에 **as**를 덧붙여서 **might as well ... as~** '~하느니 차라리 …하는 게 낫다'라고 쓸 수도 있다.

어휘_ **damage** 피해 **severe** 심한

정답_ (c)

3.

해석_ 그는 나를 점심식사에 데리러 오기로 했던 것을 잊어버렸음에 틀림없다.

해설_ **must have + p.p.** ~했음이 틀림없다

정답_ (a)

4.

해석_ 톰은 이렇게 추운 날씨에 익숙하지 않았기 때문에 종종 두꺼운 코트를 입었다.

해설_ **be used to -ing**(= **be accustomed to -ing**) '~하는데 익숙하다'라는 표현으로 써주기 위해 **-ing**형으로 고쳐 주어야 한다.

정답_ (c)

5.

해석_ 그 부서진 유리창이 많은 사고를 초래했다. 그것은 오래 전에 수리되었어야 했다.

해설_ **should have p.p. :** ~했어야 했는데(하지 않았다). 창문은 수리되는 것이므로 수동형이 되어야 한다.

정답_ (d)

6.

해석_ 당신의 비자가 만료되기 전에 연장을 하는 것이 좋을 겁니다.

해설_ **had better + 동사원형 :** ~하는 것이 좋다

정답_ (a)

7.

해석_ 이 계획은 시작되지 말았어야 했었다는 결론을 피하기 어렵다.

해설_ 조동사 다음에는 동사원형이 와야 하기 때문에 (c) 혹은 (d) 중에 답이 있다. 여기서는 **shouldn't have p.p.~** 구문으로 '~하지 말았어야 했다'는 표현을 쓰는 것이 적절하다, **not** 부정어는 조동사 뒤에 위치한다는 것이 기본 원칙이다.

정답_ (d)

8.

해석_ 북풍이 불면 무덤 위에 장미가 흩날릴 그런 장소에 내 무덤을 둘 것이다.

해설_ 무생물은 의인화된 경우를 제외하고는 능동적인 동작을 취하거나 의지를 가질 수 없다. 이 문장의 주어인 **my tomb**(내 무덤)도 무생물 주어이므로 주어의 의지가 아닌 말하는 사람의 의지를 나타내는 미래 조동사와 쓰여야 한다. 3인칭 주어에서 말하는 사람의 의지를 나타내는 조동사는 **shall**이다. **where the north ~ over it**는 관계부사절로서 **a spot**을 수식하고 있다. **over it**에서 **it**은 **my tomb**을 받는다.

어휘_ **tomb** 무덤 **spot** (특정한) 지점, 장소 **north wind** 북풍 **scatter** 흩뿌리다

정답_ (b)

9.

해석_ A: 오른쪽 볼에 멍이 들었네. 무슨 일이야?
B: 욕실 문에 부딪혔어.
A: 저런! 아팠겠다.
B: 응. 그랬어.

해설_ (d)의 'They have'는 A의 'That must have hurt'에 대한 답으로 적당하지 않다. '상처가 아팠겠구나'라는 A의 말의 주어를 그대로 받으려면 **That**이나 **It**이 와야 하며, 동사는 **has hurt**가 되어야 한다.

어휘_ **bruise** 타박상 **cheek** 뺨 **walk into** ~에 부딪히다

정답_ (d)

Chapter 05 가정법

Exercise

1.

해석_ A: 상사의 질문에 캐서린이 어떻게 대답했니?

B: 전혀 위축되지 않았어. 캐서린은 자기가 우월한 입장에 있는 것처럼 대답했어.

해설_ 문맥에 알맞은 시제가 되도록 빈칸을 채우는 문제이다. **as if** 다음에는 가정법 시제가 와야만 한다. 문장의 동사인 **responded**와 같은 시점에 일어난 일에 대한 것이므로 가정법 과거를 쓰면 된다.

어휘_ boss 상사 flinch (아픔, 무서움으로) 주춤[움찔]하다, (위험, 불쾌한 것에서) 꽁무니 빼다, 물러서다

cf. flinch from a task (임무에서 꽁무니 빼다)

flinch at the sight of (~을 보기만 해도 질리다)

have the upper hand 우위를 점하다

정답_ (b)

2.

해석_ A: 우산 안 가져왔어? 밖에 비가 퍼붓는데.

B: 가져왔을 거야, 날씨가 이렇게 될 줄 알았더라면.

해설_ 가정법 과거완료를 묻는 문제이다. '비가 올 줄 알았다면 우산을 가져왔을 것이다' 라는 의미가 되어야 하므로 과거의 사실을 역으로 표현하는 가정법 과거완료(if +주어 +had p.p, 주어 + would[could] have p.p.)를 써야 한다. 그러므로 if절에는 **had p.p.** 형태가 와야 한다.

어휘_ umbrella 우산 pour (비가) 억수같이 퍼붓다, 엎지르다

정답_ (a)

3.

해석_ A: 그 파티는 정말 끔찍했어.

B: 글쎄, 그보다 더 나쁠 수도 있었어.

해설_ 가정법이라고 해서 늘 **if**절이 있는 것은 아니다. 파티가 끔찍했다는 **A**의 말에 대한 **B**의 대답, **it could have been worse**는 '더 끔찍할 수도 있었으니 그 정도인 걸 다행으로 알아라' 정도의 뜻이다. **must have been**은 '~였음에 틀림없다' 는 뜻으로 이 문맥에서는 어울리지 않고 **could be**는 현재에 대한 추측이므로 이미 끝난 파티에 대해 쓰기에는 시제가 맞지 않다.

어휘_ awful 몹시 나쁜

정답_ (c)

4.

해석_ A: 예상치 못한 일이 발생하면 내게 알려주세요.

B: 꼭 그럴게요. 고마워요.

해설_ 접속사 **if**가 생략된 가정법 미래에 관한 문제이다. 아직 일어나지 않은 일에 대한 가정으로서 가능성이 약한 상황을 나타낼 때는, 조동사 **should**를 써서 가정법 미래를 쓴다. **if**절로 나

타내는 것보다 '**Should ~**'가 더 정중한 표현이다.

어휘_ unexpected 예상 밖의(unforeseen), 돌발적인

정답_ (b)

5.

해석_ A: 숙제 다 했니, 샐리야?

B: 시간이 충분히 있었으면 다 했을 텐데요.

해설_ 가정법 과거완료에 관한 문제이다. 주절이 **I would have**이므로, **if**절은 **had had enough time**이 되어야 한다.

어휘_ homework 숙제

정답_ (d)

6.

해석_ A: Cox가 평행봉을 하다가 허리를 다쳤어.

B: 안됐군. 좀 더 주의했어야지.

해설_ 과거의 일에 대해 '~했어야만 했는데 그렇게 하지 못했다' 라는 아쉬움을 나타낼 때 쓰는 구문이 '**should have p.p.**'이다. (c)의 **must have been**은 '~했음에 틀림없다' 는 뜻이므로 이 대화에서는 의미가 통하지 않는다. (d)도 '~할 필요가 없었는데' 라는 의미이므로 역시 맥락이 통하지 않는다.

정답_ (a)

7.

해석_ 나는 내 후원아동이 평생 행복하게 살았으면 좋겠다.

해설_ **I wish** 가정법 구문이므로, 과거형을 써야 한다.

정답_ (b)

8.

해석_ 내가 감사할 수 없는 것을 소유하기보다, 가질 수 없는 것을 감사하는 것이 더 좋았을 것이다.

해설_ **would rather** + 동사의 과거형 또는 **had** + **p.p.**가 와야 한다. **could not have** (가질 수 없었던 것)이라는 표현에서 '~하면 좋을 텐데' 보다는 '~했다면 좋았을 텐데' 라고 해석하는 것이 보다 나은 해석이고, 따라서 **had** + **p.p.**가 가장 적절하다.

정답_ (d)

9.

해석_ 내 도움이 없다면, 너는 결국 실패할 것이다.

해설_ '**but for**' 는 '현재 ~이 없다면, 미래에 ~할 것이다' 의 의미를 지니고 있다. 따라서 조동사의 과거형 + 동사원형이 와야 한다.

정답_ (d)

10.

해석_ 그는 마치 이제까지 그녀를 본 적이 없는 듯한 표정으로 쳐다
보았다.

해설_ as if 가정법 : 마치 ~이었던 것처럼

정답_ (c)

11.

해석_ 우리의 컴퓨터 프로그램을 표현하기 위해 가상현실 기술을 사
용할 때이다.

해설_ It is (high/about) time + 동사의 과거형 (should + 동
사원형): ~해야 할 때이다

정답_ (c)

12.

해석_ 세포가 완전히 막혔다면, 그 환자는 사망했을 것이다.

해설_ the patient would have died에서 가정법 과거완료 구
문임을 알 수 있다. 따라서, if절은 had+p.p.가 와야 한다. 접
속사 if가 생략된 형태인 (b) Had the cell이 정답이다.

어휘_ cell 세포, (수도원의) 독실, (교도소의) 독방
block (통로 · 교통 등을) 막다, (신경을) 마비시키다

정답_ (b)

13.

해석_ 그가 사임하지 않았더라면 위원회는 그를 해고하지 않을 수 없
었을 것이다.

해설_ 가정법 과거완료 형태를 묻는 질문이다. If + 주어 + 과거완료,
주어+조동사(would/should/could/might) + 현재완료
가 원래 문장이지만, 가정법에서 if를 생략할 경우, had + 주
어 + p.p.의 순서가 된다.

정답_ (a)

14.

해석_ (a) 내 친구는 내가 산꼭대기에서 스키타고 내려갈 준비가 되
었다고 말했다. (b) 나는 별로 자신이 없다고 말했지만 그는 같
이 정상에 올라가자고 나를 계속 설득했다. (c) 그래서, 결국은
동의했지만 내려오다 균형을 잃고 결국 다리가 부러지고야 말
았다. (d) 그의 말을 듣지 않았더라면 이런 지경에 처하지는 않
았을 텐데.

해설_ (d) If I hadn't listened to him, I wouldn't have
been in this situation.에서 wouldn't have been을
wouldn't be로 바꿔야 한다. 과거의 가정이 현재에까지 영
향을 미치는 혼합가정법이기 때문이다.

어휘_ confident 자신 있는 persuade 설득하다
end up -ing 결국 ~하게 되다

정답_ (d)

Actual Test 2

1.

해석_ **A:** 아들이 드디어 피아노 경연 대회에서 우승했어요.
B: 정말요? 소식을 듣고 기쁘시겠군요.

해설_ 조동사에 관한 문제이다. 문맥상 '~임에 틀림없다'는 표현이
므로 **(a)**가 정답이다. **(b)**는 '~일 리가 없다'는 뜻으로 반대되
는 표현이다.

어휘_ competition 시합, 대회

정답_ (a)

2.

해석_ **A:** 왜 Cox가 여태 안 오지?
B: 글쎄. 어머니가 또 아프신 건 아닐까.

해설_ B의 대답이 I'm not sure라고 시작되는 점에 유의하자. 확
실치 않다고 하였으므로 이어질 내용은 막연한 추측의 의미가
되어야 한다. 답은 (c)이다.

정답_ (c)

3.

해석_ **A:** 그는 새 직장에 들어가지 말았어야 했어.
B: 부인의 충고를 들었더라면 좋았을 걸.

해설_ 가정법의 시제에 대한 문제이다. A의 말에서 should have
p.p.는 과거에 일어난 일에 대한 유감을 표현하는 표현이다.
부인의 충고를 듣지 않고 취직을 하여 안 좋은 결과가 발생한
모양이다. 따라서 과거에 일어난 일에 대한 반대되는 가정이므
로, 빈칸에는 가정법 과거완료가 와야 한다. 정답은 (a)이다.

어휘_ job 일자리, 일 *ex.* You did a good job on my
watch. (제 시계를 정말 잘 고쳤네요.)

정답_ (a)

4.

해석_ **A:** 우리는 창립 기념일을 위해 연극을 무대에 올리기로 결정
했어.
B: 어떤 연극을 공연할지를 누가 결정하지?

해설_ 의문사의 올바른 쓰임새와 **be to** 용법을 묻는 문제이다. 가까
운 미래, 예정, 운명적인 일 등에 쓰이는 **be to** 용법은 그 자체
로 미래의 의미가 있으므로 **will**과 함께 쓰지 않는다. 문장의
주어가 없으므로 **whose**가 아니라 주격 **who**를 써야 옳다.
따라서 정답은 **(d) Who is**이다.

어휘_ stage a play 연극을 (무대에) 올리다 foundation day
(재단, 회사 등의) 창립 기념일 perform 공연하다

정답_ (d)

5.

해석_ 내가 바라는 대로 만약 Cox씨가 승진한다면 그는 시카고로
이사해야 할 것이다.

해설_ 'as I ~'로 시작하는 삽입절을 빼고 생각해 보자. 'If Mr.
Cox ~, he will ~'이라는, 조건절이 있는 문장이 된다. 즉

Cox 씨의 승진은 미래의 사항인 것이다. 그러므로 삽입절 안의 빈칸은 그가 승진될 것이다(**he will be promoted**)의 형태가 와야 한다. 답은 **(b)**이다.

정답 (b)

6.

해석 그 여자는 화랑에서 본 그림을 갖기 위해서라면 무엇이든 아낌없이 주었을 것이다.

해설 가정법의 조건절이 **to**부정사로 대체된 형태의 구문이다. 'she saw'라는 부분으로 보아 과거의 상황을 가정하는 것이므로, 가정법 과거완료의 주절을 구성하도록 '조동사 + have p.p.'를 쓰면 된다.

어휘 gallery 화랑

정답 (d)

7.

해석 화학제품을 만들기 위한 석유의 광범위한 사용은 20세기 초에 시작되었다.

해설 명확한 과거의 시점을 나타내는 부사가 등장할 경우 시제는 과거형을 써야 한다. 완료형은 항상 일정 기간에 걸친 일을 표현하기 때문에 특정 시점을 나타내는 부사와 함께 쓰일 수 없다.

어휘 widespread 광범위하게 퍼진

cf. a widespread superstition 널리 퍼진 미신
petroleum 석유 chemical 화학제품

정답 (c)

8.

해석 방학이 다음 주 금요일에 시작된다. 9월 중순까지는 학교에 갈 필요가 없다.

해설 need는 부정문에서 **need not** 혹은 **don't need to** 둘 중 하나의 형태를 취한다. 그러므로 보기 중에서 옳은 것은 **(c)**이다.

어휘 mid 중앙의 (주로 복합어를 만드는 데 사용된다)

cf. midsummer 한여름 midterm exam 중간고사

정답 (c)

9.

해석 A: 주말에 뭐 했니?
B: 아버지가 졸업하신 대학에 갔었어.
A: 근처에 있니?
B: 아니, 그렇지 않아. 여기서 40마일이나 떨어져 있는걸.

해설 과거의 일보다 더 이전에 일어난 사건에 대해서는 'had + 과거분사' 형태의 대과거를 쓴다. 보기 **(b)**에서 대학을 방문했던 주말보다 아버지가 대학을 졸업한 것이 시간적으로 훨씬 전의 일이므로 대과거를 써야 한다.

어휘 graduate 졸업하다 locate 위치시키다

cf. They located the capital in Seoul. (그들은 수도를 서울에 두었다.)

정답 (b) graduated → had graduated

10.

해석 (a) 내가 실수를 저지를 때마다, 아무리 작은 일이라도 우리 아버지는 심하게 벌을 주곤 하셨다. (b) 아버지에게는 내가 맞춰줘야만 하는 엄청난 기대가 있었고 절대로 자신의 태도를 바꾸지 않으려 했다. (c) 대학에 들어간 이후에도 아버지는 여전히 내 인생을 좌지우지하려고 했다. (d) 내 스스로 결정을 하도록 놔두려 하지 않는 것이었다.

해설 과거의 과거(대과거)가 나타나 있지 않으므로 과거완료를 쓰지 않고 과거형을 쓰면 된다. (a)에서 **would had punished**를 punished로 바꿔야 한다.

어휘 attitude 태도 run 운영하다

정답 (a) would had 삭제

Chapter 06 부정사

Exercise

1.

해석_ A: 좀 조용히 하지 못해 이 녀석들!
B: Cox, 너무 열 받지 마.

해설_ **let it upset you** 하면 '그것이 너를 화나게 하도록 두다'라는 말이므로 그를 부정하는 **not**이 앞에 오는 **(b)**가 답이 된다. '그것이 너를 화나게 하지 못하도록(네가 그것 때문에 화나지 않도록) 노력하여야 해'라는 의미의 명령문이다. **(a)**를 쓰면 '네가 화나도록 노력하지 말아야 한다'는 의미가 되므로 뜻이 달라진다.

정답_ (b)

2.

해석_ A: 이 일을 가능한 한 빨리 끝내야 합니다.
B: 하지만 전 지금 정말 쉬어야 해요.

해설_ **need**는 긍정문에서는 본동사로 쓰여 **to**부정사를 목적어로 취하며, 부정문/의문문에서는 조동사로 쓰여, 'Need I do....?', 'need not' 등의 형태로 쓰인다. 문제에서는 부정문/의문문에서 본동사로 쓰였으므로 정답은 **(d) need to take**.

어휘_ **take a break** 쉬다, 잠시 휴식을 취하다

정답_ (d)

3.

해석_ 당신은 그 건물에 들어가려면 회전문을 사용하면 됩니다.

해설_ **to**부정사의 목적을 나타내는 부사적 용법이다.

정답_ (b)

4.

해석_ 기말고사 전에 일주일밖에 안 남았다.

해설_ **to**부정사의 형용사적 용법이다.

정답_ (d)

5.

해석_ 나는 그를 시장에 임명하는 것에 강력히 반대합니다.

해설_ **to**부정사와 전치사 **to**의 목적어로 동명사를 쓰는 경우를 구별해야 한다. **object to -ing** '~ 하는 것을 반대하다'

정답_ (a)

6.

해석_ 그녀는 자신이 다른 사람들을 돕는 데 익숙하다고 말했다.

해설_ **used to** + 부정사(~하곤 했다)와 **be used to** + (동)명사(~에 익숙하다)를 구별할 수 있어야 풀 수 있는 문제이다. 용법에 맞게 쓰인 어구는 **(a) was used to helping**밖에 없다.

정답_ (a)

7.

해석_ 밀러 씨는 많은 청중 앞에서 공연하도록 요청받는 걸 싫어한다.

해설_ '밀러 씨가 많은 청중 앞에서 공연하도록 (요청받는다)'는 의미이므로 수동 부정사가 와야 한다. 정답은 **(d)**이다.

어휘_ **perform** 공연하다, 연주하다   **audience** (영화 · 연극 등의) 관객 ,청취자, 시청자

정답_ (d)

8.

해석_ 야채상들은 상점 문을 닫기 전에 모든 것을 처분하기 위해 마지막 30분 간 가격을 내리곤 했다.

해설_ '~하기 위하여, ~할 목적으로'라는 뜻의 **so as to do** 구문을 이용하면 된다. **would**는 과거의 불규칙적인 습관을 나타내는 조동사이다.

어휘_ **green grocer** 야채상   **bring down** 내리다
get rid of ~을 없애다, 처치하다
so as to ~하기 위하여

정답_ (c)

9.

해석_ 그 차고는 차 두 대가 충분히 들어갈 만큼 컸다.

해설_ **enough for ~ to ~** 구문이 '~가 ~할 수 있을 정도로 충분히 ~한'이라는 의미임을 우선 알아야 한다. '차 두 대가 들어갈 만큼 충분히 큰'이라는 의미가 되므로 차가 들어가는 주체인지 아닌지 살펴보고 만약 능동적인 주체라면 수동태가 아니어야 한다. **to**부정사의 형태를 취하고 수동형이 아닌 것은 **(c)**이다.

정답_ (c)

10.

해석_ A: 어떻게 지내셨습니까?
B: 잘 지냈습니다, 고맙습니다. 사실 저는 올해 안에 은퇴할까 생각하고 있어요.
A: 진짜에요? 당신 나이에 은퇴하는 건 꽤 이르다고 생각되는데요.
B: 맞아요. 하지만 저는 제 여생을 아내와 함께 여행을 하면서 보내고 싶어요.

해설_ **think**는 뒤에 곧바로 **that**절 등을 취해 타동사로 쓰이기도 하지만 명사를 목적어로 취할 경우는 보통 **of**나 **about**을 함께 쓴다. 'think of[about] -ing'는 '~할까 생각 중이다(consider)'의 의미이고, **think to** 부정사는 '계획, 의도(anticipate or expect)'를 나타낸다.

어휘_ **treat** 다루다, 대접하다   **retire** 은퇴하다

정답_ (b)to retire → of[about] retiring

Chapter 07 동명사

Exercise

1.

해석_ A: '스타워즈' 최신작 봤어?

B: 아직. 하지만 정말 보고 싶어.

해설_ look forward to는 '～를 고대하다'라는 뜻의 관용구이다. 주의할 점은 이때 to는 to부정사가 아니라 전치사이기 때문에 뒤에 명사나 동명사가 와야 한다는 것이다. 같은 방법으로 전치사 to가 들어가는 대표적인 관용구로는 **with a view to**(～할 목적으로), **be used to**(～에 익숙하다) 등이 있다.

어휘_ latest 가장 최근의 *cf.* the latest issue of the magazine(잡지 최신호) sequel 속편

look forward to -ing ～를 고대하다

정답_ (a)

2.

해석_ A: 야, 우리랑 같이 한잔 하자.

B: 그러고 싶지만 다음 수업에 벌써 지각이야. 가야겠어.

해설_ get은 동작을 나타내는 동사의 -ing 형태와 같이 써서 '～하기 시작하다'라는 의미를 나타낸다. 목적어와 -ing를 써서 '～를 …하게 하다'라는 의미도 나타낸다. **Let's get going.**(갑시다.) **Get the machine working.**(기계를 돌려라.)

어휘_ join 함께하다 I'm afraid (부정적인 내용 앞에) 내 생각엔 ～인 것 같아

정답_ (c)

3.

해석_ 시인들은 영감을 언어로 변환하는 일에 전념한다.

해설_ 빈칸에 알맞은 단어를 찾아 넣어 문장을 완성하는 문제이다. 이 경우는, **devote oneself to**(～에 헌신하다)의 to가 동명사를 이끄는 전치사인지, 부정사를 이끄는 전치사인지를 알아내는 것이 관건이다. 여기서는 동명사를 이끄는 전치사이므로 **(a) transforming**이 정답이다.

어휘_ devote oneself to ～에 전념하다, ～에 몰두하다

inspiration 창조적 자극, 영감, 영감에 의한 착상, 계시적인 착상 transform ～의 모양을 (～로) 바꾸다, ～을 변형[변태]시키다(into, to)

정답_ (a)

4.

해석_ 정부는 잠시 동안 어떠한 발표도 유보할 것이다.

해설_ delay는 동명사를 목적어로 취하는 동사이다.

정답_ (c)

5.

해석_ 네가 나에게 돌아왔을 때, 나는 울기 직전이었다.

해설_ be on the verge of -ing 막 ～하려 하다

정답_ (d)

6.

해석_ 그는 자신의 일에 대해 불평할 줄밖에 모른다.

해설_ **do nothing but** + 동사원형 = **do no other than** + 동사원형

정답_ (a)

7.

해석_ 나는 요전 날 밤 뱀파이어 영화를 보았는데, 피로 얼룩진 것들을 보는 것이 두려웠다.

해설_ **be afraid of -ing**의 구문이다.

정답_ (a)

8.

해석_ A: 당신 지금 질이 어디 있는지 알고 있나요?

B: 네, 아마 아래층 식당에서 식사를 하고 있을 거예요. 무슨 일이시죠?

A: 음, 전에 질에게 말하는 것을 잊었는데, 오늘밤 질을 만나기로 한 게 기억이 났거든요.

B: 제가 질을 보면 알려줄게요.

해설_ forgot talking →forgot to talk

정답_ (c)

9.

해석_ A: 당신 꽤 기분 좋아 보이네요. 무슨 일 있어요?

B: 글쎄요, 우리 모두를 위한 큰 소식이 있죠.

A: 우리 회사의 이익이나 그런 거 말씀하시는 거예요?

B: 그래요. 새로운 규정이 우리 수출의 증가를 향상시킬 것 같아요.

해설_ lead to improve →lead to improving

정답_ (d)

10.

해석_ (a) 고기나 유제품을 먹지 않는 채식주의자들에게는 영양 보조제가 필요할지도 모른다. (b) 그러나 그들은 비타민제를 복용하기 전에 신중해야 한다. (c) 비타민을 다량으로 복용하면 여러 가지 부작용이 유발되기 때문이다. (d) 다시 말해, 먼저 의사와 상담해야 한다.

해설_ 전치사 뒤에는 동명사가 오기 때문에, **(b)**에서 **before** 다음에 동사원형 **take**가 아닌 동명사 **taking**을 써야 한다.

어휘_ vegetarian 채식주의자, 채식자 supplement 보조제

dose (1회분의 약의) 복용량 side effect 부작용

정답_ (b) take →taking

Chapter 08 분사

Exercise

1.

해석_ A: 여보, 우리 사랑스러운 아기들이 잠자고 있는 것 좀 보세요.

B: 조용히 해요, 여보. 아기들을 깨우지 않기 위해서 우리는 아기들 모르게 나가야 해요.

해설_ unnoticed가 동사 뒤에서 주어의 상태를 설명하는 역할을 하고 있으며, 이때 과거분사를 쓴다.

어휘_ come out unnoticed 들키지 않고 나가다

정답_ (c)

2.

해석_ A: 캐시 생일에 깜짝 파티를 열어 주자.

B: 좋은 생각이야! 하지만 우리 계획이 들키지 않도록 조심해야 돼.

해설_ '들키지 말자'는 뜻이므로, 맥락에 따라 수동태를 써야만 한다. (be + 과거분사)가 수동태의 상태(state)를 나타내는 반면 (get + 과거분사)가 수동태의 동작(action)을 의미하므로, 이 경우에는 get 다음에 과거분사인 caught가 와야 올바른 문장이 된다.

어휘_ surprise party 깜짝 파티

정답_ (d)

3.

해석_ 유머러스한 어조로 쓰여진 그 이야기는 단번에 독자의 주목을 끌었다.

해설_ 분사구문의 태를 묻는 문제이다. 주절의 주어인 the story는 쓰여지는 것이므로, 수동태를 사용해야 한다. 따라서 정답은 (b)이다.

어휘_ catch one's attention ~의 주목을 끌다

정답_ (b)

4.

해석_ 차기 대통령의 취임사가 있은 뒤에 20분간의 휴식시간이 있을 예정이다.

해설_ Following은 '~ 후에'라는 뜻이다.

정답_ (b)

5.

해석_ 유명한 여배우 Nicole의 운전기사가 그녀의 다음 스케줄을 위해 차를 미리 대기시켜 놓았다.

해설_ have the car waiting 차를 대기시키다

정답_ (d)

6.

해석_ 데이트 신청을 받았을 때, 그녀는 너무 기뻐 환희의 노래를 불렀다.

해설_ 수동형 분사구문이다. 종속절의 시제가 과거형이므로, 그 이전의 과거를 나타내기 위해서 완료형인 having been asked out으로 쓰는 것이 적절하다. 보통 being이나 having been은 생략되므로 답은 asked out이다.

정답_ (d)

7.

해석_ 스키 실력을 향상시키는 방법은 끊임없는 연습뿐이다.

해설_ 빈칸에 올 어구는 your skiing skills와 함께 주어부를 이루어야 한다. 따라서 명사구가 와야 하며, 술부의 continuous practice를 보어로 취했을 때 자연스러워야 한다. 정답은 (c)이다.

어휘_ continuous 끊임없는

정답_ (c)

8.

해석_ 코뿔소는 사냥으로 거의 멸종위기에까지 갔으나 또다시 이 지역에서 흔한 동물이 되었다.

해설_ 전체의 주어가 rhino이므로, 사냥을 당하는 대상이지 능동적인 주체가 아니다. 그러므로 빈칸에는 수동태 형태가 와야 한다. 풀어쓰면 (As it was hunted ~)가 될 것이다. 이것을 분사구문으로 바꾸려면 주절의 동사(is)보다 앞서는 시제, 즉 Having been hunted ~로 해야 한다.

정답_ (d)

9.

해석_ 그가 나한테 거짓말했다는 것을 알게 되니까 너무 실망스럽다.

해설_ much는 과거분사(비교급)를 강조할 때 쓰이고 very는 진행형이나 원급을 강조할 때 쓰인다. 답은 (a). 그러나 surprised, pleased, delighted, excited 등 독립적인 형용사가 된 과거분사는 very로 수식하는 경향이 있다. *cf*. She was much surprised. → She was very surprised.

정답_ (a)

10.

해석_ A: 실례하지만, 당신께 벌금이 부과될 것입니다.

B: 그럴 리가 있나요. 저는 잘못한 게 없는데요.

A: 당신은 과속하셨어요. 여기 속도 위반 딱지입니다.

B: 이번만 좀 봐주세요, 경찰관님.

해설_ charging → charged

정답_ (a)

11.

해석_ (a) 캠퍼드에서 우리 회사가 들어설 새로운 부지에 지금 건설 공사가 진행되고 있는 중이다. (b) 이 도시의 외곽지역은 우리 회사 같은 곳에게는 이상적인 지역이다. (c) 미국 내 우리 직원들 중 일부는 이주를 요구받고 있고, 결국 미국 내 우리 직원의 10퍼센트 가량이 영국으로 옮겨갈 예정이다. (d) 그러나 새로

운 직원의 대부분은 그 지역에서 모집할 것이며, 우리 생각에
그 지역은 개발로 인해 많은 혜택을 볼 것이라 본다.

해설 주어와 동사의 역할을 살펴보면 (d)에서 주어가 **the majority of our new employees**라고 했으므로 직원들인데, 동사가 **is to recruit**로, (단수인) 직원이 모집에 나선다는 뜻이므로 이상하다는 것을 알 수 있다. 따라서 (복수인) 직원들이 모집되는 것이므로 수동태인 **are to be recruited**로 바뀌어야 한다.

정답 (d)

Actual Test 3

1.

해석 A: 파티에 뭘 입고 갈지 결정을 못 하겠어.
　　B: 어제 산 새 정장 어때?

해설 의문사와 **to**부정사가 함께 쓰여 명사구를 이루는 표현에 대한 문제이다. A는 파티에 '무엇을' 입고 가야 할지 모르겠다며 난감해하고 있다. '무엇을'에 해당하는 의문사 (b) **what**이 와야 한다.

어휘 suit (정장) 한 벌

정답 (b)

2.

해석 A: 그녀가 왜 오늘 그렇게 화난 표정을 하고 있는지 아니?
　　B: 이상하게 들릴지 모르지만, 그녀는 그 제안을 받고 나서 아주 우울해했어.

해설 **to**부정사가 다른 어구들과 함께 문장 앞에 쓰여, 일종의 문장 부사 역할을 하는 것을 독립부정사라 하는데, 숙어적인 표현이므로 표현 그대로 암기하고 알맞은 문맥에서 활용하면 된다. 정답은 (a) **Strange to say**이다.

어휘 **Strange to say** 이상한 얘기지만　 **depressed** 기운이 없는, 의기소침한

정답 (a)

3.

해석 A: 어떤 스포츠를 좋아하니?
　　B: 스키와 스쿠버다이빙을 좋아해.

해설 스키와 스쿠버다이빙은 모두 **like**의 목적어로서 병렬 관계에 있으므로 문법적인 형태도 같아야 한다. 또한, 지금 당장 무엇을 하고 싶다는 것이 아니라 일반적으로 좋아한다는 의미이므로 동명사가 바람직하다. 정답은 (a)이다.

정답 (a)

4.

해석 A: 최소한 20킬로그램 더 뺄 때까지 다이어트를 계속 할 거야.
　　B: 글쎄, 그 속도대로라면 한참 걸리겠는 걸.

해설 'It takes 사람+시간+to-V'의 구문은 '사람이 ~할 때까지 (시간이) 걸린다'라는 의미. 여기서는 시간이 명확히 나와 있지 않고 **a while**이 대신 나와 있다. 그러한 구문을 따르고 있는 것은 (d)이다.

정답 (d)

5.

해석 무슨 말을 해야 할지 몰라서, 그는 몇 마디를 혼자 중얼거렸다.

해설 분사구문에 관한 문제이다. '무엇을 말해야 할지 몰라서'에 해당하는 영어 표현은 (b) **Not knowing what to say**이다. 분사를 부정하려면 분사 앞에 부정어 **not**을 쓴다.

어휘 **mutter** 중얼중얼 말하다

정답 (b)

6.

해석_ 그녀는 이번 학기에 피아노를 정말 열심히 연습한 모양이다.

해설_ **to**부정사의 시제 문제. 이번 학기 동안 이미 피아노를 열심히 연습해 왔기 때문에 지금 실력이 좋아졌다는 뜻이므로, **seems** 다음에 나올 부정사구는 현재완료 시제가 되어야 한다. 정답은 **(a)**이다.

어휘_ **practice** ~을 연습하다, (의사등 전문직을) 개업하다
semester (대학) 학기 (9-1월, 2-6월의 두 학기. 미국에선 4학기제의 **quarter system**도 많음. 영국 등의 3학기제에서는 **term**을 사용)

정답_ **(a)**

7.

해석_ 맘모스 동굴로 알려진 그 동굴은 독특한 구조로 유명하다.

해설_ 과거분사를 이용한 수식 어구에 대한 문제이다. **be known as**는 '~로서 알려져 있다'는 뜻을 가진 관용 표현. 정답은 **(a)**이다.

어휘_ **be known as** ~으로 알려져 있다
structure (생물 · 지질) 구조

정답_ **(a)**

8.

해석_ 새로운 컴퓨터 시스템은 다음 달 설치될 예정이다.

해설_ 사람에 의해 컴퓨터가 설치될 것이므로 수동태가 와야 하며 가까운 미래에 있을 일을 말할 때에는 '**be to**부정사' 형태를 쓰므로 정답은 **(b)**이다.

정답_ **(b)**

9.

해석_ A: 밖에서 젊은 아가씨 둘이 너를 찾고 있는데.
B: 무슨 용건인지 말하든?
A: 네 저녁식사를 가지고 왔다고 했어.
B: 내 여동생과 그 애 친구일 거야.

해설_ **two young ladies**를 수식하는 분사의 형태는 수동의 의미를 나타내는 과거분사가 아닌 능동의 의미를 지닌 현재분사이어야 한다.

어휘_ **ask for** ~ ~를 찾다 **bring ~ over** ~을 가져오다

정답_ **(a)** asked → asking

10.

해석_ **(a)** Bill은 사람들에게 못된 장난을 하는 경향이 있었다. **(b)** 어느 날, 그는 경찰에 장난 전화를 걸어 동네에 강도가 들었다고 신고했다. **(c)** 집에 돌아온 그는 자기 집에 누군가 침입한 사실을 발견했다. **(d)** 그 사건이 있은 후로 그는 다시는 그런 짓을 하지 않았다.

해설_ **(b)**의 **to reporting**이 잘못된 부분이다. 목적의 의미를 나타내는 **to**부정사의 부사적 용법이므로 **to report**로 고쳐야 한다.

어휘_ **crank call** 장난 전화 **burglary** 강도

break into 침입하다

정답_ **(b)**

Chapter 09 접속사, 관계사, 전치사

Exercise

1.

해석_ A: 너 요새 무슨 문제 있니? 요즘 네가 얼마나 무례하고 성가시게 구는지 알고 있니?

B: 요즘 그렇게 굴어서 정말 미안해.

해설_ 'What's eating you?'라는 말은 '무슨 근심 걱정이 (너를 괴롭히고) 있니?'라는 뜻으로 계속 이어지는 A의 말은 B의 최근 행동을 비난하고 있다. 이에 대해 적절한 B의 응답은 사과하는 내용일 것이다.

정답_ (c)

2.

해석_ A: 이 연립 주택은 어떠세요?

B: 바로 제가 찾던 집이네요.

해설_ (내가 찾던 것)에 해당하는 영어 표현이 되어야 하므로, (~하는 것)으로 해석되는, 선행사를 포함하는 관계대명사 **what**이 와야 한다.

어휘_ townhouse 벽을 서로 공유하고 있는 주택. 주로 4집 정도가 붙어 있으며 각자 현관이 따로 나 있다.

정답_ (d)

3.

해석_ A: 두 시간 동안이나 이 리포트를 가지고 씨름했어. 뭔가 좀 먹으면 어떨까?

B: 그러고 보니 배가 좀 고프네요.

해설_ 'now (that)은 since'라는 의미로, '~라고 하니, ~이고 보니'라는 의미를 가진다. (b), (c)는 문맥에 맞지 않는다. (a)의 경우, 우리말로는 그럴듯해 보이지만, **because**는 인과관계를 의미하는 접속사이다. 그것을 언급했기 때문에 배가 고픈 것은 아니므로 답이 되지 못한다.

정답_ (d)

4.

해석_ A: 집을 둘러보아도 될까요?

B: 물론이죠. 어디든지 보십시오.

해설_ 당신이 원하면 어디든지 둘러보라는 내용이 빈칸에 와야 한다. 그러므로 **want to (go)**의 형태인 **(c)**가 적절하다.

정답_ (c)

5.

해석_ A: Jane이 언제 방문할지 아니?

B: 응, 다음 주에 올 거야.

해설_ 다른 전치사 없이 명사구 **next week**가 부사처럼 쓰여 시제를 나타낸다. 이때 **next**라는 표현이 명확한 때를 나타내므로 전치사 for, in, till과 같이 쓰이면 어색하다. 만약 이러한 전치사를 써주고자 한다면 **in one week**식으로 고쳐 주어야

한다.

정답_ (a)

6.

해석_ 지난 주말에 우리는 모든 사람들이 걸작이라고 부르는 것을 보러 갔고, 그것을 본 뒤에 실망했다.

해설_ see의 목적어 역할을 하면서 선행사를 포함하고 있는 **what**이 적절하다.

정답_ (c)

7.

해석_ 너는 항상 너를 사랑해 줄 남자친구가 있으니 행복하겠구나.

해설_ such A as B: B하는 그런 A

정답_ (d)

8.

해석_ 우리 회사는 파산의 위기에 몰려 있는 상태이고, 설상가상으로 나의 집이 자연 재해로 인하여 황폐해졌다.

해설_ what을 포함한 관용표현으로 **what makes the matter worse**는 '설상가상으로'라는 뜻이다.

정답_ (b)

9.

해석_ 우리는 회기를 연장하고 대표들이 한자리에 모여 합의를 도출할 수 있는 절차가 필요하다.

해설_ be extended in에서 전치사 **in**이 목적격 관계대명사 **which** 앞에 와야 한다.

정답_ (a)

10.

해석_ 어떤 사람의 생일은 탄생의 기쁨과 행복으로 축복받는 때이다.

해설_ 관계부사 **when**의 선행사는 생략할 수 있으므로 답은 때를 나타내는 관계부사 **when**이다.

정답_ (a)

11.

해석_ 그녀는 영화를 보자마자 울음을 터뜨렸다.

해설_ No sooner A than B: A 하자마자 B하다

정답_ (b)

12.

해석_ Jennifer는 그가 듣지 않도록 내게 귓속말로 말했다.

해설_ lest(for fear) ... (should) ~하지 않도록 / so that이나 in order that은 문법상 옳지만 문맥상 적합하지 않다.

정답_ (a)

13.

해석_ 너의 스캔들이 드러나는 것은 시간 문제이다.

해설_ '~하기 전까지는'을 나타내는 표현이다.

정답_ (b)

14.

해석_ 이러한 문제가 여름에 종종 발생하기 때문에, 사람들은 그들의 피부를 보호할 수 있는 무언가를 가지고 와야 한다.

해설_ (a) because는 종속절을 이끄는 접속사로 주절이 필요하다. 반면 for는 주절이 필요하지 않다.

정답_ (a)

15.

해석_ 너는 비행기를 타려면 한 시간 이내에 공항에 있어야만 한다.

해설_ in (지금부터) ~ 후에 / after (어떠한 일) 후에

정답_ (c)

16.

해석_ Shane은 빠른 기술과 정보를 따라잡기 위해 정기적으로 새로운 자료를 업데이트할 필요가 있다.

해설_ on a regular basis 정기적으로

정답_ (b)

17.

해석_ Jack은 계속해서 나에게 돈을 요구했는데, 그것으로 인해 나는 그에게 질렸다.

해설_ 관계대명사 that은 제한적 용법의 모든 주격 및 목적격 관계대명사를 대신할 수 있다. 그러나 comma 뒤, whose 대신, 전치사 뒤에는 주격, 목적격 that을 사용할 수 없다.

정답_ (b)

18.

해석_ A: 이제 그만 떠나는 게 좋겠어요.
B: 뭐가 그렇게 바빠요?
A: 10시에 지도교수를 만나야 하거든요.
B: 그건 불가능해요. 벌써 10시 30분인 걸요.

해설_ 관사(the)가 들어가느냐, 들어가지 않느냐에 따라 의미가 달라지므로, 문맥상 적절한 것을 택해야 한다. out of question은 '틀림없이, 분명히'라는 뜻으로, 의심이나 의문을 가질 여지가 전혀 없음을 의미한다. out of the question은 '생각할 수 없는, 불가능한'이라는 뜻으로, 전혀 있을 수 없는 불가능한 일이라는 의미이다. 여기서는, 벌써 10시 30분인데 어떻게 10시에 지도교수를 만날 수 있겠느냐는 문맥이므로, '불가능하다'는 의미의 out of the question이 알맞다.

어휘_ rush (일에 쫓기거나 하여) 분망한 상태
out of question 틀림없이, 분명히
out of the question 생각할 수 없는, 불가능한

정답_ (d)

19.

해석_ (a) 행운은 흔히 도박을 연상시킨다. (b) 그러나 '운'에만 의지한다면 대부분의 전문 도박꾼들은 망할 것이다. (c) 그들은 게임을 안팎으로 잘 안다. (d) 그럼에도 불구하고, 그들은 항상 그것에 의지한다.

해설_ 접속사에 관한 문제이다. (b)에서 주절과 even 다음에 나온 종속절 사이에는 역접이나 양보의 관계는 없다. 그냥 '운에만 전적으로 의지한다면'이라는 조건의 의미로 족하다. 따라서 even을 if로 고쳐야 한다.

어휘_ out of business 파산하여   inside and out 안팎으로, 완전히

정답_ (b)

Chapter 10 형용사, 부사, 비교

Exercise

1.

해석_ A: 도와드릴까요?

B: ‘뉴욕 타임즈’를 찾고 있어요. 여기서 살 수 있나요?

해설_ 2어동사의 경우 목적어를 두 단어 사이에 넣기도 하고 부사 다음에 쓰기도 한다. 그러나, 특히 목적어가 대명사인 경우는 동사와 부사 사이에 넣어야 한다. 정답은 **(b) pick it up**이다.

어휘_ copy (책·잡지 등의) 1부, 1권 **pick up** …을 사다

정답_ (b)

2.

해석_ A: 새 역사 선생님 어떻게 생각하니?

B: 좋아요, 그렇죠?

해설_ 여기서 ‘어떻게’에 해당하는 단어는 **how**가 아니라 **what**이다. 동사구 **think of**의 목적어이기 때문이다. 굳이 **how**를 쓰고 싶다면, “**How do you like your new history teacher?**”라고 할 수 있을 것이나, “**How do you like your steak?**”(스테이크를 어떻게 해 드릴까요?)와 같은 문맥에서 사용되는 것이 보통이다. 정답은 **(d)**이다.

어휘_ terrific 굉장한(= excessive); 훌륭한

정답_ (d)

3.

해석_ A: 왜 운전하는 것보다 걷는 걸 더 좋아하세요?

B: 걷는 게 운전하는 것보다 기운을 북돋워 주니까요.

해설_ invigorating같이 3음절 이상인 단어의 비교급은 그 앞에 **more**를 덧붙여 주며, 뒤에는 접속사 **than**이 나온다. 정답은 **(a)**이다. **as**는 동등비교를 할 때 쓰인다.

어휘_ invigorating 기운나게 하는, 기분을 돋우는

정답_ (a)

4.

해석_ 그 집은 아주 안락하지만 사치스럽지는 않다.

해설_ enough가 부사로 쓰일 때의 위치를 묻는 문제이다. enough가 형용사/부사 다음에 오면 통상적으로 ‘충분히, 필요한 만큼’이라는 의미를 가진다. 그러므로 답은 **(a)**. 만약 **(b)**처럼 enough to ‘~할 정도로 충분히 ~한’ 구문을 쓰고자 한다면 뒤에 동사가 와야 한다.

정답_ (a)

5.

해석_ Newbury 가의 양쪽에는 많은 상점들이 있다.

해설_ 빈칸 다음에 나오는 **sides**가 복수이므로, ‘길 양쪽’이라는 표현으로 **both sides**라고 해야 한다. **either side**라고도 할 수 있다.

어휘_ side (길·강 등의) 한쪽, 가장자리

6.

해석_ A: 요즘 일본과 중국의 가장 큰 차이점은 무엇입니까?

B: 중국 경제가 일본 경제보다 더 빠르게 성장하고 있어요.

해설_ 비교의 대상은 서로 대등 관계를 이루어야 한다. 여기서 비교 대상은 중국의 경제와 일본의 경제이다. 경제가 두 번 반복되므로, 뒤에 나오는 말은 대명사 **that**으로 받을 수 있다. 정답은 **(b)**이다.

어휘_ rapidly 급속히

정답_ (b)

7.

해석_ 크리스마스가 가까워질수록, 대부분의 아이들은 더 행복해진다.

해설_ ‘the + 비교급, the + 비교급’ 표현에 관한 문제이다. 앞의 **the** + 비교급은 접속사 역할을, 뒤의 **the** + 비교급은 부사 역할을 한다. 정답은 **(c) the happier**이다.

어휘_ the + 비교급, the + 비교급: ~하면 할수록 더 …하다

정답_ (c)

8.

해석_ **Jason**이 Jack 대신에 위험을 무릅쓰는 것은 꽤 어려웠다.

해설_ 난이도나 당위성을 나타내는 형용사는 사람을 주어로 하는 문장에 사용할 수 없고, ‘It is + 형용사 + for + 목적격 + to 동사원형’ 구문을 사용해야 한다.

정답_ (b)

9.

해석_ 나는 머지않아 삼촌의 재산을 상속받고 부자가 될 것이다.

해설_ before long 머지않아, 곧

정답_ (c)

10.

해석_ 당신이 왜 제게 터무니없는 것을 계속 주문하시는지 이해할 수 없군요.

해설_ the + 형용사·분사 → 추상명사

어휘_ the ridiculous 터무니 없는 것

정답_ (a)

11.

해석_ A: 이봐, 다른 거 볼 만한 거 없어?

B: 채널 11번에서 다큐멘터리를 해.

A: 음, 난 차라리 축구경기를 볼래.

B: 그럼 그러자.

해설_ worth는 뒤에 동명사를 써서 ‘~할 가치가 있다’라는 뜻을 나타낸다. to부정사를 쓰려면 worthwhile to부정사로 써야 한다. 따라서 **Hey, isn't there anything else worth watching?**이 올바른 표현이다.

어휘_ channel 채널, 경로 had rather 차라리 ~하다

     cf. I had rather stay at home.(난 차라리 집에 있을래.)

정답_ (a) to watch → watching

Chapter 11 명사, 관사, 대명사

Exercise

1.

해석_ A: 사회당이 지난번 성명에서 뭔가 새로운 것을 제시했나요?

    B: 아뇨, 그런 것 같지 않은데요.

해설_ B가 하는 말을 풀어쓰자면 **it**(the Socialist Party) **would not appear to offer anything new**이다. 이 문장을 올바로 줄이면 **it would not appear so**가 되지만 **so**를 없애면 **not**이 **appear** 뒤로 가야 한다.

정답_ (b)

2.

해석_ A: Cox가 새로 머리한 것을 가지고 왜 그리 놀리는 거야?

    B: 맘 상하게 할 뜻은 없었어. 단지 자기 나이에 비해 요란하다는 걸 말하려는 거였어.

해설_ 머리 스타일이 **elaborate**하다는 것은 화려하고 장식적인 스타일이라는 의미이다. 따라서 어린 나이에 비해 머리 모양이 지나치다는 의미를 담고 있는 내용이다. 여기서의 **for**는 '~로서는, ~에 비해서'라는 의미로 '그 나이의 소녀로서는'이라는 의미를 가진 것은 (c)이다.

정답_ (c)

3.

해석_ 사람들은 가끔 자신들의 경험을 통해 첫인상이 오래 지속된다는 사실을 알고 있다.

해설_ 문장의 구성 요소 중 빠진 부분을 찾으면 된다. **the first**는 수사로서 '첫 번째'라는 뜻의 수식어이다. **last**는 자동사로서 '계속되다, 지속되다'는 뜻이며, **a long time**은 '오래'라는 뜻의 수식어이다. 따라서 빠진 부분은 바로 주어, 주어가 될 수 있는 말은 '인상'이라는 뜻의 명사 **impression**뿐이다.

어휘_ last 지속되다 impress 감동시키다 impressively 인상적으로 impressive 인상적인 impression 인상

정답_ (d)

4.

해석_ 활자의 크기가 매우 작기 때문에 신문을 읽기가 어렵다.

해설_ **paper**는 종이를 나타내며, **a paper**나 **the paper**는 신문을 나타낸다.

정답_ (b)

5.

해석_ 우리 회사의 관례에 따라, 우리는 노동자에게 시간 당이 아닌 일 건수 당 임금을 지급해 왔다.

해설_ **by the** 단위: '~ 단위로'

정답_ (a)

6.

해석_ San Diego에서 새로 건설되는 16마일 거리의 궤도 전차 노선은 San Diego와 멕시코 접경 도시인 Tijuana를 연결시킬 것이다.

해설_ 3인칭 주어의 단순미래는 will로 나타낸다.

어휘_ trolley line 궤도 전차 노선 border 국경
link A with B A와 B를 연결하다

정답_ (b)

7.

해석_ 부모가 아이들의 삶에서 얼마나 중요한 역할을 하는지 많은 아이들은 깨닫지 못한다.

해설_ 'how + 형용사 + a + 명사' 형태를 묻는 문제이다. 이때 how는 '얼마만큼, 얼마나'라는 의미로, 바로 뒤에 형용사/부사를 수반한다. 'parents play a very significant role ~' 같은 표현을 강조하여 (c)와 같이 바꿀 수 있다. how 외에도 quite, so 등이 '형용사 + a(n) + 명사' 형태를 취한다.

정답_ (c)

8.

해석_ A: 엄마, 엄마를 위해서 제가 무엇을 해드릴까요?
B: 신선한 야채와 과일을 씻는 것을 좀 도와주겠니?
A: 네, 그럴게요. 그 뒤에 뭘 해야 하죠?
B: 그럼, 마루를 청소하고 내가 빨래하는 것 좀 도와주렴.

해설_ fruits →fruit, vegetable은 셀 수 있는 명사이지만, fruit은 셀 수 없는 명사이다.

정답_ (b) fruits→fruit

9.

해석_ A: 저녁식사 다 되었어요! 와서 식사하세요!
B: 음, 정말 맛있는 냄새가 나는걸요. 그리고 모든 음식이 멋져 보여요.
A: 이 케이크는 맛이 어때요?
B: 진짜 맛있어요.

해설_ 전치사 of의 목적어에 해당하므로 보어에 대응하는 how가 아닌 전치사의 목적어에 대응하는 what이 와야 한다.

정답_ (c) How →What

10.

해석_ A: 이 당근 케이크 들어보세요.
B: 괜찮습니다. 단 것 안 좋아하는 것 아시잖아요.
A: 하지만, 당신을 위해서 구웠는걸요.
B: 음, 그럼 한 조각만 먹을게요.

해설_ (c)에서 음식을 yours '당신의 것'를 위해 만들었다고 하면 의미가 통하지 않는다. '당신을 위해'(for you) 만들었다고 해야 한다. have a sweet tooth란 '단 것을 좋아한다'는 뜻의 관용표현이다.

어휘_ have a sweet tooth 단 것을 좋아하다

정답_ (c) yours →you

11.

해석_ A: 알약과 크림은 어디에 쓰는 거죠?
B: 알약은 부기를 빼는 것이고요, 크림은 발진을 낫게 해줄 겁니다.
A: 발진은 언제쯤이면 깨끗해질까요?
B: 두 주 안에 없어지지 않으면 다시 오십시오.

해설_ '어떤 용도인가' 혹은 '어떻게 하는 것인가' 하는 의미는 우리말로 보아 how로 시작할 것이라 착각하기 쉽다. 반드시 what ~ for?라고 써야 한다.

정답_ (a) How→What

12.

해석_ (a) 오늘밤 중서부 지방 날씨입니다. (b) 밤에 산발적인 소나기와 천둥 번개가 계속되겠습니다. (c) 번개, 큰 우박과 토네이도가 일어날 가능성도 있으니 조심하십시오. (d) 이러한 기상은 주변 지역에도 영향을 미칠 것입니다.

해설_ (b)에서 명사 night 앞에 정관사 the가 들어가야 한다. through the night 또는 all through the night, during the night 하면 '밤 동안 내내, 밤새 죽'이라는 뜻이다.

어휘_ scattered showers 산발적인 소나기, 때때로 내리는 강우 thunderstorm 심한 뇌우 system 기상 배치 (상황)

정답_ (b) night →the night

Chapter 12 일치 · 특수구문

Exercise

1.

해석 A: 당신은 내일 피로연에 오실 수 있어요?
　　　 B: 아무래도 안 될 것 같아요.

해설 possible은 사람이 주어인 문장의 보어로 쓰일 수 없고, 반대로 able과 capable은 주어가 사람인 경우에 보어로 쓰일 수가 있다. to come을 진주어로 하는 가주어 it이 필요하다. 일반적으로 부정사의 의미상 주어는 'for+목적격'으로 나타낸다.

어휘 reception 환영회, 피로연　able 재능이 있는
　　　 capable 유능한

정답 (d)

2.

해석 내가 건물에 들어가자마자 비가 내리기 시작했다.

해설 부정어구를 문두에 강조할 때 주어와 동사가 도치된다. 종속절이 과거이므로 주절은 그 이전의 과거를 나타내기 위해 과거완료를 사용해야 한다.

정답 (d)

3.

해석 그녀는 내가 대학에 돌아가서, 열심히 공부하고 학위를 취득하도록 하였다.

해설 대등접속사의 앞, 뒤에는 같은 품사의 단어를 나열해야 한다.

정답 (b)

4.

해석 많은 사람들이 내 최근 소식에 관하여 질문했다.

해설 many + a + 명사 → 단수 취급

정답 (b)

5.

해석 6시 5분에 출발하게 되어 있으나 지연이 될 것이다.

해설 There is ~ 구문의 미래형은 There will be ~이다.

어휘 be scheduled to do ~할 일정이 잡혀 있다, ~하기로 되어 있다　depart 출발하다　delay 지연, 연기

정답 (a)

6.

해석 그 프로젝트의 1/4이 그 팀에 의해 완료되었다.

해설 분수 표현은 분자를 기수로 앞에 써주고, 뒤에 분모를 서수로 써주되, 분자가 2이상이면 분모에 -s를 붙여 준다. the project는 단수이므로 One-fourth도 단수 취급한다.

어휘 projoot 기획, 안(案), (대규모의) 계획 사업

정답 (b)

7.

해석 과거에는 이와 비슷한 상황에서 대통령이 사임한 적이 한 번도 없었다.

해설 never와 같은 부정어가 문장의 맨 앞에 오면, 주어와 동사가 도치된다. 의미상 과거의 경험을 말하는 것이므로, 현재완료 시제를 쓰면 된다. 따라서 정답은 (b) has the president resigned이다.

어휘 resign 사임하다, 사직하다
　　　 under ~ circumstances ~한 상황에서

정답 (b)

8.

해석 수잔은 아카펠라를 잘 부르지만, 악기를 연주하는 것에는 관심이 없다.

해설 여기에서는 동사가 빠졌음을 쉽게 알 수 있다. '~에 흥미가 있다'라는 표현으로는 have interest in ~과 be interested in~이 있고, have no interest in ~은 '~에 흥미가 없다'라는 뜻임을 쉽게 알 수 있을 것이다. but으로 이어지므로 문맥상 '악기를 연주하는 것에는 관심이 없다'라는 뜻의 표현이 와야 적절하다.

어휘 interest 흥미, 관심; 흥미를 갖게 하다
　　　 interested 흥미 있는, 관심이 있는
　　　 interestingly 흥미 있게

정답 (a)

9.

해석 A: 표 사느라 오전이 다 가 버렸어.
　　　 B: 그랬어? 몇 시간이나 줄 서서 기다렸는데?
　　　 A: 3시간.
　　　 B: 너무 했다!

해설 얼마나 오래 기다렸냐는 질문에 대한 대답이므로, (c)에는 기간을 나타내는 전치사 for가 와야 한다. 정답은 (c)이다.

어휘 wait in line 줄 서서 기다리다

정답 (c) To → For

10.

해석 A: 그는 게으를 뿐만 아니라 매우 이기적이에요.
　　　 B: 누가 아니래요. 저는 그와 함께 일하는 것이 지겨워요.
　　　 A: 게다가, 그는 이 프로젝트의 중요성을 조금도 깨닫지 못하고 있죠.
　　　 B: 그리고 우리들은 지쳐 쓰러져 죽기 직전에 있고요.

해설 (a) 문두에 부정어가 왔으므로, 주어와 동사가 도치되어야 한다. 즉, Not only is he lazy but also very selfish. 로 고쳐야 한다.

정답 (a) he is → is he

11.

해석 (a) 제 2차 세계대전 이후 세계 경제는 놀라운 속도로 성장했다. (b) 경제와 함께 세계무역도 전에 없이 팽창했다. (c) 세계

무역의 확대는 운송기술과 정보통신, 국제 금융 제도의 발전에
힘입었다고 할 수 있다. **(d)** 세계 무역의 증가가 전후 경제성장
을 도왔다는 것은 분명하다.

해설_ (d)에서 **that**절 속의 주어는 **the increase**이다. 그러므로
동사는 복수형인 **have supported**가 아니라 **has
supported**로 고쳐야 옳다.

어휘_ incredible 믿을 수 없는, 굉장한 **expand** 팽창하다
attribute ... to ~ …을 ~의 덕으로 (탓으로) 돌리다
transport 운송 **telecommunications** 정보통신
financial 금융의

정답_ (d) have → has

12.

해석_ (a) 매기와 콜린이 저녁식사에 올 예정이라 빨리 집에 가는 게
나한테 중요했다. **(b)** 그러나 역에 들어서자 악천후로 지연된
기차를 기다리는 사람들로 붐비고 있음을 알았다. **(c)** 바로 그
때 차 한 대가 서더니 그 안의 남자가 나에게 타라고 외쳤다.
(d) 처음에는 그가 의심스러웠으나 곧 매기의 오빠임을 알았
다.

해설_ 동사가 여럿 연결되다 보면 동사들 간의 관계가 동일한지 살펴
보아야 한다. 선택지 **(c)**의 경우 (**a man**) 이하의 동사가 두
개 있으나 그 연결 관계가 다름을 알 수 있다. 첫 번째 동사가
shouted라고 되었으므로 뒤의 동사도 과거형으로 써서
and offered라고 쓰든가(**and he offered**도 됨), 아니면
분사형이나 부정사형으로 고쳐서 **offering/to offer**라고 해
야 옳다.

정답_ (c) offer → and offered

1.

해석_ A: 당신에게 내 휴가 계획을 써 보냈는데요.
　　　B: 그랬죠. 하지만 날짜는 언급하지 않았어요.

해설_ ‘**So** 주어+동사’는 ‘**Yes**, 주어+동사’, ‘**So** 동사+주어’는
‘주어+동사, **too**’의 의미이다.
I am rich.— So you are. (=Yes, you are rich.)
I feel lonely.— So do I. (=I feel lonely, too.)
그러므로 답은 **Yes, you wrote.**를 의미하는 **So you did.**
이다.

정답_ (b)

2.

해석_ A: 전화 온 데 없었나요?
　　　B: 오늘 아침 어떤 친구 분이 전화했어요.

해설_ a/an, this/that, some, any, no 등의 한정사와 소유격은
연속적으로 함께 사용하지 못한다. 따라서, 이러한 경우에는
‘**a my friend**’가 아니라 ‘**a friend of mine**’의 형태, 즉
이중소유격의 형태로 표현해야 한다. 정답은 **(b)**이다.

어휘_ message 메시지, 전보

정답_ (b)

3.

해석_ A: 그녀가 모든 학생들 중에서 가장 재주가 많은 것 같아요.
　　　B: 저도 그렇게 생각해요. 그녀는 정말 천재예요.

해설_ 동의를 뜻하는 표현 ‘**so + do/be**동사/조동사+주어’에 관한
문제이다. **A**의 본동사가 일반동사 **think**이므로, **do**로 받아
야 한다. 정답은 **(b)**이다. 참고로 ‘**Neither + do +** 주어’는
‘~ 역시 그렇게 ~하지 않다’라는 뜻이다.

어휘_ talented 재능이 있는, 유능한 **genius** 천재

정답_ (b)

4.

해석_ A: 요즘 어떻게 지내세요?
　　　B: 더 없이 좋아요. 새 직장이 아주 마음에 들거든요.

해설_ 비교급을 사용한 최상급 표현이다. 새 직장에 매우 만족한다는
것으로 보아 요즘 어느 때보다도 잘 지내고 있다는 말이 빈칸
에 들어가야 한다. **I've never done better than I'm
doing these days** 또는 **It has never been better
than it is these days** 등이 적절하다. 따라서 **Never
been better**가 적절한 답이 된다.

정답_ (a)

5.

해석_ 그 예비 직원은 의료 보험 혜택을 받을 수 있는지 물어보았다.

해설_ ‘~인지 아닌지’ 묻는 것이므로 **that**절이 아니라 **if**절이 와야
하며, 주절의 시제와 일치해야 하므로 **(a)**가 정답이다.

어휘_ prospective 장래의, 예비의

cf. **prospective employee** 직원 후보(아직 입사가 결정된 것은 아니지만 될 가능성이 있는 사람)

coverage (보험) 보상 범위

정답 (a)

6.

해석 이 지역에는 세계에서 가장 아름다운 종류의 나비들이 서식한다.

해설 부사구가 도치되어 문장 맨 앞으로 나올 때는 '동사 + 주어'의 어순이고, 강조를 나타내는 조동사 **do**를 쓰는 경우는 'do + 주어 + 본동사'의 어순이 되기도 한다. 정답은 **(a) are some of**이다.

어휘 **corner** 지역, 지방(region)

species 종(種); 종류(sort, kind)

정답 (a)

7.

해석 이 바위는 저것보다 네 배 더 크다.

해설 배수사 표현에 대한 문제이다. '기수 + **time(s)** + **as** + 원급 + **as**' 나 **twice the size/ number/ amount/ depth/ width/ height/ length/ weight of** 등으로 나타낼 수 있다. "This rock is four times the size of that one" 이라고도 할 수 있다.

정답 (d)

8.

해석 잭슨 씨는 새로운 종류의 비행기의 설계도를 그렸으나, 그의 발명품은 결코 완성되지 않았다.

해설 접속사 **Though**가 이끄는 종속절 이후에 나오는 주절에 주어가 빠져 있으므로 **(b) his invention**이 알맞다.

어휘 **draw** 스케치하다, 묘사하다

정답 (b)

9.

해석 A: 안녕하세요, 손님. 무엇을 도와 드릴까요?

B: 도시 관광 프로그램 때문에 왔어요.

A: 죄송하지만, 취소되었는데요.

B: 정말입니까? 정말 유감이네요.

해설 B가 그냥 처음 찾아와 도시 관광을 하고 싶다고 말한다면, **I'm here for a city tour**가 알맞다. 그러나, 관광 프로그램이 취소되었다고 하는 것을 보면, 그냥 일반적인 관광이 아니라 이미 계획되어 있던 특정 관광 프로그램을 지칭하는 것임을 알 수 있다. 따라서 **the**를 사용해야 한다.

어휘 **cancel** 취소하다, (주문·계약 따위를) 무효로 하다

정답 (b) a → the

10.

해석 **(a)** 인간의 여러 활동들은 대기 중 이산화탄소의 양을 증가시켰다. **(b)** 과학자들은 이러한 증가가 향후 수십 년간 지구의 기온을 높일 것으로 예상한다. **(c)** 한 가지 가능한 해결책은 숲에서 과다한 이산화탄소를 흡수하는 것일 것이다. **(d)** 그러나, 새로운 연구에 따르면, 숲은 온실 효과 문제의 장기적인 해결책은 될 수 없다.

해설 **(b)**에서 **what**을 **that**으로 바꾸거나 없애야 알맞다. **what** 이하에 나오는 **this buildup will warm ~ decades**는 완전한 하나의 절이다. 따라서 이 절을 이끄는 접속사는 관계대명사가 아니라 명사절을 이끄는 **that**이 와야 한다. 또한 이 때 **that**은 생략할 수도 있다.

어휘 **buildup** 강화, 집중, (교통의) 체증

soak up 흡수하다, 빨아들이다, 이해하다

정답 (b) what → that

Final Test 1

1.

해석_ A: Sarah가 정말 화난 것 같은데. 왜 그런지 아니?

B: 오늘 아침에 소매치기를 당했다고 들었어.

해설_ 소매치기를 '당한' 것이므로 동사는 **get**이 적절하며, **pick**의 형태는 수동태가 알맞다.

어휘_ **pick** 소매치기하다

정답_ (a)

2.

해석_ A: 새로운 상사의 나이를 아니?

B: 이제 갓 30살이 되었다고 들었어.

해설_ 어순 문제이다. **just**의 위치는 동사 **turned**의 바로 앞에 와야 한다. 또한 '나이가 몇 살이 되었다'라고 할 때는 **turn**의 목적어로 숫자가 온다.

어휘_ **turn** (나이가) ~살이 되다

정답_ (c)

3.

해석_ A: 실례합니다, 야구 글러브를 사려면 어디로 가야 하죠?

B: 5층에 가시면 많은 스포츠 용품들이 있습니다.

해설_ **a range of** 뒤에는 가산명사가 올 경우 반드시 관사 없이 복수형이 사용되어야 한다. **equipment**와 같이 불가산명사가 올 경우에도 관사는 생략한다.

어휘_ **a range of** 광범위한 **equipment** 장비, 용품

정답_ (b)

4.

해석_ A: 맙소사! 오븐 끄는 걸 깜빡했어!

B: 걱정 마, 내가 껐어.

해설_ **forget**, **remember**의 목적어로 **to**부정사가 올 경우 '~ 할 것을 잊어버리다/기억하다'가 되며, 동명사가 올 경우 '~한 사실을 잊어버리다/기억하다'가 된다.

정답_ (c)

5.

해석_ A: 청년실업자 수가 줄고 있다는 것은 절대 좋은 신호가 아닙니다.

B: 이해할 수 없군요. 이유를 설명해 주십시오.

해설_ 주어가 **the number of**이므로 단수동사가 와야 한다. 또한 문장 전체의 주어는 **That the number of younger workers is falling**이므로 문장 전체의 동사 또한 단수동사 **is**가 와야 한다.

어휘_ **definitely** 명확히, 반드시

정답_ (a)

6.

해석_ A: 주문하셨습니까?

B: 아니요. 메뉴판 좀 가져다 주세요.

해설_ 현재진행 수동태가 와야 한다.

정답_ (c)

7.

해석_ A: 미 대통령 선거에서 누가 가장 유력한 후보라고 생각하니?

B: 사람들은 McIves가 가장 유력하다고 말하지만, 난 Kingstone이 선거에서 이길 거라 생각해.

해설_ 어순 문제. 주절의 동사가 **think**일 경우 목적절의 의문사는 문두에 위치한다.

어휘_ **likely** 유망한 **candidate** 선거 후보

정답_ (b)

8.

해석_ A: 난 이 **TV** 프로가 정말 싫어.

B: 나도 그래. 역겹고 전혀 재미없어!

해설_ 의미는 부정이지만 문장 형태는 긍정인 경우, 대답하는 문장 또한 긍정문이어야 한다. **I do, either**는 잘못된 표현이고 **I don't, either**로 써야 하며 그 의미는 '나 또한 그러하지 않다'이다.

정답_ (a)

9.

해석_ A: Jessica가 Paul과 사귀니?

B: 내가 아는 한은 아니야.

해설_ 부정어가 문두에 나오면 주어, 동사가 도치된다.

정답_ (d)

10.

해석_ A: Jason이 여기 오면, 제게 좀 알려주시겠어요?

B: Jason이 동의할 경우에만 그럴게요, 죄송합니다.

해설_ 조건의 부사절은 내용상 미래의 일이더라도 현재시제를 사용한다.

정답_ (b)

11.

해석_ A: Joe를 언제 만날 수 있나요?

B: 3시까지 여기에 오기로 되어 있어요.

해설_ 'be supposed to'는 가까운 미래를 나타내는 용법이다.

정답_ (b)

12.

해석_ A: 운전면허 시험에 또 떨어졌어.

B: 네가 조금이라도 연습했더라면 지금쯤 면허를 땄을 텐데.

해설_ 혼합가정법. If절은 과거의 일을 가정하는 것이므로 가정법 과거완료를 쓰나, 주절은 현재의 일을 가정하므로 가정법 과거를 쓴다.

어휘_ **driver's license test** 운전면허 시험

정답_ (d)

13.

해석_ A: 여행 준비물로 또 무엇을 챙겨야 하지?
B: 짧은 바지 한 벌도 필요해.

해설_ a pair of ~는 단수 취급한다.

정답_ (a)

14.

해석_ A: 당신과 이야기하면서 즐거웠어요.
B: 저도요. 우리 다시 만날 수 있을까요?

해설_ time + 현재분사는 '~하느라 보내는 시간'이란 뜻이다. 따라서 빈칸엔 talking이 와야 한다. 또한 동사 talk은 자동사이므로 목적어 앞에 전치사를 반드시 필요로 한다.

정답_ (d)

15.

해석_ A: 엄마, 이 숙제 좀 도와주세요.
B: 미안하다, Jacob. 그건 네 일이고 너 스스로 해야 해.

해설_ help는 준사역동사이므로 목적보어에 to부정사와 동사원형 모두 올 수 있다.

어휘_ by yourself 혼자, 스스로

정답_ (a)

16.

해석_ A: 이 립스틱이 손님 피부색과 잘 어울리는 것 같아요.
B: 그럼 그걸로 할게요. 얼마죠?

해설_ go with는 '~와 어울리다'란 뜻으로, go를 수식하는 부사가 들어가는 것이 알맞다.

어휘_ go with ~와 어울리다

정답_ (b)

17.

해석_ A: Mr. Kim의 나이를 듣고 깜짝 놀랐어.
B: 나도. 그는 머리가 벗겨져서 실제보다 훨씬 더 나이들어 보이는 것 같아.

해설_ 여기서의 go는 '특정 상태가 되다'란 뜻이므로 형용사 보어가 필요하다.

정답_ (a)

18.

해석_ A: 너랑 너희 오빠 서로 화해했니?
B: 응, 화해했어. 우린 이제 서로 사이가 좋아.

해설_ be on good terms with '~와 사이가 좋다'의 경우 명사 term은 항상 복수로 쓴다.

어휘_ bury the hatchet 화해하다

정답_ (c)

19.

해석_ A: 이번 프로젝트에서 200달러밖에 벌지 못했어.

B: 기운 내! 200달러도 여전히 큰 돈이야.

해설_ '200달러라는 금액'이 주어이므로 단수 취급해야 한다.

정답_ (c)

20.

해석_ A: 저 앵커가 몇 살쯤 될 것 같니?
B: 맞히기 어려운 걸. 음... 아마 40에서 45세 정도?

해설_ 어순 문제. 목적절에 의문문이 올 경우, 주절의 동사로 think가 오면 목적절의 의문사는 문두에 온다. 또한 how old는 같이 붙어 다닌다.

어휘_ anchorman 앵커, 뉴스 진행자

정답_ (d)

21.

해석_ 방 안에 혼자 있으면서, 그는 자신의 유서를 작성했다.

해설_ 분사구문 문제이다. When he was in the room alone, he made his testament.인 원래 문장에서 접속사, 주어를 생략하고 was를 being으로 바꾸었다.

어휘_ testament 유서

정답_ (b)

22.

해석_ 외세의 개입은 반드시 "총질"을 초래한다고 그는 생각한다.

해설_ 시제 문제이다. 주절이 목적절 중간에 삽입된 형태인데, 이때 시제가 일치되려면 주절 동사는 현재시제를 취해야 한다.

어휘_ intervention (타국의 내정 등에 대한) 개입, (내정) 간섭
invariably 반드시

정답_ (a)

23.

해석_ 이 프로그램은 당신이 가장 유용한 컴퓨터 기술을 익히는 것을 도와줄 것입니다.

해설_ 동사 acquaint는 'acquaint + 사람/yourself + with + 사물'의 형태로 사용된다.

어휘_ acquaint 잘 알게 하다

정답_ (d)

24.

해석_ 그녀는 나와 똑같은 치마를 입고 있다.

해설_ 유사관계대명사 as는 관계대명사 절을 이끈다. 관계대명사 절은 원래 'as I am wearing'이므로 대동사는 'am'을 사용해야 한다.

정답_ (a)

25.

해석_ 중소기업과 공공부문 취업자 수는 증가하고 있다.

해설_ 주어가 the number of이므로 단수동사가 와야 한다.

어휘_ small businesses 중소기업
public service 공공부문

정답_ (a)

26.

해석_ 중립적이고 전문성을 갖춘 학자들로 구성된 독립된 조사기관에 모든 것을 위임해야 한다.

해설_ consist of 는 '~으로 구성되다'이므로 빈칸에는 현재분사형이 적합하다.

어휘_ delegate 위임하다   academic 대학생, 대학교수, 학자   neutrality 중립   expertise 전문 기술, 전문 지식

정답_ (c)

27.

해석_ 일련의 조직적 부정행위가 후에 발각되었다.

해설_ a series of 뒤에는 복수명사를 쓴다. 그러나 'a series of + 복수명사'는 전체적으로 단수 취급한다.

어휘_ a series of 일련의   later on 나중에

정답_ (c)

28.

해석_ 그의 더러운 성질을 진작 알았더라면, 그와 절대 사귀지 않았을 텐데.

해설_ 과거의 일을 가정하는 것이므로 가정법 과거완료 문제이다. if 절의 동사는 had + p.p. 형태를 쓴다. 이때 if 생략 시 had가 문두에 위치한다.

어휘_ go out with ~와 사귀다

정답_ (c)

29.

해석_ 당신이 그녀라면 누구를 선택하겠어요?

해설_ 가정법에서 suppose는 if를 대신한다. 가정법 현재이므로 조건절의 동사는 과거형을 취해야 한다.

정답_ (c)

30.

해석_ 아이들이 도착할 때면 이 케이크가 다 구워질 거예요.

해설_ 미래완료시제 문제이다. 'will + have + p.p.'의 형태를 사용하되, 케이크는 '구워지는' 대상이므로 수동태를 쓴다.

정답_ (d)

31.

해석_ 이 와인은 더할 나위 없이 훌륭합니다.

해설_ 어순 문제이다. highly는 원래 recommended 앞에 위치하나, enough와 함께 쓰였으므로 recommended 뒤로 이동하게 된다.

정답_ (c)

32.

해석_ 최종 점수를 듣고, Jackie와 그녀의 코치는 기뻐서 눈물을 흘렸다.

해설_ 전치사가 앞에 있으므로 동명사가 와야 한다. 태는 능동, 시제는 주절과 일치된 시제이므로 (a) hearing이 오는 것이 바람직하다.

정답_ (a)

33.

해석_ 그는 자살의 이유를 쓴 유서를 남겼다.

해설_ note를 수식하는 분사구문은 giving으로 시작해야 한다.

어휘_ suicide 자살

정답_ (d)

34.

해석_ 그가 파산하자마자 그녀는 그를 떠났다.

해설_ 어순 문제이다. No sooner로 문장을 시작할 경우 주어와 동사의 위치가 바뀐다.

어휘_ go bankrupt 파산하다

정답_ (d)

35.

해석_ 세관은 3주 후에 결정을 내릴 것으로 예상된다.

해설_ custom은 '관습'이지만 customs는 문맥에 따라 custom의 복수형이 아니라 '관세, 세관'의 뜻이 되며, 이때는 단수 취급한다.

정답_ (c)

36.

해석_ 그가 죽고 나서야 그들은 그의 결백을 깨달았다.

해설_ 어순 문제이다. 부정어를 문두에 오도록 할 경우 주어, 동사가 도치된다.

어휘_ innocence 무죄, 결백

정답_ (b)

37.

해석_ 지금은 매우 늙었지만, 그녀는 젊었을 적에 대단한 미녀였던 것 같다.

해설_ 시제문제이다. 미인이었던 것은 과거이고 보이는 것은 현재이므로 완료부정사를 사용한다.

정답_ (c)

38.

해석_ 그룹 B는 6살짜리 12명으로 구성되어 있습니다.

해설_ '6살짜리 아이'는 a six-year-old이고, 이의 복수형은 old에 s를 붙인다.

어휘_ consist of ~로 구성되다.

정답_ (c)

39.

해석_ 그 재산소유권은 그들에게서 당신에게로 이전되었습니다.

해설_ 전치사 문제이다. title이 '법적인 소유권'의 의미를 지닐 때

title to Sth 또는 **to do Sth**의 형태를 쓴다.

어휘_ **property** 재산 **convey** 이전하다

정답_ (c)

40.

해석_ 23,000명이 넘는 신용불량자들이 올해 9월까지 개인파산을 신청했다.

해설_ 서수 **first**는 정관사를 필요로 한다. 또한 1월~9월을 모두 포함하는 개념이므로 **month**는 복수로 써야 한다.

어휘_ **delinquent** 채무 불이행자, 신용불량자
file for ~을 신청하다 **bankruptcy** 파산

정답_ (b)

41.

해석_ A: 일에 쫓기는 것 정말 싫어.
B: 미루지 않았어야 했는데. 어제는 뭐 했는데?
A: 하루 종일 컴퓨터 게임 했지.
B: 어제 다 끝내놓았더라면 오늘 편한 마음으로 게임을 즐길 수 있을 텐데.

해설_ 과거의 일에 대한 후회나 아쉬움을 나타낼 때는 **should have + p.p**의 형태를 쓴다. 따라서 **You couldn't have put it off**를 **You shouldn't have put it off**로 고친다.

어휘_ **put off** 미루다

정답_ (b)

42.

해석_ A: 넌 거짓말 탐지기가 절대 오류가 없다고 생각해?
B: 거의 그런 셈이야. 왜?
A: 어제 신문기사를 하나 읽었는데, 탐지 테스트를 실시하는 사람들이 반드시 전문가는 아니라고 하더라고.
B: 그럼 신뢰도가 그리 높을 수 없겠군.

해설_ 'A를 B라고 생각하다'라는 표현을 할 때는 **think of A as B**를 사용한다. 따라서 **Do you think**를 **Do you think of**로 바꾼다.

어휘_ **think of A as B** A를 B라고 생각하다
lie detector 거짓말 탐지기
foolproof 잘못될 수가 없는

정답_ (a)

43.

해석_ A: Lucy와 헤어졌어? 무슨 일이 있었는데?
B: 난 이제 결혼하고 싶은데, 그녀는 나와 생각이 달랐어.
A: 결혼하자고 하지 그랬니?
B: 여러 번 청혼했지만, 그녀는 끝내 받아들이지 않았어.

해설_ **a number of** 뒤에는 복수명사가 온다. 따라서 **marriage proposals**가 올바르다.

어휘_ **marriage proposal** 청혼

정답_ (d)

44.

해석_ A: Katie가 우리 계획을 눈치챈 것 같아.
B: 이런, 그럼 그녀의 생일파티가 깜짝 파티가 될 수 없잖아.
A: 내 생각에 Alex가 우리 계획을 그녀에게 말한 것 같아.
B: 그가 알아차리게 하지 말았어야 했는데. 모두 내 잘못이야.

해설_ 동사 **tell**의 대상을 간접목적어로 쓸 수 있으므로 전치사 **to**는 불필요하다.

정답_ (c)

45.

해석_ A: 정말 죄송하지만, 우리 약속을 오는 목요일로 연기할 수 있을까요?
B: 왜죠? Wien에 아직 도착하지 않으셨나요?
A: 비행기를 놓쳤어요. 다음 비행기는 수요일에 있고요.
B: 전 괜찮지만, 당신이 도착할 때쯤 나머지 사람들은 모두 Paris로 떠난 상태일 거예요.

해설_ 완료시제는 **when**절과 함께 쓰이지 않는다. 따라서 **when you arrive**를 **by the time you arrive**로 고친다.

어휘_ **postpone** 연기하다

정답_ (d)

46.

해석_ (a) 오늘밤, 우리는 우리나라의 위대함을 확인하기 위해 모였습니다. (b) 그것은 고층 빌딩의 높이, 우리의 군사력, 우리의 경제 규모에 기인한 것이 아닙니다. (c) 우리의 자부심은 아주 간단한 전제에 바탕을 두고 있습니다. (d) 그 전제는 200년도 넘은 과거에 만들어진 선언문에 요약되어 있습니다.

해설_ 태에 관한 문제이다. **premise**는 '요약된' 것이므로 (d)의 **sum up**을 수동태로 바꿔서 **summed up**으로 쓴다.

어휘_ **affirm** 단언하다 **skyscraper** 고층 빌딩 **premise** 전제 **sum up** 요약하다 **declaration** 선언(문)

정답_ (d)

47.

해석_ (a) 나는 여전히 낙관적인 결과가 가능하다고 믿는다. (b) 세계는 전후 가장 심각한 불경기를 겪고 있다. (c) 그리고 경기회복은 더딜 것이며 인플레이션이 회복을 방해할 것이다. (d) 그럼에도 불구하고, 불황과 디플레이션의 종말론적 시나리오는 억지스러운 측면이 있다.

해설_ **outcome**은 반드시 관사를 필요로 하는 단어이다. 따라서 **a bullish outcome**으로 써야 한다.

어휘_ **bullish** 낙관적인 **severe** 심한 **recession** 불경기, 경기후퇴 **sluggish** 둔한, 느린 **plague** 괴롭히다 **doomsday** 지구 종말의 날 **depression** 불황 **farfetched** 억지스러운

정답_ (a)

48.

해석_ (a) 내가 9살쯤 되었을 때, 엄마는 멋진 자기 사진을 원하는 여자들에게 사진을 찍어주는 사업을 시작했어요. **(b)** 난 엄마의 광도계, 반사경 등을 들었죠. **(c)** 엄마는 나를 우리 집 뒷베란다에 있는 암실로 데려가서 사진을 현상하곤 했어요. **(d)** 반짝이는 붉은 빛과 함께 사진 속의 형상이 나타나는 모습을 넋을 놓고 쳐다봤죠.

해설_ watch가 지각동사이므로 목적보어는 동사원형이 와야 한다. 따라서 **the pictures appeared**를 **the pictures appear**로 바꾼다.

어휘_ light meter 노출계, 광도계 **reflector** 반사경, 반사 장치 **darkroom** 암실 **porch** 현관, 베란다 **develop** (사진) 현상하다

정답_ (d)

49.

해석_ (a) 모델일은 무척 고독합니다. **(b)** 여배우들이나 가수들은 측근들, 헤어 및 메이크업 담당자들, 그리고 투어 매니저들과 함께 다니지만, 모델들은 혼자입니다. **(c)** 심지어 전 세계에서 가장 잘나가는 슈퍼모델들도 혼자 다닙니다. **(d)** 그래서 전 가능한 한 자주 L.A.에 가서 제 고교 친구들과 어울리려고 합니다.

해설_ as often as I can을 **as often as I could**로 고친다.

어휘_ modeling (패션) 모델업 **entourage** 측근자, 주위 사람들

정답_ (d)

50.

해석_ (a) 모든 사람들이 비관적인 전망을 하고 그런 전망에 따라 행동할 때 주식 매수량을 점진적으로 늘리면 반드시 잘된다는 사실을 나는 지난 40년간의 경험에서 깨달았다. **(b)** 정의에 의하면, 주가 사이클의 바닥은 비관적 전망이 최대에 이른 지점이다. **(c)** 가격이 반등하기 위해 호재가 있어야 할 필요는 없다 **(d)** 그저 이미 시장에 반영된 것보다 덜 나쁘기만 하면 된다.

해설_ 진주어·가주어 용법이므로 가주어 **it**을 사용한다. 따라서 **that is**를 **it is**로 바꾼다.

어휘_ bearish (증시가) 약세인, 약세를 예상하는 **invariably** 변함없이, 늘 **rally** (증권 등이)시세를 회복하다

정답_ (a)

Final Test 2

1.

해석_ A: 이봐, 왜 여기 있는 거야? 지금쯤 뉴욕행 비행기 안에 있어야 하는 거 아니야?

B: 맞아, 근데 공항 가는 길에, 사무실에 여권을 두고 온 게 생각났지 뭐야.

해설_ forget, remember의 목적어로 **to**부정사가 올 경우 '~ 할 것을 잊어버리다/기억하다'가 되며, 동명사가 올 경우 '~한 사실을 잊어버리다/기억하다'가 된다.

정답_ (a)

2.

해석_ A: 내가 오늘 죽는다면, 내 가족의 미래는 어떻게 될까?

B: 헛소리 그만해! 그건 생명보험회사가 제일 좋아하는 질문일 뿐이고 넌 절대 오늘 안 죽어.

해설_ 복수형 명사의 소유격을 만들 때, 명사가 **-s**로 끝나므로 소유격의 **s**는 생략하고 **apostrophe(')**만 붙인다.

어휘_ cut the crap 쓸데없는 소리 그만해 **life insurance** 생명보험

정답_ (d)

3.

해석_ A: 저 스케이트 선수에게 있어서 놀라운 것은 우아함과 열정을 모두 갖고 있다는 것이죠.

B: 맞습니다. 우리가 가졌던 큰 기대를 하나도 빠짐없이 충족시켰습니다.

해설_ every single one of 다음의 대명사가 받는 것은 **expectations**이므로 복수형인 **them**이 와야 한다. 또한 **single**은 'every one'을 강조하기 위해 사용된 것이므로, **one**이 생략되면 틀린다.

어휘_ deliver on (약속 등을) 이행하다

정답_ (b)

4.

해석_ A: 핸드폰을 어디에 뒀는지 기억이 나질 않아.

B: 저기 울리고 있는 것이 네가 찾는 거 아니니?

해설_ 주절 **is that ringing one**에 선행사가 없으므로, 관계대명사로 **what**이 와야 한다.

정답_ (c)

5.

해석_ A: 아이스크림 좋아하니?

B: 물론이야. 누가 싫어하겠어?

해설_ Who doesn't like it에서 **like it**이 생략된 것이다. **who**를 3인칭 단수로 받는 것에 주의한다.

정답_ (b)

6.

해석_ A: 국회가 대통령의 선택을 인준할 가능성이 큽니다.

B: 국회는 자신의 존재 이유를 재고해야만 한다고 생각합니다.

해설_ Chances are (that) ~은 '아마 ~일 것이다'라는 관용 표현이다.

어휘_ the National Assembly 국회
endorse 재가하다, 승인하다 **the Assembly** 국회

정답_ (c)

7.

해석_ A: 저녁 먹을 시간이야.

B: 전혀 배고프지 않아. 한 시간만 늦게 먹으면 안 될까?

해설_ 'time for dinner'와 같은 경우 **dinner**는 무관사명사로 쓴다. 또한 'time to eat dinner'가 맞는 표현이다.

정답_ (b)

8.

해석_ A: Sally를 데리러 공항으로 가야 해.

B: 나는 네가 이런 폭풍우 속에서 돌아다니지 말고 집 안에 머물렀으면 좋겠어. Sally도 혼자 올 수 있어.

해설_ Sally가 혼자 올 수 있다는 말로 미루어 B가 A에게 나가지 말라고 권유하는 것임을 알 수 있다. 따라서 **I'd rather stay/styed**는 답이 될 수 없다. **would rather** 뒤에 절이 올 경우 동사는 과거시제를 쓴다.

정답_ (d)

9.

해석_ A: Chris가 Mr. Jenkins에게 Amy를 해고하도록 시켰다는 걸 알고 있었니?

B: 정말? 그럼 Chris가 그랑 바람을 피우고 있다는 게 사실인가 보군.

해설_ 'have +목적어 + 목적보어' 구문이다. **have**가 사역동사이므로 목적보어 자리에 동사원형이 온다.

어휘_ have an affair with …와 바람피우다

정답_ (a)

10.

해석_ A: '치즈 케이크와 함께 한 가난'이란 에세이 읽어봤니?

B: 아니. 누가 쓴 건데?

해설_ 동사의 시제를 묻는 문제이다. 질문은 완료시제지만 대답은 단순시제로 함에 주의한다.

정답_ (b)

11.

해석_ A: 만일 네가 내일 죽는다면, 오늘을 어떻게 보낼 거야?

B: 대답하기 무척 어렵구나.

해설_ 가정법 문제. 주절이 '...**would you spend**...'이므로 가정법 과거임을 알 수 있다. 따라서 단순과거형인 **died**가 알맞다.

정답_ (b)

12.

해석_ A: 나는 그가 한 말을 거의 이해할 수 없었어요.

B: 동감이에요. 그는 훌륭한 수학자일지는 모르나, 교사로는 낙제예요.

해설_ 대화의 내용상 '거의 이해하지 못했다'라는 부정의 의미가 되도록 빈칸을 채워야 하므로 **a little**은 적합하지 않다. 또한 **what**은 여기서 (관계)대명사이므로 전치사 **of** 뒤에 오는 것이 옳다.

어휘_ mathematician 수학자

정답_ (b)

13.

해석_ A: 인터넷으로는 신발을 절대 사지 말아야 한다는 것을 마침내 깨달았어. 얼마나 돈 낭비인지!

B: 괜찮아. 현명한 사람은 실수를 통해서 배우는 법이야.

해설_ profit은 자동사로 '이익을 얻다', '얻는 바가 있다'란 뜻이며, 이때 전치사 **from, by**와 같이 쓴다.

정답_ (b)

14.

해석_ A: 성공한 사람들은 어떤 공통적인 자질이 있나요?

B: 제가 인터뷰한 사람들은 포기하는 대신에 실패를 분석하고 그들이 뭘 잘못했는지를 파악하더라고요.

해설_ 시제 문제이다. 과거시제인 **figured out**보다 앞서 일어난 일이므로 대과거 시제인 '**what they had done wrong**'이 와야 한다.

어휘_ trait 특성, 특징

정답_ (d)

15.

해석_ A: 제 아내가 저보다 9살 더 많아요.

B: 와, 정말 흔치 않은 경우인데!

해설_ 어순 문제이다. '~보다 나이가 많다'는 '**senior to~**'를 쓰고, 구체적인 나이 차는 **by**를 사용해서 나타낸다.

정답_ (a)

16.

해석_ A: 이 책의 해적판은 지금까지 십만 권 이상 팔렸다고 들었어요.

B: 그렇다면 올해의 베스트셀러는 단연 이 책이겠군요.

해설_ sell은 타동사 '~을 팔다'의 뜻으로 쓰이기도 하지만 자동사 '팔리다'로도 쓰일 수 있다. 빈칸에는 주어가 '책'이므로 목적어 없이 자동사 **sell**의 과거형이 오는 것이 타당하다.

어휘_ pirated version 해적판

정답_ (a)

17.

해석_ A: 정말 아름다운 풍경이네요!

　　　B: 네. 이곳의 아름다움은 말로 표현하기가 어렵죠.

해설_ 감탄문의 어순은 'what + (a/an) + 형용사 +명사'이다. **scenery**(경치)는 무관사명사이다.

어휘_ description 설명, 묘사

정답_ (b)

18.

해석_ A: 올해 하반기에도 세계 경제 전망이 악화될 것으로 보십니까?

　　　B: 물론이죠. 주식시장과 투자심리 모두 현재 매우 비관적입니다.

해설_ deteriorate은 자동사이다. 완료시제는 명확한 시점을 나타내는 부사구와는 함께 쓰이지 않는다.

어휘_ outlook 전망　the latter half of this year 올해 하반기

정답_ (a)

19.

해석_ A: 어지러워요.

　　　B: 저쪽에 가서 누워 있지 그래요?

해설_ lay는 타동사(눕히다)임을 유의한다. and가 등위접속사이므로 lying은 부적합하다.

어휘_ dizzy 어지러운, 현기증이 나는

정답_ (c)

20.

해석_ A: 이 스위치는 우리가 이 집에 이사 올 때부터 여기에 있었어요.

　　　B: 그럼 내가 전엔 이걸 왜 못 봤을까?

해설_ how come은 why의 뜻이며, 'how come+주어+동사'의 순서로 쓴다.

정답_ (b)

21.

해석_ 통계는 청소년 흡연자 수가 증가하고 있음을 보여주고 있다.

해설_ that절의 주어는 the number of이므로 단수동사가 와야 한다. a number of는 many와 같은 뜻인데, 문장의 빈칸에는 의미상 적절하지 않다.

어휘_ juvenile 청소년, 청소년의

정답_ (a)

22.

해석_ 시장은 부동산 투기 억제를 위한 강력한 정부규제정책이 발표된 이래로 침체를 겪어 왔다.

해설_ 시제 문제, since~절이 있으므로 주절은 현재완료가 타당하다.

어휘_ mired in ~의 곤경에 빠진, 진흙탕에 빠진

　　　slump 침체　regulation 규제　curb 억제하다

property 재산　speculation 추측, 투기

정답_ (c)

23.

해석_ 심각한 재정 압박에도 불구하고, 그는 올해 하반기에 새로운 브랜드를 출시하는 것을 고집했다.

해설_ persist는 자동사이고, 전치사 in을 목적어 앞에 사용한다.

어휘_ financial 금융의, 재정의　pressure 압박　persist 고집하다, 주장하다　launch (신제품을) 시장에 내다

정답_ (b)

24.

해석_ 그는 이 고전을 옥중에서 집필했다.

해설_ behind bars는 '옥중에(서), 감옥에 갇힌'이라는 관용 표현이다. 이때 bars는 무관사 복수명사로 쓰임을 주의한다.

어휘_ classic 일류의, 고전의

정답_ (b)

25.

해석_ 만일 초기 투자자들이 '2 더하기 2는 4'라는 것만 기억했다면, 재앙은 피할 수도 있었을 것이다.

해설_ 가정법 과거완료이므로 '조동사 과거형 + have + p.p' 형태가 와야 한다. 또한 avert는 '피하다'란 뜻이므로 여기서는 수동형으로 쓰여야 한다.

어휘_ primitive 원시의, 초기의

정답_ (d)

26.

해석_ 이 젊은 요리사들이 음식에 대한 열정은 물론 높은 수준의 기술과 자신감을 충분히 갖춰서 앞으로 나아가며 스스로의 미래를 개척할 수 있기를 희망합니다.

해설_ that these young chefs ~ their own future가 진주어이므로 가주어 it뒤의 동사 hope는 수동태가 되어야 한다. hopeful은 주로 사람 주어를 사용하므로 정답이 아니다.

어휘_ equip 갖추게 하다, …할 능력을 기르다

　　　self-confidence 자신감　carve out 잘라내다, 개척하다

정답_ (a)

27.

해석_ 우리 주(州)는 30개의 군으로 구성되어 있다.

해설_ consist of는 '~로 구성되다'이므로 빈칸에 능동태가 와야 한다. 시제가 현재이고 주어 our state가 단수이므로 동사 consist 뒤에 s를 붙인다.

어휘_ county 군(행정구역 단위 중 하나)

정답_ (b)

28.

해석_ 우리 대학의 영문학과 교수진은 모든 시대의 영문학을 아우르는 뛰어난 연구 및 교수의 경력을 소유하고 있습니다.

해설_ 분사 문제이다. **all periods of English Literature**가 **cover**의 목적어이므로 빈칸에는 능동형 분사가 와야 알맞다.

어휘_ **faculty** 교수진 **distinguished** 뛰어난

정답_ (d)

29.

해석_ 올 12월에 시작하는 영어훈련 코스에 대한 정보를 알고 싶습니다.

해설_ **information**은 셀 수 없는 명사이다. 따라서 복수형은 불가능하다. 다만 **some**으로 수식할 수는 있다.

정답_ (b)

30.

해석_ 그 가격은 우리가 감당할 수 있는 것을 훨씬 넘는다.

해설_ 선행사를 포함하는 관계대명사가 와야 한다. 참고로 **way**는 부사나 전치사를 강조할 수 있다.

정답_ (a)

31.

해석_ 그가 그 1캐럿짜리 다이아몬드 반지를 훔친 것으로 추정되었다.

해설_ 시제 문제이다. 훔친 시점이 추정되는 시점보다 앞서므로 **to** 부정사절에는 현재완료 시제를 써주어야 한다.

어휘_ **carat** 캐럿 (보석의 무게, 단위; 200 mg)

정답_ (b)

32.

해석_ 이 기업은 또한 캐나다의 한 에너지 기업과 연대하여 러시아의 원자력 발전소 두 곳에 주요 장비를 공급하기도 했다.

해설_ **alliance**가 '동맹'의 뜻으로 쓰일 때는 가산명사이며 관사를 필요로 하지만, **in alliance with**(~와 연합, 연대하여)로 쓰일 때는 무관사로 사용한다.

어휘_ **equipment** 장비

정답_ (a)

33.

해석_ 자본주의에서 거대 생산업체들은 제품을 판매할 더 큰 시장 및 새로운 국가들을 지속적으로 필요로 한다.

해설_ **product**는 가산명사이므로 '**their products**'가 알맞다. 또한 '**to sell their products to larger markets and new countries**'에서 **larger markets and new countries**가 생략된 것이므로 **products**뒤에 **to**가 필요하다.

정답_ (d)

34.

해석_ 가장 좋은 다이어트 방법은 열량 섭취를 획기적으로 줄이는 것이라는 사실을 학자들은 발견했다.

해설_ 선행사와 관계대명사 모두 필요하다. 또한 동사 **reduce**는 시

제일치를 위해 과거형으로 써야 한다.

어휘_ **intake** 섭취

정답_ (c)

35.

해석_ 누구나 총감독님을 만날 수 있는 것은 아니다.

해설_ '접근할 수 있는, 만날 수 있는'의 뜻은 **accessible to**로 표현한다. 전치사 사용에 주의한다.

정답_ (b)

36.

해석_ 그녀는 모든 것이 제시간에 준비되도록 하기 위해 열심히 일했다.

해설_ **so that**은 **in order that**(~하기 위해)의 뜻을 가진다. 모든 것이 준비되는 것은 **work**의 시점에서 미래이나, 말하는 시점에서는 과거이므로 **would**가 적절하다. 완료시제는 필요없다.

정답_ (a)

37.

해석_ 전국 아파트 시가 총액은 올해 984억 달러 늘어났다.

해설_ 전치사 문제, '(숫자가) 얼마만큼 증가하다'라고 쓸 때는 '**rise by**'를 쓴다.

어휘_ **aggregate market value** 시가 총액

정답_ (a)

38.

해석_ 정부의 강력한 가격억제 정책은 효과를 거두고 있다.

해설_ 능동형이 알맞고, 주어 **The government's intensive efforts**는 복수이므로 **are working**이 답이다.

어휘_ **curb** 재갈을 물리다, 억제하다

정답_ (b)

39.

해석_ 금융 공황과 세계 경제의 붕괴는 관계 당국의 허를 찔렀다.

해설_ **by surprise**는 '불시에, 느닷없이'의 뜻이다. 전치사 **by**를 사용하고, **surprise**는 무관사 명사로 사용함을 기억한다.

어휘_ **the authorities** 관계 당국

정답_ (c)

40.

해석_ 그 거리의 양쪽에 플라타너스 가로수가 있다.

해설_ '길 양쪽에'란 뜻으로 **both sides of the street, each side of the street**이 바른 표현이다. **every side of the street**란 표현은 쓰지 않는다.

어휘_ **sycamore** 플라타너스

정답_ (b)

41.

해석_ **A:** 나는 할 수 있는 모든 것을 했고, 이젠 탈모를 막기가 불가

능하다는 것을 깨달았어.

B: 걱정을 더 할수록 머리는 더 빠져. 그러니 마음 편히 먹어.

A: 알아. 하지만 나이보다 늙어 보이는 게 무척 속상해.

B: 탈모는 네가 지니고 살아야 할 유전적 조건이라는 사실을 받아들여.

해설_ concern (걱정시키다)은 수동형으로 쓰는 것이 바람직하다.

어휘_ lose one's hair 머리카락이 빠지다, 머리가 벗겨지다
hereditary 유전적인

정답_ (b) The more you concern → The more concerned you are

42.

해설_ A: 어제는 왜 가게 문을 닫았었나요?

B: 아이들과 아내가 독감으로 매우 아팠거든요.

A: 이런, 안됐군요. 당신도 몸조심해야 해요. 요즘 독감이 유행이래요.

B: 걱정해줘서 고마워요.

해설_ '~를 걱정하다'라는 뜻은 'worry about'으로 표현한다.
worry 뒤에 사람 목적어가 오면 '~를 걱정시키다'란 뜻이다.

어휘_ flu 독감

정답_ (d) Thanks for worrying me → Thanks for worrying 또는 Thanks for worrying about me

43.

해설_ A: 왜 이렇게 늦었어? 2시간이나 기다렸는데!

B: 정말 미안해. 오는 길에 문 잠그는 걸 깜빡한 게 생각나서 집에 다시 갔거든.

A: 그렇지만 적어도 전화라도 해줬어야지.

B: 어제 핸드폰을 잃어버려서 할 수가 없었어.

해설_ '~ 했어야 했는데'는 should + have + p.p.를 쓴다.

정답_ (c) you should give → you should have given

44.

해설_ A: 우리가 익히 아는 사실, 즉 '적게 먹어야 체중이 준다'는 원칙론을 연구자들이 확인했어.

B: 그래도 탄수화물, 지방, 단백질을 어떤 비율로 섭취하느냐가 중요하다고 들었어.

A: 이 기사에는 가장 좋은 다이어트는 열량 섭취를 크게 줄이는 것이라고 나와 있어.

B: 그러나 적어도 하루에 1200 칼로리는 섭취해야 해.

해설_ 비교급에는 than이 필요하다.

어휘_ confirm 확인하다   carbohydrate 탄수화물
protein 단백질   intake 섭취

정답_ (d) no less → no less than

45.

해설_ A: 어떻게 도와드릴까요?

B: 이 사진에 있는 붉은 재킷을 사고 싶어요.

A: 죄송합니다, 그건 다 팔렸어요. 다른 건 어떠세요? 이것들이 우리 매장에서 제일 잘 나가는 것들이에요.

B: 어느 것도 제 스타일은 아니네요.

해설_ none of them is   다음에 보어가 필요하므로 명사보어 'my style'이 와야 한다. none of them은 단/복수 어떤 것으로 보아도 무방하다.

정답_ (d) none of them is in my style   → none of them is my style

46.

해설_ (a) 포장에 있는 엉터리 사용설명서가 그 품질 문제를 악화시킨다고 전문가들은 말한다. (b) 가령 싸구려 전구를 열이 잘 받는 장치에다 끼워놓는 것과 같은 잘못된 사용은 전구 수명을 급격하게 감소시킨다. (c) 이 문제를 연구하는 몇몇 과학자들은 품질 문제에 있어서 정부를 비난한다. (d) 그들은 연방정부가 가격인하를 지나치게 강요한 것이 결국 제조업자들로 하여금 저가 부품을 쓰게 만든 역효과를 가져왔다고 한다.

해설_ fixtures를 수식하는 절은 문장 주요 성분이 빠짐없이 있으므로 부사절로 보아야 맞다.

어휘_ compound 악화시키다   instruction 사용설명서
bulb 전구   low-end 싸구려, 저가의
fixture 설비, 시설   be prone to ~하기 쉽다
backfire 기대에 어긋난 결과가 되다
component 성분, 구성요소

정답_ (b) which heat is prone to →where heat is prone to

47.

해설_ (a) 계란은 (흰자와 노른자로) 분리하고, 흰자와 노른자를 각각 다른 그릇에 담아 놓습니다. (b) 밀가루, 베이킹파우더, 우유를 노른자에 넣고 섞어서 부드럽고 걸죽한 반죽을 만듭니다. (c) 흰자는 소금과 함께 탁탁 저어서 뻣뻣하게 솟아오르도록 만듭니다. (d) 그 흰자를 반죽에 부드럽게 섞어줍니다 — 이제 사용할 준비가 되었습니다.

해설_ bowl이 단 두 개라고 글 어디에도 언급되지 않았다. 따라서 the other는 적합하지 않은 표현이다.

어휘_ yolk 계란 노른자   batter 반죽   whisk 재빨리 움직이다,
빠르게 휘저어 거품을 만들다   stiff 뻣뻣한
fold A into B (요리에서) 한데 모아 부드럽게 섞다

정답_ (a) the yolks into the other → the yolks into another

48.

해설_ (a) 투자 심리는 믿을 수 없을 만큼 위축되어 있다. (b) 나는 이런 경우는 본 적이 없었다. 심지어 전망이 매우 암울했던 1974년조차 이렇진 않았다. (c) 그때, 미국은 베트남전에서 패배한

직후였고 대통령은 거의 탄핵될 뻔했다. (d) 그럼에도, 그때의 우울함은 우리가 현재 목격하고 있는 수준까지는 아니었다.

해설 impeach는 '탄핵되다'가 아니라 '탄핵하다'이므로, **the president**가 목적어로 와야 한다.

어휘 **incredibly** 놀라우리만큼, 믿을 수 없게
grim 잔인한, 냉혹한   **impeach** 탄핵하다

정답 (c) the president nearly impeached → nearly impeached the president

49.

해설 (a) 우리 정치인들은 해야 할 일이 더 있다. (b) 공장이 멕시코로 이전하는 바람에 일자리를 잃고 이제는 시간당 7달러짜리 일자리를 놓고 자기 자식과 경쟁해야 하는 노동자들을 위해서이다. (c) 직업을 잃고 나서 어떻게 의료비 혜택 없이 매달 4,500달러의 아들 약값을 어떻게 감당해야 할지 걱정하며 눈물을 삼키던 한 아버지를 위해서이다. (d) 우수한 성적, 동기, 의지는 있지만 대학에 갈 돈이 없는 젊은 여성을 위해서이다.

해설 '해야 할 일'의 뜻으로 쓰일 때 **work**는 불가산명사이다.

어휘 **choke back** (감정, 눈물 등을) 억누르다
benefit 혜택   **drive** 추진력, 동기

정답 (a) more works → more work

50.

해설 (a) Fifteen의 2층엔 예약하지 않고도 맛있는 음식과 환상적인 칵테일을 즐길 수 있는 비스트로가 있습니다. (b) 편안한 분위기와 친절한 서비스가 있는 이곳은 친구들과 아침, 점심, 저녁식사 혹은 그저 술 한 잔과 함께 대화를 나누기에 아주 좋습니다. (c) 이 레스토랑의 1층은 편안한 분위기의 현대적인 디자인으로 꾸며져 있으며 친한 이들과의 식사 및 사업상 접대를 하기에 최적의 장소입니다. (d) 우리 레스토랑의 홈페이지 www.fifteenrestaurant.com를 방문해 보세요.

해설 making it ~ 으로 된 분사구문이므로 관계대명사 **which**는 필요 없다. 굳이 관계대명사를 쓸 경우 앞 문장 전체를 선행사로 받아, 'which makes it ~'으로 써주면 된다.

어휘 **upstairs** 2층에, 위층에

정답 (b) which making it → making it

Final Test 3

1.

해설 A: 우리 점심 먹을 때가 지났네.
　　B: 너무 바빠서 적당한 시간을 놓쳤어.

해설 B의 말로 미루어 볼 때 점심시간이 지났음을 알 수 있다. 'it's high time~'은 과거시제와 함께 쓰여서 '~할 때가 지났는데 아직도 안 하고 있다'는 의미로 사용된다.

정답 (d)

2.

해설 A: 오늘날, 기업들이 종업원을 일시 또는 완전 해고하기는 그리 어렵지 않다.
　　B: 그러니까 종업원들은 해고되지 않기 위해 열심히 일할 수밖에 없다.

해설 lest는 '...하지 않기 위해'의 뜻이므로 문장 의미상 부정어 **not**은 필요없다. **lest**가 이끄는 절은 **should**가 생략되었다고 보므로, 동사원형이 오는 것이 타당하다.

어휘 **lay off** 일시 해고하다

정답 (c)

3.

해설 A: 그의 빠른 구조가 없었더라면, 나는 죽었을 거야.
　　B: 우리 모두 Jones 씨에게 얼마나 감사한지 모른단다, 얘야.

해설 주절의 문장으로 보아 가정법 과거완료가 와야 한다.

정답 (d)

4.

해설 A: 우리 가족은 모두 채식주의자야.
　　B: 말도 안 돼. 며칠 전에 네 동생이 햄 샌드위치를 먹는 걸 봤어.

해설 문제의 **family**는 개개인을 지칭하는 군집명사로 쓰인 것이므로 복수 취급한다. 또한 대화의 내용으로 미루어 A가 칭하는 시점은 현재이다.

어휘 **vegetarian** 채식주의자

정답 (b)

5.

해설 A: Joe, 방을 깨끗이 하라고 몇 번을 말해야 하니!
　　B: 지금 막 청소하려던 참이었어요!

해설 어순 문제, '막 ~하려 하다'는 'be about to'로 쓰고, **just**는 **about** 앞에 쓰여 의미를 강조한다.

정답 (d)

6.

해설 A: 그녀가 Jamie를 좋아하는 것 같아. 이해할 수가 없어.
　　B: 뭐, 취향은 제각각이니까.

해설 '취향은 다양하다'란 표현은 'there's no accounting for tastes'라고 한다. 이 때 **taste**는 무관사 명사이며, 주로

복수로 씀에 유의한다.

정답_ (b)

7.

해석_ A: 라흐마니노프의 피아노 협주곡 2번을 연주하고 싶어요.

B: 네 수준을 훨씬 넘어서는 것을 연주하려고 하지 마.

해설_ 전치사 **above**를 강조할 수 있는 어휘를 골라야 한다. **way** 이외에도 **far**, **much** 등이 있다.

정답_ (b)

8.

해석_ A: 도서관은 몇 개나 있나요?

B: 캠퍼스 내에 5개가 있고, 걸어갈 수 있는 거리에 2개가 더 있습니다.

해설_ **within walking distance**는 '걸어갈 수 있는 거리에'라는 관용 표현이다. 이때 **distance**는 불가산명사임을 주의해야 한다.

정답_ (a)

9.

해석_ A: 지진으로 인해 수백만 달러의 피해가 발생했어요.

B: 긴급 구호 자금 및 특별 재난 지역으로의 지정이 요구됩니다.

해설_ **worth**(~의 가치가 있는)는 앞에 있는 명사를 꾸며주는 형용사이므로, **worth** 앞에는 명사가 와야 한다. **millions of dollars** (수백만 달러)는 **million**과 **dollar** 모두에 **-s**를 붙임에 유의한다.

어휘_ emergency aid fund 긴급 구호 자금

designate 지정하다

정답_ (d)

10.

해석_ A: 그는 그 일에 기가 죽은 것 같아요.

B: 그를 도울 수 없어서 매우 유감이군요.

해설_ 빈칸에는 수동태가 와야 하며, **seems**로 보아 **to**부정사가 오는 것이 적합하다.

어휘_ daunt 위압하다, 기세를 꺾다

정답_ (c)

11.

해석_ A: 이 건물의 주인인데요, 10분만 있다 갈게요.

B: 누구의 차이건 간에, 똑바로 주차되어야 합니다.

해설_ **whoever**의 소유격이 와야 한다.

정답_ (d)

12.

해석_ A: 산업 구조가 크게 변했습니다.

B: 맞아요. 가령 국내 영화 산업의 매출은 국내 신발 산업의 매출액의 거의 2배에 달합니다.

해설_ '두 배의 돈'은 **double the money**라고 쓴다.

정답_ (b)

13.

해석_ A: 내가 그녀와 같이 있기를 원하세요?

B: 아니요. 그녀는 혼자 있는 것을 더 좋아해요.

해설_ **prefer** 다음에 **to**부정사 뿐 아니라 동명사도 올 수 있음을 기억한다. 대화의 내용으로 보아 완료시제의 사용은 불필요하다.

정답_ (a)

14.

해석_ A: 사인을 밝혀냈습니까?

B: 아직 아닙니다만, 오늘 오후에 경찰이 부검을 실시할 예정입니다.

해설_ '부검하다'는 '**perform an autopsy**'라고 표현한다. **autopsy** 앞에 부정관사를 씀을 유의한다.

어휘_ autopsy 검시, 부검

정답_ (a)

15.

해석_ A: 악천후 때문에, 유감스럽지만 연기가 필요합니다.

B: 안 돼. 그 사업은 2월 완공일자를 맞출 것이야. 알겠나?

해설_ 완료시제는 명확한 시점과 함께 쓰이지 않는다. 또한 **completion**은 원래 무관사 명사이나, 여기서는 '**completion date**'이므로 정관사가 필요하다.

어휘_ severe 맹렬한, 가혹한

정답_ (a)

16.

해석_ A: 시드니의 기후가 제주도의 기후보다 온화한가요?

B: 확실하진 않지만, 비슷할 것 같군요.

해설_ 비교문에서 동등 대상을 지칭할 경우 대명사 **that**을 쓴다.

정답_ (b)

17.

해석_ A: 통계청 조사에 따르면 3월에는 국내외의 일련의 불확실성으로 인해 소비심리가 악화되었다고 합니다.

B: 경기침체를 겪고 있음을 아무도 부인할 수 없습니다.

해설_ **a range of** 뒤에 가산명사는 복수형, 불가산명사가 오면 단수형을 쓴다. **uncertainty**는 '불확실성'이란 의미일 때는 불가산명사이다. 그러나 '불확실한 일, 불확실한 것'의 의미일 때는 복수로 사용되며, 문제의 경우 우리말로 옮길 때는 '불확실성'이 자연스러울지라도 그 실제적 의미는 '불확실한 일, 불확실한 것'이다. 따라서 복수형 **uncertainties**가 적합하다.

어휘_ National Statistical Office 통계청

sentiment 감정 deteriorate 악화되다

정답_ (c)

in ruins라고 쓴다. ruin이 복수형임을 주의한다.

정답_ (c)

24.

해석_ 내 개인 트레이너는 내게 몸무게가 80**kg** 이하가 되어야 한다고 권유했다.

해설_ 주절의 동사가 **recommend**이므로 **that**절에는 **should**가 생략된 동사원형이 올 수 있다.

정답_ (b)

25.

해석_ 시체를 보자마자 그들은 눈을 감았다.

해설_ 'Hardly[Scarecely] + have + 주어 + 과거분사' 또는 'Hardly[Scarecely] + had + 주어 + 과거분사'의 어순을 따른다. 과거의 일을 서술하고 있으므로 문제에서는 **Scarcely** 다음에 **had**가 오는 것이 맞다.

정답_ (c)

26.

해석_ 많은 다른 사람들도 그 감정에 공감했다.

해설_ 'a good (great) many +복수명사 +복수동사'의 형태로 쓴다.

어휘_ sentiment 감상, 감정

정답_ (a)

27.

해석_ 앞 자리 표를 확보하려면 일찍 와야 한다.

해설_ assure + A + of + B 구문은 'A에게 B를 보장하다'의 뜻이다. **assure**의 사람 목적어는 문장의 주어 **you**와 동일하므로 재귀대명사 **yourself**가 와야 맞다.

정답_ (c)

28.

해석_ 주식 시장에서 조달된 자금은 총 2,000달러가 되었다.

해설_ aggregate은 타동사로 '총계가 ~가 되다'란 뜻이 있다. 따라서 전치사 없이 능동형으로 쓰이는 것이 알맞다.

정답_ (a)

29.

해석_ 투표율을 높이기 위해, 중앙 선거관리위원회는 유권자들에게 적극적으로 이번 선거에 참가하여 줄 것을 권유했다.

해설_ participate는 자동사이므로 수동태로 쓰이지 않는다. 또한 전치사를 필요로 하며, 이때 가장 알맞은 전치사는 **in**이다.

어휘_ in a bid to ~하기 위해 bolster 지지하다, 보강하다 voter turnout 투표수 The National Election Commission 중앙 선거관리위원회

정답_ (d)

18.

해석_ A: 사실, 코 성형을 생각 중이야.

　　　B: 내버려두는 게 좋을 걸. 네 얼굴 전체의 균형을 잃을 거야.

해설_ 보어의 의미상의 주어가 **it**(=nose)이므로, **undo**의 과거분사가 오는 것이 적합하다.

어휘_ plastic surgery 성형수술

정답_ (c)

19.

해석_ A: 폭로는 곧 죽음이다.

　　　B: 무슨 일이 일어나도 이것을 비밀로 지키겠다.

해설_ whatsoever는 whatever의 강조형이다. 빈칸엔 주어가 될 수 있는 것이 들어가야 하는데, 보기 중에서는 의미상 **whatsoever**만 가능하다.

어휘_ disclosure 발각, 폭로

정답_ (c)

20.

해석_ A: 프리지아는 장미와 백합 다음으로 우리 꽃집에서 가장 많이 팔리는 품목입니다.

　　　B: 모두 제가 가장 좋아하는 꽃들이에요.

해설_ 어순 문제, '몇 번째로 많이 팔리는'이란 표현은 'the + 서수 + top + selling'을 쓴다.

정답_ (a)

21.

해석_ 이 천연 밀랍으로 만든 초들은 저급 양초들처럼 유리잔에 검댕을 남기지 않고 깔끔하게 연소합니다.

해설_ 유사관계대명사 **as**의 용법을 묻는 문제이다. **as**의 선행사가 'leaving black marks on the glass'이므로 동사 **happen**은 단수형으로 쓰여야 한다.

어휘_ inferior 열등한, 하위의

정답_ (d)

22.

해석_ 그들은 여성 노동자들과는 연대하고 있지 않은데, 이 여성노동자들이 원하는 바는 자본주의의 폐지를 통해서만 얻어질 수 있는 것이다.

해설_ 어순 문제. 소유격 관계대명사 **whose**가 와야 하며, 'whose needs'가 관계대명사절의 주어이고 **serve**는 수동태로 와야 한다.

어휘_ abolition 폐지

정답_ (a)

23.

해석_ 3년간의 전쟁 후 나라 전체기 폐허가 되었다.

해설_ 전치사 문제. '폐허가 되어'란 표현은 전치사 'in'을 사용하여

30.

해석_ 양사는 사용자가 이미지 파일을 온라인으로 저장하고 그것을 컴퓨터와 카메라폰 그리고 기타 장비로 전송할 수 있도록 하는 사진공유 서비스를 개발할 계획이다.

해설_ 어순 문제이다. 주격 관계대명사 **that**절이 **service**를 수식하고 있다.

어휘_ **camera-equipped** 카메라가 내장된

정답_ (a)

31.

해석_ 그녀는 부채 규모가 더 증가하지 않는다면, 별도의 국가 부채 관리 기관은 필요하지 않을 것이라고 덧붙였다.

해설_ 문장의 의미상 빈칸에는 '만약 ~하지 않는다면'의 뜻을 가지는 접속사가 들어가야 알맞다. **while**과 **whereas**는 '반면에'란 의미로, 빈칸에 들어갈 경우 각 절의 연결이 부자연스러워진다.

어휘_ **volume** 규모

정답_ (c)

32.

해석_ 그의 기억력이 일반인보다 뛰어나다는 것은 거의 말할 필요도 없다.

해설_ 어순 문제이다. **need**가 조동사로 쓰여 주어 바로 다음에 위치하고 그 뒤에는 동사원형이 온다. 또한 빈도부사 **hardly**의 위치는 조동사 뒤, 본동사 앞이다.

정답_ (b)

33.

해석_ 어제 올 들어 가장 심한 황사가 한반도 전역을 강타했다.

해설_ 산맥, 강, 바다, 반도 등은 정관사 **the**를 붙인다. 또한 고유명사이므로 첫글자를 대문자로 쓴다.

어휘_ **yellow dust** 황사

정답_ (c)

34.

해석_ 인터뷰에 늦지 말아야 합니다.

해설_ 주절의 동사가 **insist**, **recommend**, **advise** 등인 경우 뿐만 아니라 주절에 형용사 **necessary**, **advisable**, **desirable** 등이 올 때도 **that**절에는 **should**가 생략된 동사원형이 올 수 있다.

정답_ (a)

35.

해석_ 그 회사가 갑자기 쓰러질 가능성은 매우 희박하다.

해설_ '~할 가능성은 ~하다'란 표현은 '**chances are ~**'라고 쓴다. **chance**를 무관사 복수명사로 씀을 유의한다.

정답_ (c)

36.

해석_ 제 제안을 그녀가 받아들이기를 촉구할 예정입니다.

해설_ **urge**는 목적보어로 **to**부정사를 취한다.

어휘_ **urge** 촉구하다

정답_ (b)

37.

해석_ 법인카드를 사용한 사람들은 모든 출장경비를 되돌려받게 될 것입니다.

해설_ 단수형인 **expense**는 '지출, 비용', 복수형인 **expenses**는 '소요되는 경비'를 의미한다. 따라서 문장의 의미상 빈칸에는 복수형 **expenses**가 적합하다.

어휘_ **reimburse** 변상 · 상환 · 변제하다
company credit card 법인카드

정답_ (d)

38.

해석_ 전세계가 경기 침체, 불황, 그리고 자산 가치 붕괴의 장기 사이클에 직면할 확률이 50퍼센트이다.

해설_ 관사와 어순문제이다. 관사가 필요하며, 그 위치는 50 **percent**의 앞이다.

어휘_ **recession** 경기 침체 **depression** 불황
destruction 붕괴

정답_ (a)

39.

해석_ 요즘 우편물이 너무 많아서 미치겠어!

해설_ **mail**은 불가산명사이므로 **much**로 수식하고, 동사에는 **-s**를 붙인다.

정답_ (d)

40.

해석_ 해외 화교 기업계의 자산은 총 2조 달러로 추정된다.

해설_ **estimate**(추정하다)의 수동형이 와야 한다. 또한 주어 **assets**이 복수이므로 **are estimated**가 된다.

어휘_ **asset** 자산 **trillion** 1조

정답_ (d)

41.

해석_ **A:** 어떻게 가정주부가 연봉 4만 달러의 전문직 여성이 되었지요?
B: 그녀는 변호사가 되기 위해 혹독한 훈련기간을 보냈어요.
A: 이제 그러한 노력이 결실을 맺고 있군요.
B: 그렇지만 대신 가정을 잃었지요.

해설_ 주격관계대명사는 **be**동사와 같이 생략할 수 있고, 단독으로 생략하면 틀린다. **train**은 타동사(훈련시키다)도 되지만, 자동사(훈련되다)도 될 수 있음을 유의한다.

어휘_ **pay off** 성과를 거두다

정답_ (a) a professional woman makes →
a professional woman who makes

42.

해석_ A: 이 상자 안에 있는 게 뭐 같아?

B: 전혀 모르겠어. 어쨌든 열어선 안 된다고 했어.

A: 뭔지 알고 싶어 죽겠어. 넌 안 그래?

B: 사실 그렇진 않아.

해설_ (c)에서는 **Are you not anxious to know what it is**?
의 줄임말이 와야 한다.

정답_ (c) Don't you → Aren't you

43.

해석_ A: 그녀에게 무슨 일이 일어난 거야?

B: 그녀의 아버지가 오늘 아침 교통사고를 당하셨대요.

A: 저런, 그녀는 좀 어때?

B: 정신이 없는 것 같았어요.

어휘_ That's tragic 저런, 안 됐군요.

해설_ happen은 자동사이므로 수동태로 쓰이지 않는다.

정답_ (a) What was happened → What happened

44.

해석_ A: 급하게 쓰였기 때문에, 그 책에 오류가 많다는 사실을 우리
는 부정할 수 없어요.

B: 맞아요. 우리 모두 그 점에 대해서는 유감스럽습니다만, 다
른 대안이 없었어요.

A: 어쨌든 적어도 기한을 지켰다는 점은 만족스럽습니다.

B: 다음엔 더 잘할 수 있을 거예요.

해설_ 분사구문의 의미상 주어는 **the book**인데, 주절의 주어는
we이므로 분사구문의 의미상 주어를 생략할 수 없다. 굳이 주
어를 생략하려면 분사구문의 주어를 **we**로 하여 재작성하여야
한다.

어휘_ option 선택권 gratifying 즐거운, 만족스러운

정답_ (a) Written in haste → Having written the book in
haste

45.

해석_ A: 태어날 아기를 위해 이 방을 새로 도배하고 싶어요.

B: 좋은 생각이에요. 무엇부터 해야 하죠?

A: 방 크기는 가로 세로 12피트예요.

B: 그런데 도배 대신에 페인트를 칠하는 건 어때요?

해설_ 치수, 길이 등을 나타낼 때는 복수형 **measurements**를 쓴
다. 단수형 **measurement**는 '측량' '측정'의 뜻이다.

어휘_ repaper (새로) 도배하다

정답_ (c)

46.

해석_ (a) 현재 우리가 겪는 극심한 경기 침체가 일반적인 불황과 다
른 점은 경제 전반에 대한 신뢰가 사라졌다는 사실이다. (b)
우리는 지금 공황 상태에 빠져 있고, 그 두려움이 가라앉기 전
에는 경기 침체가 더욱 맹위를 떨칠 수밖에 없다. (c) 투자자
신뢰도의 최고 잣대는 '실시간 경제 성적표'라고 불리는 다우

존스 공업 평균 지수다. (d) 이 지수는 가끔씩 상승하지만 그것
이 곧바로 불황의 끝을 의미하진 않으며, 이 불황은 다우 지수
가 상승세를 계속 유지할 때까지 끝나지 않을 것이다.

해설_ 시간/조건의 부사절에서는 현재시제가 미래시제를 대신한다.
until the Dow will turn up and stay up은 시간의 부
사절이므로 **will**이 생략되어야 한다.

어휘_ recession 불황 downturn 침체, 하락
panic ~에 공포(공황)을 일으키다 (변화형은 -icked; -
icking) quell 진압하다, 억누르다
rage 맹위를 떨치다 signify 의미하다

정답_ (d) until the Dow will turn up and stay up → until
the Dow turns up and stays up

47.

해석_ (a) 연구결과에 따르면 남자들은 대개 외모보다는 건강상의 이
유나 질병에 대한 두려움 때문에 다이어트를 하는 경향이 있
다. (b) 반면 여성은 사회적 압력 때문에 다이어트를 하는 경향
이 훨씬 강하다. (c) 우리는 배가 불룩 나오고 몸무게가 300파
운드나 나가는 미식축구 공격수들을 흔히 보지만, 그들은 한결
같이 자신의 거대한 몸집과 그 몸집으로 인해 얻은 직업에 만
족한다. (d) 남자가 과체중 때문에 비난받는 경우는 적다.

해설_ 적절한 대명사 사용에 관한 문제다. 원래 명사구는 **the job
(that) their size earned the linemen**이고, 대명사로
대체하면 **the job it earned them**이 된다.

어휘_ lineman [미식축구] 라인맨 (공격선 · 방어선에 있는 선수)
stigmatize 비난하다

정답_ (c) the job they earned it → the job it earned
them

48.

해석_ (a) 20년 전만 해도 그의 저술은 소수의 학자만을 겨냥한 것
들이었다. (b) 그러다가 1990년대 초부터 '기대 체감의 시대
(**The Age of Diminished Expectations**)'나 '경제학
의 향연(**Peddling Prosperity**)' 등 대중적인 경제서적들
을 출간하였다. (c) 1996년에 한 웹사이트에 기고되기 시작
한 그의 칼럼은 뉴욕 타임즈의 눈길을 끌었고, 결국 뉴욕 타임
즈 외부평론 면에 그의 칼럼이 실리기 시작했다. (d) 그러나
그는 칼럼의 주제를 자신의 전문 분야(경제학)에만 국한시키
지 않았고, 지난 8년 동안 그의 칼럼 대부분은 부시 행정부의
이라크 전쟁과 대외 정책에 대한 통렬한 비판으로 가득했다.

해설_ 문맥상 '스스로에게 제약을 두지 않았다'라는 의미이므로, 재
귀대명사가 오는 것이 적절하다.

어휘_ a /the handful of 소량의, 소수의 pen 저술하다
accessible 접근 가능한
op-ed (opposite editorial page의 준말)로, 신문에서
일종의 외부인 기고란에 해당함.

정답_ (d) he hasn't limited him → he hasn't limited
himself

49.

해석 (a) 사실 휴대전화는 일종의 감지장치다: 문자메시지를 보내거나 통화를 할 때마다 무선통신기지국이 사용자의 위치를 정확히 파악한다. (b) 전 지구상에 40억 대의 휴대전화가 있으니까, 매달 수조 개의 데이터 포인트가 네트워크상을 흐르는 것이 되며 이것은 사용자의 움직임을 보여주는 디지털 그래프를 만든다. (c) 그 개별 움직임을 종합하면 한 구역, 한 지역, 한 도시, 심지어 한 사회 전체의 움직임을 하나의 그림으로 보여준다. (d) 휴대전화는 '글로벌 신경계의 뉴런(신경세포)'이 된 것이다.

해설 create의 의미상 주어는 **trillions of data points**이다. 따라서 **flowing**과 일치되려면 능동형분사 **creating**으로 써야 한다.

어휘 **cellular tower** 무선통신 기지국
pinpoint 위치를 정확하게 파악하다
handset 단말기 **aggregate** 집합하다, 모이다
convey 전달하다 **neuron** 신경세포 단위

정답 (b) **create digital graphs of** → **creating digital graphs of**

50.

해석 (a) 지금쯤 시금치가 다 식었을 테니까, 여분의 물기를 짜내서 그릇에 다시 담으세요. (b) 시금치를 잘게 썰어서 그릇에 담으세요. (c) 잘게 썬 시금치를 아까 짜낸 물기와 섞고 리코타 치즈와 약간의 파마산 치즈를 더하세요, 그 다음 짤주머니를 이용해 반죽을 카넬로니에 채우세요. (d) 샌드위치 백의 모서리 부분에 시금치 반죽을 넣어서 사용하면 짤주머니 대용이 됩니다.

해설 handful이 '한 움큼(의 양)'이란 뜻의 명사이므로, **amount**는 필요가 없다.

어휘 **spinach** 시금치 **chop** 자르다, 잘게 썰다
handful 한 움큼 **ricotta** 리코타(이탈리아산 치즈의 일종)
Parmesan 파마산 (이탈리아산 치즈의 일종)
piping bag 파이핑백(고깔모양의 짤주머니)
cannelloni 카넬로니 (원통형 대형 파스타(**pasta**) 또는 그 요리)

정답 (c) **a handful amount of the Parmesan** → **a handful of the Parmesan**

GRAMMAR CLIP

01

〈뜻에 주의할 완전자동사〉

- count(중요하다), make(움직이다), last(계속되다), do(만족하다), be(존재하다)

〈형용사보어를 갖는 불완전자동사〉

- turn/go/come/run/fall/grow/get(~가 되다), seem/appear/look(~하게 보이다), sound(~하게 들리다), feel(~하게 느껴지다), smell(~한 냄새가 나다), taste(~한 맛이 나다)

〈자동사로 착각하기 쉬운 타동사〉

- marry, accompany, obey, enter, answer, influence, discuss

〈3형식으로의 전환〉

- to를 쓰는 경우: give, show, teach, tell, write, lend 등
- for를 쓰는 경우: make, buy, get, leave, read 등
- of를 쓰는 경우: ask, inquire 등

〈조동사의 의미〉

- may well: ~하는 것도 당연하다
- so that+주어+may: ~하기 위하여
- may as well ~ as...: ...하느니 차라리 ~하는 편이 낫다
- cannot have p.p.: ~했을 리가 없다
- must have p.p.: ~했음에 틀림없다
- may have p.p.: ~했을지도 모른다
- should have p.p.: ~했어야 했다
- would rather A than B: B하느니 차라리 A하겠다

〈that절에 쓰이는 should〉

- suggest[propose, insist, order] that+주어+(should)
- It is natural[necessary, important] that+주어+(should)
- It is strange[surprising, a pity] that+주어+(should)

02

〈현재가 미래를 대신하는 경우〉

- come, go, arrive, start, leave 동사가 쓰이는 가까운 미래
- 시간, 조건을 나타내는 부사절

〈과거완료 대신 과거시제를 쓰는 경우〉

- when, after, before, till, as soon as 등에 의해 전후 관계의 시간이 명백할 경우

〈진행형이 없는 동사〉

- see, hear, feel, smell, taste, love, like, hate, want, know, believe, be, have, resemble, belong to

〈주의해야 할 현재완료 용법〉

- ago, when, last, yesterday 등과 같이 쓰지 않는다.
- just는 현재완료에, just now는 과거시제에 쓴다.

03

- 형용사[부사]+enough+to부정사: ~하기에 충분할 만큼
- too+형용사[부사]+to부정사: 너무 ~해서 ...할 수 없다

〈of를 써서 의미상의 주어를 표현하는 경우〉

- kind, foolish, nice, careful 등이 올 때
- 지각동사: see, watch, look at, notice, hear, listen to, feel 등
- 사역동사: let, make, have
- 관용구문: cannot but+동사원형=cannot help+동명사 =cannot have no choice but+to부정사(~하지 않을 수 없다)

04

- 동명사를 목적어로 취하는 동사: finish, enjoy, mind, avoid, deny, keep, promise, give up, put off
- remember[forget, regret]: 동명사 목적어(과거의 일), 부정사 목적어(미래의 일)

〈동명사 구문〉

- It is no use -ing: ~하는 것은 소용없다
- There is no -ing: ~하는 것은 불가능하다
- cannot help -ing: 어쩔 수 없이 ~하다(=cannot but 동사

원형)

- **feel like -ing**: ~하고 싶다(=**feel inclined to**부정사)
- **prevent A from -ing**: A가 ~하는 것을 못하게 하다
- **never ... without -ing**: ~할 때는 언제나 ...한다
- **look forward to -ing**: ~을 고대하다
- **be used[accustomed] to -ing**: ~에 익숙하다
- **It goes without saying.**: 두 말할 필요가 없다.

05

- 분사구문의 의미상 주어는 주절의 주어와 일치해야 한다.
- **Being** 또는 **Having been**으로 시작하는 분사구문은 **Being** 또는 **Having been**을 생략할 수 있다.
- 분사구문을 부정할 경우에는 부정어구를 분사 앞에 둔다.
- **with**+명사+분사: 동시 동작을 나타냄

〈비인칭 독립분사구문〉

- **Judging from**: ~로 판단하건데
- **Generally speaking**: 일반적으로 말해서
- **Frankly speaking**: 솔직히 말해서
- **Strictly speaking**: 엄격히 말해서

06

〈목적어가 that절인 문장의 수동태 전환〉

- 주절의 시제와 일치하는 경우

  People say that he is rich.

  →It is said that he is rich.

  →He is said to be rich.

- 주절의 시제가 that절의 시제보다 늦는 경우

  People say that he was rich.

  →It is said that he was rich.

  →He is said to have been rich.

- 직접목적어만 주어로 변환할 수 있는 4형식동사: **do, make, buy, sell, get, bring, send, write, read, sing, pass** 등
- 사역동사나 지각동사를 수동태로 전환할 때는 원형부정사를 to부정사로 바꾸어 준다.

- 긍정명령문 수동태: **Let**+목적어+과거분사
- 부정명령문 수동태: **Let**+목적어+**not be**+과거분사

  Don't let+목적어+**be**+과거분사

〈by 이외의 전치사를 쓰는 수동태〉

- **be covered with, be surprised at, be filled with, be known to**

07

- 가정법 문장에서 **if**가 생략되면 주어와 동사의 위치가 바뀐다.
- **I wish**+가정법 과거: ~한다면 좋겠는데

  I wish+가정법 과거완료: ~했더라면 좋았을 텐데

- **as if**+가정법 과거: 마치 ~인 것처럼
- **as if**+가정법 과거완료: 마치 ~였던 것처럼

〈관용 표현〉

- **It's (high) time**+가정법 과거: ~할 시간이다
- **If it were not for~**: ~가 없었다면
- **If it had not been for~**: ~가 없었더라면
- **as it were**: 말하자면

08

〈수의 일치〉

- 언제나 단수: 단위를 나타내는 수사 / **each, every** / **lots of, much**
- **a number of**: 복수 / **the number of**: 단수
- 별개의 사물이 **and**로 연결되어 하나의 사물을 나타낼 때: 단수
- 복수형의 학과명: 단수
- 상관접속사: 모두 B에 일치시킨다(**not only A but also B, B as well as A, either A or B, neither A nor B**)

〈시제의 일치 예외〉

- 언제나 현재: 진리나 진실, 속담이나 격언, 현재의 습관
- 언제나 과거: 역사적 사실〈화법 전환〉
- 부사와 지시대명사의 전환: **here→there, now→then, ago→before, today→that day, yesterday→the day before tomorrow→the next day, the**

following day, these→those,
last night→the night before, this→that

- 의문사가 없는 의문문은 if나 whether를 접속사로 쓴다.
- 명령문을 전환할 때는 원형동사를 to부정사로 쓴다.
- Let's로 시작하는 명령문은 전달동사를 suggest, propose 등을 쓰고 that절의 동사는 should+원형동사를 쓴다.

09

〈부정관사(a, an)의 다양한 뜻〉
- 하나의(=one), 종류 전체를 대표, 어떤(=certain), 매~(=per), 동일한(=of the same)

〈정관사(the)를 쓰는 경우〉
- the+앞에 나온 명사[유일무이한 명사, 서수, 최상급, only, same, very]
- 단위를 나타낼 때: by the+(시간, 수량) 단위
- the+형용사: ~한 사람들(=~ people)
- 소유격 대신: hit[strike]+사람+on the+신체 일부
  catch[take]+사람+by the+신체 일부
  look[stare]+사람+in the+신체 일부

〈관용적 표현〉
- A is one thing, B is another: A와 B는 별개이다〈물질명사의 수량 표시법〉
- a cup of coffee, a glass of milk[water, juice], a cake of soap, a piece of paper[chalk, advice, furniture]

〈a+물질명사=구체적인 제품이나 사건〉
- a glass(유리잔), a silk(비단옷), a fire(화재 사건)

〈a+추상명사=그 성질의 소유자, 구체적인 행동 및 사물〉
- a bearty(미인), a youth(젊은이), many kindnesses(많은 선행들), a necessity of life(생활 필수품)

〈a+고유명사=~하는 사람, ~의 작품〉
- I bough a Ford.(나는 포드 자동차 한 대를 샀다.)
- I want to be an Einstein.(나는 아인슈타인 같은 사람이 되고 싶다.)

- I read a Hemingway. (나는 헤밍웨이 작품 한 편을 읽었다.)

10

〈관계대명사 that을 꼭 써야 하는 경우〉
- 최상급/서수사/the very/the only/the same/the first/the last 등이 선행사를 수식할 때
- all/any/every/no 등이 선행사를 수식할 때
- anything/everything/nothing이 선행사일 때
- 사람+동물/사람+사물이 선행사일 때
- who/what/which 등의 의문사가 선행사일 때

〈유사관계대명사〉
- as: such, the same, as 등이 선행할 때
- but: not no 등이 선행할 때
- than: 비교 구문이 선행할 때

〈관계대명사 what의 관용적 표현〉
- what 주어+동사: 주어의 사람됨
- Reading is to the mind what exercise is to the body.(독서와 정신의 관계는 운동과 신체의 관계와 같다.)

〈관계대명사의 생략〉
- 목적격 관계대명사는 생략할 수 있다.
- 주격 관계대명사+be동사는 생략할 수 있다.
- There is 뒤의 주격관계대명사는 생략할 수 있다.

〈복합관계사〉
- whatever=no matter what, whenever=no matter when, wherever=no matter where

11

〈부사의 위치〉
- 빈도부사: 일반동사 앞에, 조동사 뒤에, be동사 뒤에
- 목적어가 명사이면 부사는 명사 앞이나 뒤에 올 수 있다. 하지만 목적어가 대명사일 경우 부사는 반드시 대명사 뒤에 와야 한다.
- 자동사+전치사의 경우에 목적어는 명사이든 대명사이든 모두 전치사 뒤에 둔다.

- **as** 원급 **as**: ~만큼 ...하다
- **as** 원급 **as possible**: 가능한 한 ~하게(=**as** 원급 **as**+주어 +**can**)
- **not so much A as B**: A라기보다는 차라리 B이다
- **not so much as**: ~조차 ...않다 〈비교급 표현〉
- 동일인의 이질적인 성질을 비교할 때는 **more**+원급+**than**을 쓴다.
- **the**+비교급+**of the two**: 둘 중에서 더 ~하다
- **the**+비교급+**for[because]**: ~ 때문에 그만큼 더 ...
- **the**+비교급~, **the**+비교급...: ~하면 할수록 더 ...하다
- 비교급 강조: **much still, far, even, by far** 등을 비교급 앞에 쓴다.
- **than** 대신 **to**를 쓰는 경우: **superior, inferior, senior, junior, major, minor**
- **no more A than B**: A가 아닌 것은 B가 아닌 것과 같다

〈최상급 표현〉

- 동일인을 비교할 때는 최상급에서 **the**를 생략한다.
- **the last ~**: 결코 ~할 것 같지 않은, 부적당한

12

〈등위접속사〉

- 명령문+**and**: ~해라, 그러면 / 명령문+**or**: ~해라, 그렇지 않으면

〈상관접속사〉

- **both A and B**: A와 B 모두
- **not only A but also B**: A뿐만 아니라 B도(=**B as well as A**)
- **either A or B**: A 혹은 B
- **neither A nor B**: A도 아니고 B도 아니다
- 때를 나타내는 접속사: **while, until, since, as soon as, once**
- 이유, 원인을 나타내는 접속사: **because, since, as, now that**
- 조건을 나타내는 접속사: **if, unless, suppose, provided that**
- 양보를 나타내는 접속사: **although, even though,**

whether ... or not, no matter what, 명사[형용사]+**as**+주어+동사

- 목적을 나타내는 접속사: **so that, in order that**
- 결과를 나타내는 접속사: **so**+형용사+**that, such**+명사+**that**

13

〈부분 부정〉

- **all[every, both]+not**: 모두 ~하는 것은 아니다
- **not+always[necessarily, completely]**: 언제나[반드시, 완전히] ~하는 것은 아니다

〈이중 부정〉

- **never ~ without...**: ~하면 반드시 ...한다
- **cannot ~ too...**: 아무리 ...해도 지나치지 않다
- **nothing but**: 겨우(=**only**)
- **far from**: 결코 ~아닌(=**anything but, by no means**)〈강조 구문〉
- **It is ~ tnat** 구문: 동사를 제외한 문장의 일부를 강조할 때
- 동사를 강조할 때: 동사 앞에 **do**를 쓴다.
- 의문문, 부정문 강조: **at all, on earth, in the world** 삽입

〈도치 구문〉

- 부정 부사구+조동사+주어+일반동사
- 보어+자동사+주어
- 목적어+주어+타동사 (단, 부정어구가 들어간 목적어의 도치는 목적어+조동사+주어+일반동사의 어순이다.)